LISTENING IN

Horse Mountain Press publishes works that affirm the human spirit,
promoting individual, community and global awareness.
This book is printed on recycled paper. A portion of the proceeds will be donated for
replanting of trees in states where paper is produced.

LISTENING IN
Dialogues with the Wiser Self

Ellen Meredith

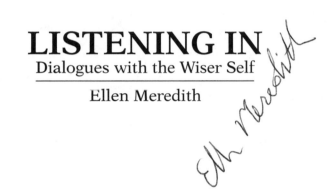

HORSE MOUNTAIN PRESS
Haydenville, Massachusetts

Horse Mountain Press
P.O. Box 446
Haydenville, Massachusetts 01039-0446

9   8   7   6   5   4   3   2   1

First Edition

Printed in the United States of America

Library of Congress Cataloging in Publication Data
Meredith, Ellen, 1955—
    Listening in: dialogues with the wiser self
    p.   cm.
    includes bibliographical references (p.   ) and index.
    1. New Age movement. 2. Spirit writings. 3. Spiritual life.
    4. Channeling (Spiritualism).
I. Title.
Library of Congress Catalog Card Number 93-77564
ISBN 0-9636073-5-9 $14.95 Softcover

Book Design, Page Illustrations: Maureen Scanlon
Cover Art: Mary Frank; detail from *Persephone*, oil on metal, 1986
             Courtesy of Midtown Payson Galleries, New York
Electronic Page Composition: William L. McNaughten
Printed and bound by Malloy Lithographing, Ann Arbor, Michigan

To Judith
who awakened me, reminds me, and keeps me working

Contents

Groundings

Acknowledgments

During the four years it took to write and refine *Listening In*, many people were instrumental in its creation.

My council not only taught me the perspectives presented in these pages, but also encouraged me to use my own love for language to give voice to their teachings in ways that I hope can do them justice. I am grateful to these teachers for their wisdom, their friendship in times of need, and their partnership in writing these dialogues.

My clients and students in California, Switzerland and elsewhere asked the right questions at the right times. Their interest, diversity, need and willingness to listen gave me new understanding of the council teachings and of the role inner teachers can play in guiding us.

Sandy Boucher contributed to the shaping of this book with her intelligent, respectful consultation and editing. She helped me to cut excess material with minimum pain, and used just the right combination of praise and critique to keep me enthused about the rewriting process.

Joan Halsey, a wise crone in her own right, had the patience to copy-edit the manuscript with her fine-toothed comb. She worked valiantly with my quirky and rarely consistent punctuating tendencies. Any mistakes that remain in the text are determined miscreants that deserve to enjoy their survival.

Several friends and friends-of-friends read portions of the manuscript in its evolution, and gave me much-needed encouragement and response. Patricia Yeghissian deserves recognition as the first and only person (besides me) to wade through the original transcripts of talks and to reassure me that she could see valuable material in them. She later re-read and responded to the second draft. Judith Evans gave me thoughtful critiques, section by section, as I produced the second draft, and helped me to develop confidence in the voice I was using. Edith Sullwold read a post-edited version of the book and reassured me just as I was losing my perspective on this project. Thanks also are due to Jill Lippitt, Sara Hostetler, and Audrey Rubin.

I am grateful to Bob Silverstein of Quicksilver Books, who generously read and critiqued the manuscript in one of its earlier forms and gave me valuable advice about publishing.

Maureen Scanlon is a wonderful designer and I am fortunate to have had her design this book. Her work speaks for itself. In addition, she assembled a talented and supportive team of production people: Will McNaughten on computer, Susan Bergeron-West on design and layout, Mary Lawler for calligraphy. Thanks to Horse Mountain Press for a delightful venture and for seeing this project through its many stages of production.

Those are the people who assisted me directly in producing this book. There are some others to whom I am grateful for their influence. Thanks to Nancy Manyí-ten Williamson, Ruth Denison, Diane Vreuls, Stuart Friebert, Pat Ikeda, Deborah Berman, Chandrama Jaeger, Cleo, Chloë and Pudge. Their teaching, emotional support, encouragement, and in the case of the last three, purring and physical warmth enabled me to stay aware of my connections in the web.

A note about pronouns. The council has allowed me, as messenger, to shape the information I received so that it makes sense in my own culture and context. In an effort to avoid the awkwardness of using "she/he", I used "she" or "he" as generic terms, according to my whim.

The Dialogue Begins

As a child, I was quite taken with a fairy tale about a stupid man and his peevish wife. They were destitute, and were walking along the road to market, searching the gutters for something they might sell. The man found an old lamp, crusted with dirt, and rubbed it to see what might lie beneath the grime.

It was a magical lamp, of course, and a genie appeared, granting the man three wishes. Without thinking he blurted out, "I wish I had a sausage to eat, I'm so hungry!" Immediately a succulent Kielbasa appeared in his hand.

His wife was incensed. "How could you waste a wish on a sausage, you stupid oaf?" she cried.

And in the strangely translated dialect of fairy tales he hollered back, "I wish you had a sausage on your nose, you old cow!"

Immediately, his precious sausage flew from his hands and stuck to his wife's nose! They were both horrified, and chastened. In an act of great sacrifice, the man decided he must use his final wish to remove the sausage from his wife's nose. This led to a reconciliation of sorts, and they proceeded down the road, somewhat wiser, still hungry, and with a worthless, dirty old lamp to sell at market.

My young friends and I were greatly dissatisfied by the course of events in this story. We discussed it at length, and agreed that the first thing we would wish for would be unlimited wishes. We would never be so stupid as to wish for a sausage.

For several nights I lay in bed practicing how I would deal with the genie and his three wishes. After my first wish for unlimited wishes, my second would be that I could never accidentally wish for something bad. That would avoid the sausage-on-the-nose problem. Even at that young age my friends and I, while not able to understand the pressures of hunger and poverty, did realize one truth. You needed more than the good luck to find a magic lamp and get a genie: you had to use the gift wisely.

Years later, I did find a kind of magic lamp. It was not a genie offering me wishes, but rather a group of inner teachers offering me insights, perspective, emotional healing and guidance. Luckily, they did not limit their offer to three responses, or like the stupid man and his peevish wife, I might well have wasted the opportunity. It took me a while to realize that the value of this gift lay in how I used it.

I found my magic lamp in a corner of my own mind. On an early spring day, fourteen years ago, I sat at my desk waiting for inspiration. I was a graduate student at a large midwestern university, trying to be a Writer, with a capital W. I believed great insight and inspiration lurked just at the edge of my awareness. My dubious and not very original aspiration was to write the great American novel, then go on the Johnny Carson Show to be interviewed about it.

This goal was clearly not sustaining me. The draft of a novel I had just completed (not the greatest book ever written) did not buoy my spirits. Furthermore, the fact that I had won a prize with my writing and received an excellent job offer did not make me happy either. I was depressed. Looking back, I realize that the cracks and fissures of a rocky childhood were opening in my foundation.

My family, like many in the fifties and sixties, had tried hard to look like Ozzie and Harriet, while sweeping differences and difficulties under the rug. When my parents' recent messy divorce brought the structure tumbling down, all my feelings and beliefs shook loose. I was, like many in my generation, desperately searching for the meaning of life while pretending I already knew.

So I sat at my desk, straining to write my way to redemption. I listened and waited for ideas for the next book, like that stupid man and his peevish wife scouring the gutters for something to sell at market. Then a peculiar thing happened. I sensed my grandmother, ten years dead, standing behind me with her hands laid comfortingly on my shoulders. She said, "Don't wrap yourself up in expectations, Ellen, or they will stifle you." It seemed like good advice, so I wrote it down.

Her message was actually far more complicated than the words I recorded. I felt her sorrow because she had been obese during her lifetime, and trapped by the limitations of her cumbersome body. I felt her thinking, "Don't hem yourself in like I did." The messenger wasn't *quite* my grandmother: it was a loving presence, clearer and more articulate than my grandmother had ever been.

This was not the kind of visitation you read about in books. For instance, I did not think there was someone actually standing there. I felt no cold fog, heard no distinct voice or strange bells tinkling. In fact I didn't know until later that I had had a visitation. I was always having imaginary dialogues in my mind, hearing people tell me what I wanted to hear. This appearance of my grandmother felt familiar and pleasant in a bittersweet kind of way. She had been the closest, most affectionate of all my family.

The event would have faded into the murky oblivion of my journal if it hadn't been for what happened two days later. An adventurous friend dropped by on her way to a "psychic tea" at a spiritualist church in a nearby small town. She invited me to come along and get a fifteen-minute psychic reading.

It sounded like a good diversion. I'd never seen a psychic before or even given much thought to the phenomenon. My stereotypes were fairly conventional: I expected this person to wear flowing robes, speak with a strange foreign accent, and have an unearthly light in her eyes. The reality gave me quite a chuckle. The church was a newly-built rectangular house with aluminum siding. The tea was held in the large basement recreation room, its cinderblock walls decorated with children's drawings from Sunday School, and crepe paper Easter bunnies. Forty to fifty people, typical country midwesterners, sat around long folding tables, gossiping about events in their families.

There was a certain hush in the atmosphere, in deference to the eighteen psychics up at one end of the room, who sat at small, numbered card tables talking earnestly to what were obviously clients sitting across from them. At first glance the psychics were disappointingly ordinary people. Three quarters of them were women you might see in the grocery store, in flower-print dresses or stretch nylon slacks. The rest were earnest looking middle-aged or older men, with dark-rimmed glasses and hair carefully oiled in place. They reminded me of folks I used to see when I was a child at the annual chicken barbecue offered by the Junior Chamber of Commerce.

My friend and I checked in, paid our ten dollars, and chose our psychics by number. We sat down at the long tables to wait our turn. On one side of us five women whispered, exchanging zucchini recipes. On the other side a weathered older man was describing in great detail the untimely breakdown of his backhoe. It was not what we had expected, to say the least!

Then the bell rang, and it was my turn to see "number 11,"

who introduced herself as Joelle. A woman in her late thirties, Joelle was a solid, kind-faced person, the sort I might have gone to school with but wouldn't have known very well, because she lived out in the country, and was more engaged with helping out on the family farm than with academic studies. Or so I imagined. But her presence at the card table made me realize that people I knew casually and thought of as ordinary might well have dimensions I had never before perceived.

I sat down for the reading, and Joelle said with very little preamble, "Your maternal grandmother is standing behind you with a message. She does not want you to hem yourself in like she did in her life. She says not to wrap your expectations around you like a blanket or they will stifle you."

This time I *did* hear music: the theme song from "The Twilight Zone." This was long before Shirley MacLaine's books and the term "New Age" had reached the midwest. I remember thinking that either Joelle had just done an astonishing act of mind reading, or else my dead grandmother really was standing behind me. Either way, it was amazing. If it had been a question of wishes, I would have wasted my three right then. I remember sputtering a variety of meaningless comments, before coming to my senses and asking her, "How did you do that?"

She told me I had received other messages but just didn't know it. If I wanted to hear them, I should "slow down and listen."

As I told my friend about the "reading" on the way home, I puzzled over Joelle's instructions. It was probably good advice, but it made little sense to me. My life was already pretty slow-moving. As a student I wasn't exactly in the fast lane. And I had already spent years at the typewriter listening my heart out.

What I learned over the next few weeks, however, was that the quality of listening is intimately connected to the questions you ask. It had never occurred to me to ask consciously for dialogue with a source of wisdom. I had never thought about the possibility of communication with inner teachers (or dead relatives for that matter).

I had spent a lot of time tuning into my unconscious, filling my journal with images, impressions and snippets of writing that I later came to recognize as a vocabulary for what I call the *wiser self*. But my genie, in the form of my grandmother, had pointed me in a new direction, a more conscious kind of relationship where I could eventually learn the grammar and syntax of that wiser self.

About a week after the psychic tea, while cleaning my house, I noticed that a tickertape, like one of those stock brokers' market updates, was ticking through my mind, unrolling a scroll of letters. I decided to write the letters down, to see if they formed words.

What appeared on the page before me was: "**You have asked to know us, and so we are here. We have been with you for a very long time, and now you are ready to come stand with us. We will work with you. Let your wiser self which observes continue the writing at night, and we will come through with a few lines. Simply don't block the connection. Past awareness of us is imminent. Someone will give you a plant to water, be aware of the plant processes of growth. Surely you can grow plants?**"

It's a short message here, but taken down letter by letter it exhausted me. And excited me. And scared me. Who was this "we?" It certainly didn't sound like my grandmother. And if the message emerged from some weird trick of my subconscious, then why did it arrive letter by letter? The strangest part was that I had had a dream about a plant the night before, which I had written in my journal that very morning.

In the dream, my sister, with whom I didn't get along in real life, showed up at my door holding a plant. She said, "I'm leaving town for a while, and I want you to take care of this chameleon plant for me." In the dream she was affectionate and so was I. "Sure," I said. I set it on the counter next to the remains of my breakfast, a plate of scrambled eggs, and bid her a fond farewell. When I turned back to water the plant, it was gone; on the counter where I had set it was a second plate of scrambled eggs.

I realized that wherever I set the chameleon plant, it would change into its surroundings. I grew very worried about how I was going to take care of this plant, especially since I didn't know when my sister was coming back. The dream progressed, with several incidents of accidental transformation. The plant became a newspaper. It became a glass with liquid in it. Eventually the plant disappeared altogether.

I had awakened feeling anxious about what my sister would say when she realized I'd lost her plant.

As I read over my tickertape message about "the plant processes of growth" I remembered the sensations of my dream, which felt charged with meaning. The problem was that I didn't know what the significance was. Only later did I discover that that charged feeling is a common starting point for dialogue with the inner teachers. Your curiosity is piqued by a strange coincidence or seemingly significant juxtaposition of ideas. You begin to explore, to ask why, to create an opening for guidance.

When I was writing the letters from the tickertape, I felt hot. Energy coursed through me in a rush similar to sensations I had felt before in the throes of inspiration. I sensed a group of…what? People? Presences? I didn't at that time have a concept of "entity" or "spirit." These beings who seemed to gather around me as I wrote were familiar to me, on an emotional level, and I had the nagging sense in the back of my mind, like a forgotten dream, that I had known them somewhere.

Reading the message over again touched off in my mind whole pockets of meaning that had been built up in the past. Curiously, while my mind was puzzling over the details of who, what, when, where and why, some part of me felt very comfortable and easy with the whole process.

In the ensuing days, I tuned into this "we" repeatedly with questions about who they were, what the images meant that were appearing in my mind, why I was feeling what I was feeling. They soon began calling themselves "the council," in messages that contained a funny mix of clarity and further confusion. They told me that they were teachers, and that my wiser self was a member of their council. They also told me that to think of them as a council of teachers was a useful metaphor, but that I shouldn't get hung up on the hierarchy or details of their existence. The importance of their message lay in its effects on me.

I treated this communication as a game at first, playing with the messages and symbols I was given, trying to make sense of them. And my whole life seemed to explode in interaction with this dialogue I was having with the council. For example, a day after my chameleon plant dream, I received a letter in the mail from an old friend who had been deeply influential in my life. The letter began (with no greeting) "I am a chameleon." One of my fellow students decided, out of the blue, to give me a potted plant as a gift. Since I do not have much of a green thumb, I felt that the universe was trying to tell me something.

What the universe was offering me, which I couldn't quite grasp yet, was an invitation to explore the processes by which seed ideas grow into full-flowering experiences. I was being invited to learn about cultivating consciousness, which, like a chameleon, transforms in adaptation to its context. The message, the dream, the letter and the gift from my friend had many layers of meaning to them, like a good poem, some universal and some extremely personal. And because these events intrigued me, I was pulled more deeply into exploring the strange dialogue.

My relationship with the council was not formal. I would say, "Hey you guys, are you there?" and would hear a rather portentous, "We are here." Then they would begin to discuss whatever question or concern was on my mind. I learned to hear (and write) their messages more efficiently, getting past my need to take letter-by-letter dictation, receiving whole impulses and thoughts, putting them into phrases that were partly my language and partly seemed to come from them. If I distorted the thought or intent they were trying to communicate, they would correct me, often with gentle recognition of my need to hear things in certain ways.

The messages from the first several years of dialogue are garbled, and leap between wisdom and banality, the universal and the personal, in the way our minds do when we are speaking to ourselves and don't need to explain the connections to other people.

The topics were often mundane, of no interest to anyone but me. Like the man who was hungry for sausage, I was primarily hungry to understand myself and my relationships to other people. I remember, for example, asking the council if I should call a friend of mine, since she was on my mind. I got a dual message: "Isn't that something you can decide for yourself? Do you wish to call her?" Yet then they added somewhat cryptically: "You will hear your voice echo in the emptiness of her room. Her heart is sore right now."

It affirmed my inner sense that I somehow *ought* to call my friend, and when I did, I discovered that her partner had moved out on her, taking all the furniture. She was indeed sitting in an empty room, not very capable of response because of her pain.

My relationship with the council remained secret for several years as I finished school and moved through various editing and teaching jobs. It seemed so private, a kind of therapy I was conducting with myself. But I also realized that this talking with spirits might be considered very strange and perhaps even raise doubts about my sanity. The secrecy allowed me to explore more freely: I didn't have to explain myself to others or stand behind the messages, when in fact I did occasionally distort or misunderstand the teachings. I was free to learn through trial and error how to hear and articulate more clearly the multi-leveled perceptions I was being given.

On the other hand, right from the start, this council discouraged any sense of special secrets and insider information. They did not want me to think I was an initiate of some secret order, as many systems of occult exploration encourage. They repeatedly led me to test my insights in everyday reality. Their philosophy was that ordinary existence is magical: each individual is special and is an initiate in this business of living.

My life filled with events that validated the inner work I was doing. For example, I grew concerned about a pregnant friend. Although we had not spoken in a while, I got the sense that something was not quite right. An image came to me of a baby bound in tight ties. The council explained: **"Your friend is choking the child with her fears and desire to control. There is not enough room in her mind or her womb for this child to be herself."**

They continued, making a link to a group project I was leading that seemed to be going all wrong: **"You too are choking your baby project. You cannot control it with your will. You must let the energy of each individual create the ultimate shape. Let go of your "deadline" and let the "live lines" come together. We suggest you take a few days off. Let a space open for this child to gestate. Like magic, the seed you all planted in the first week will begin to realize its form."**

Emotionally, taking time off felt like the wrong strategy. I wanted to push harder and do the unfinished work myself. But when I followed the council's advice, the uncooperative members of the project group did get their work done, and the product did indeed take a shape I could not have achieved alone.

A few days later I found out that it was true that my friend's pregnancy had run into problems. Her baby had stopped growing, and appeared to be in some distress. Her doctor ordered bed rest, and soon thereafter the baby started to grow normally.

I came to see that the council was training me, using the events of my everyday life as the arena for my lessons. As they put it, they were teaching me to stand with them, to see as they saw. They were also teaching me to *travel* in consciousness: to go on imaginary journeys in my mind, meeting an amusing cast of characters and learning to develop greater compassion, flexibility and sometimes humility.

They taught me to be more flexible with language and metaphor, playing with shifts in perception. They guided me to remember my past lives and deeper connections with others. They introduced me to other councils and alternate realities. They guided me through a long illness, then taught me to do healing with others on the energetic, physical, and emotional levels. Together we explored various belief systems, both esoteric and exoteric, and they showed me how to apply these teachings to the problems and concerns of everyday life.

After my illness, the council popped into my mind one day to ask me if I would be willing to use their teachings to work with others. I agreed, somewhat tentatively. I was teaching at a state university in California at the time and couldn't imagine how I could introduce such topics into my classes.

Three days later the doctor who had helped me when I was ill called to ask me to consult on some cases with her. She had noticed that I could see what was going on in my own body, physically and energetically, and wondered if I could do that for other people as well. I agreed to try.

The first patient was a woman with a back injury that did not respond to treatment. I found, to my amazement, that I could see a hairline fracture that had not shown up on the x-ray. And to my further astonishment, I heard the council inside my head saying they had a message for her.

In some embarrassment, I explained that I had a message for her from my inner teachers. I proceeded then to speak for the council, making connections between the emotional issues that had created the imbalance in her energy and the physical habits which turned that imbalance into injury.

The patient took the situation in stride, thanking my teachers for the guidance. I, however, drove home quaking with fear, knowing I had crossed a line and gone public with something that had always been a deeply private experience. I halfway expected the gods of Normalcy to rise up and expose me as a fraud.

Instead I received a phone call from a woman I'd never met, saying she'd heard a rumor that I did psychic readings. Without thinking twice, I scheduled her for a session the next day. The council said, "Don't worry," and I felt a strange glow of certainty, even though I could hear my mind in the background gearing up to panic. I told myself that I could always share with her some of the council concepts I had learned over the years.

What happened instead was that the council arose in my mind, chatting with her as they had always chatted with me. I'd always believed that the insights I received about friends were predicated on my own knowledge of them. But sitting with that first client, I discovered to my utter surprise that the council knew details about her life that I had no way of knowing. Although I had studied with them intensively for six years, I never fully believed they existed until that moment.

Within a year I left my university job, because I was doing so many psychic readings and healing consultations that I didn't have time to grade papers. Within another year, I found myself not only doing full-time psychic counselling, but I had also joined the faculty of another California university, this time doing thesis advising for Masters degrees in Consciousness Studies.

To this day, I am not certain whether inner teachers in general and my council of entities in particular are a separate consciousness or some part of my own mind and imagination. I have decided it doesn't matter. The training and teachings I receive from them are interesting, useful and admirable. And the insights and lessons they have offered to my clients and students over the last eight years make me feel honored to be listening in.

A few years ago the council asked me, in their usual low-key way, if I would be willing to write a book, making their teaching available to a broader audience. I agreed, wondering how I would ever find the time. Shortly thereafter, my friend *the chameleon* called to invite me to join her in Switzerland. She offered to provide a financial and emotional safety net while I wrote this book.

Listening In is written in the voice of the council, because students have told me over the years that listening to the council helps them to hear their own wiser self more clearly. The material has been *channeled*, by which I mean I transcribed hundreds of pages of meandering council chats, then reorganized and rewrote the material several times in dialogue with the council, who wanted you to hear, see and feel their teachings on several levels.

The book works best when you read it slowly, perhaps just

a section or two at a time, and then let the resonance of the ideas echo in your mind and the seeds of suggestions take root in your imagination.

It is divided into two parts. The first is an exploration of what I might call the "cosmology of the self." It offers many seed ideas about finding meaningful ways to live authentically and express your deeper values. Part Two explores *wiser self* perspectives on love and change: issues the council is most frequently asked to address. Throughout the book I have included sample groundings, which the council likes to use at the beginning of group sessions in order to help listeners bring their attention into clearer focus.

The ideas in this book are not intended to be seen as rules or precepts for living. They are suggestions of a way of thinking, a way of perceiving, that allow you to get in touch with your own wiser self and recognize your own understanding. The council does not want followers or disciples; they don't want to be seen as some Strange Phenomenon. Their identity, as they say, "is immaterial."

What is important in the council's teaching is the opportunity it provides for *listening in*. The true learning occurs when we, the listeners, actively tune into that wise resonant place within us, connect to the wiser self, and examine our lives and actions from that perspective. The *Dialogue* happens each time we are able to get to the heart of a matter, make connections between ideas and events, and hear the extraordinary resonance of the life force within our everyday experience.

"Allow Us To Introduce Ourselves..."

We call ourselves *the council*, and we are a group of entities who meet in a place that you might call the inner planes or a source of wisdom: the home of the wiser self.

Our goal in presenting our understandings to you is to help you come home to your own greatest truth, your own greatest good. We hope to give you some ideas about bringing your life into more meaningful constellation, becoming more awake to who you are and how you are. What we have to offer is a mix of ideas and suggestions which can perhaps help you to deepen your sense of inner authority, and to find a richer, more resonant way of living your life.

It might be important to you to know whether we are male or female. We are both and neither. Each of us has known lives in many forms, male and female, and many gradations in between, in a variety of cultures where those terms meant different things at different times. So we feel that we have insight into the spectrum of what those designations might mean, and do not at this time identify our energy as particularly male or female. We chose the name *council* because it is neutral and collective, and we feel it has a nice ring to it.

There is something in the nature of our energy that can be very useful to you in recognizing or activating your own. It is like the striking of a bell or gong. You hear the sound and you feel the sound. And by the same token, our consciousness comes to you both through hearing and through feeling. Allow us to speak to you on these levels.

Our purpose in asking Ellen to write this book is to invite you to come work with us. To come study with us, over time, when you feel comfortable tuning into our awareness.

How can we be of help to you? Imagine that you are climbing a mountain and we happen to have reached the top of that particular mountain. We're up here with walkie-talkies, and you're just setting out to climb. You each have a walkie-talkie too: this book is about how to use your walkie-talkie.

You will hear us saying, "The next half-mile has a lot of big boulders on it so you might want to be careful and conserve your energy. Take it more slowly." Or we might say, "You have three paths coming up ahead and from what we can see the left path has a lot of thorns to go through, the middle path is quite steep, and the right path is twice as long. Your choice." We're here (like other entity guides) with our walkie-talkies giving insight from our perspective. We also have our guides with their walkie-talkies, giving us guidance.

Ellen hesitates when we use the image of climbing a mountain, because in your culture higher often means better. But we see the climb up the mountain as the climb home to yourself. You are climbing home to your truest self-expression and self-awareness. You do this through the events and experiences that you create in your lives.

We are not a right-answer machine, we are not a source of all-powerful wisdom. Our guidance is not the Word of God coming down from on high and absolutely correct. But we are part of the divine as you are part of the divine. And we have a perspective on the experiences you are living that perhaps can be useful to you.

On the other hand, you still need to take each step on your path yourself. No one can take steps for you. We can say, "Watch out, there's a hole," but it's your choice whether or not you step into it. It is your choice what you do with our information. We try to give guidance in ways that are not invasive to your free will, your free choice.

The teachings we offer to you are part of a spiritual curriculum for developing greater insight and equilibrium in your life. We have tried to incorporate responses to many of the questions we have received over the years from our various students and in-body friends, so that you could see these lessons in concrete and everyday terms. As you read, let your mind wander and free-associate. Let your imagination play with the images and concepts. Let your everyday life provide the workshop for experimenting with these perspectives. As you do this, you will feel the dialogue which has produced this book reconstituting within you.

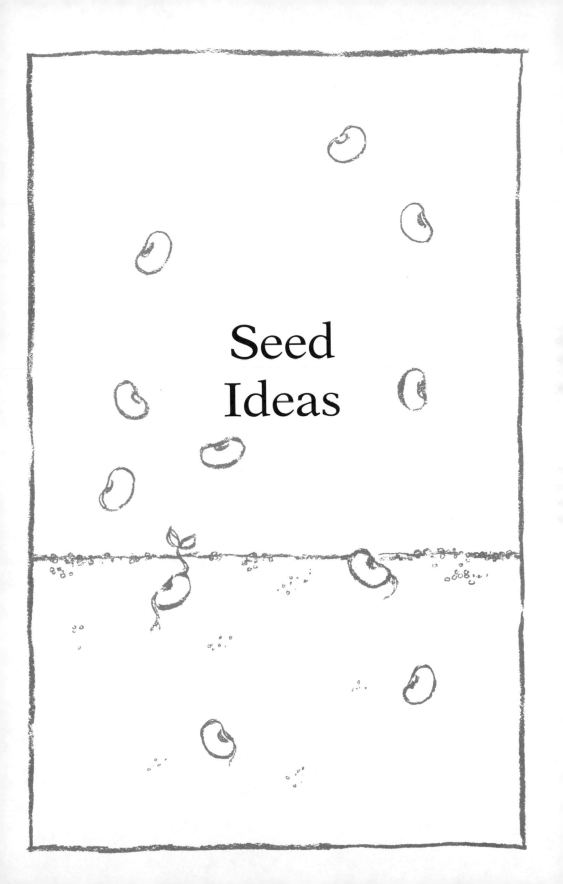

Seed
Ideas

Dimensions
of the Dream

Grounding

Seed Grounding

Shut your eyes for a moment, take a few deep breaths, and as you exhale, let go of the tensions of the day. You may need to shake a few muscles loose if they're tight. As you inhale, feel your energy gather into a tighter and tighter ball, so you are becoming more self-contained with each in-breath. With each out-breath let yourself release tensions. Do this several times.

Your consciousness, your awareness has been scattered. A little bit at work, some with your family, some with your friends, some out there in the larger world. With each in-breath, you draw your consciousness back in to you, to your center.

As you breathe, feel your energy becoming ever more dense and contained. Feel it circulating within and around your body, just there, not reaching out anywhere else. Relax and feel your own Self gathered in, becoming richer and more resonant with each in-breath.

If you find your mind reaching out to other things, gently invite it back with the in-breath, invite it to be in your body and around your body. Use your out-breath to relax.

Now imagine that you are a seed. Perhaps an apple seed. Feel the hard shell on the outside, the softer pulp inside, all the potential that is contained within you. And imagine yourself being gently and lovingly picked up by some gardener and placed into a warm little cubby, a hole or cave or cocoon that has been prepared for you in the earth. Feel the warmth and the support of the soil around you. Imagine there is a nice cushion of air all around you, so that as the soil covers you, you are not closed in. You are gently held in a womb of soil, in a protective holding place. It is dark, warm, and very safe.

And imagine as you sit there, you can feel the daytime sun coming down and warming the soil even further. As the warmth reaches you, you can feel within you a gathering. You are ready to explode forth. Ready to send down roots. You breathe in the warmth and the moisture. As you breathe out, send roots down into the soil beneath you.

Feel the roots growing and pushing farther with each exhale. And feel the joy of this growth as you are unfurling and unfolding, reaching out toward nourishment in the soil around you.

Now as you exhale, feel yourself growing upward as well, toward the sun, sending a stalk up, so that with each in–breath you draw in the nourishment of the soil and the moisture, and with each out-breath you are exploding forth with growth and new life.

Let your consciousness quicken with this unfolding of your potential, as if you were in a time-lapse photograph, so that with each exhale, your stalk grows higher and your roots spread broader and deeper, and the stalk begins the process of hardening into a trunk, thickening, pushing upward and outward. Imagine that as the seasons are turning, the leaves come out with the new light of spring. Keep breathing.

Feel also the buds...the flowers that come forth. Beautiful pink or white flowers. Feel the joyous unfolding of this. Watch as the petals drop, the flowers fall. There is a waiting period, as the buds begin to form, this time for baby fruits....

Watch in your mind's eye as this process quickens even further. The apples come, ripening, they thicken and sweeten with the nourishment of the season, and then finally fall with their own weight. Then the season turns further, and the leaves grow reddish brown. They are no longer needed to draw in chlorophyll; they drop and return to nourish the soil.

Feel that nourishment coming in at your roots, and feel the period of rest. Know that winter is coming and it is in its own way a little cocoon. Take a few breaths and remember what the cocoon of winter has been like. Feel that the days have grown shorter, and now they start to grow longer again, the light is returning and you are ready to push forth with new leaves, new growth, new buds, and start that cycle over again.

Feel the moment, the season of time present. And then open your eyes. Bring your awareness back to your room. Move around a little to get your body loosened and working and to wake yourself up.

Threes

❧

Now that we've introduced ourselves, we'd like to introduce you to your selves. We would like to give you our view of who you are and how you are constructed. It is perhaps slightly different from the way you have of seeing or understanding yourself.

Look through the window of your mind's eye at a tree that has meant something to you in your life. The tree lives in three worlds. It has the underground life of its root system, the solidity of its trunk, and the outreach into the heavens of its leaves and branches.

You, too, live in three realms. You have a portion of the Self that is hidden underground, in the realm of spirit. You have a solid trunk self, your physical body moving over the surface of the earth. And you have the outreach of your personality self, with all the plans, dreams and imagined experiences that enrich and feed the whole.

Trees are very special teachers. They are connectors between three levels of being, and we do not mean this metaphorically. There is far more to trees and the energy of trees than many people in your culture are aware.

We ask you to recognize that through your deep root system you have massive connections, energetically and spiritually speaking. Your roots feed and nourish you. They stretch out metaphorically for miles and miles, and intermingle with those of other people, sharing sources of nourishment.

Your trunk—the body—is the conduit for all the nutrients and the growth of your whole Self. It is far more contained and solid than the other two parts of your being.

Your leaves and branches are the activities, actions, projects, creative thoughts and expressions that you send out into the world. Just as a tree draws nourishment from under the ground, sends it up through the trunk, and displays it forth in branches and the expression of its foliage, you too follow a similar process.

Taking care of yourself, then, is really a matter of taking care of your three selves: what you do to care for and maintain access to your root system; how you inhabit and cultivate your body; and how well you are able to put forth the kind of projects and personality that truly express and nourish you.

There is one other aspect to a tree that is important. Not only do the water and nutrients of the soil come up into the tree, but the tree also replenishes the soil. It drops its leaves, it drops its fruits and nuts, there are droppings from the animals that live in the tree. These replenish the nutrients in the soil that then feed the root system. There's a cyclical exchange. As you contribute to your family, community, and friends, you not only improve the quality of life around you, you also nourish yourself.

As you may be aware, trees play a vital role in maintaining the physical atmosphere of your planet, in maintaining the weather and the climate. If you have done any reading about the cutting down of the Amazon Rain Forest, you will recognize the great danger and great loss as trees are destroyed. By the same token, as a tree in your own right, you are feeding and maintaining the atmosphere of the planet, on the physical, cultural and spiritual levels. We want to encourage you to play with that image over time.

You are ultimately here in life to unify these three worlds: the inner realms of spirit, the manifest reality of your everyday existence, and the extended realm of all potential and dreams. In order to do this, you have three interrelated but distinct selves. These three selves are not a metaphor. They are three types of consciousness that weave together into the identity or Self that you think of as "me."

We see you as a committee of three selves.

You have your *earth elemental self*, which is your body self, a creature, like all other creatures on the planet. You have the *talking self*, which is your personality, or the self that develops socially, has dramas, and engages in events and activities. And then there's the *wiser self*, which is the part of you connected within the realm of spirit.

Each of these three selves has its own focus, agenda, and sanctity to maintain. Your earth elemental self is trying to survive on a physical level. Its goals may not be easily reconciled with the goals of your talking self, who may or may not be in tune with the wiser self. Part of your greatest challenge, and the work of being human, is to coordinate the desires and expression of your committee of three. When things are not working in your life you will find that most likely it is because the different agendas of these selves are out of balance.

Earth Elemental Self

You know your earth elemental self from those moments when your body seems to have a mind of its own: when you want to wake up and your earth elemental insists on sleep; when you are trying to lose weight, and your earth elemental protests with a hunger that cannot be ignored. You may feel that we are making an artificial separation to describe your body as a distinct self, but we feel it is necessary to understand the sanctity of this consciousness on its own terms in order to learn to fully work with it.

Your earth elemental self is not just a vessel to inhabit; it is a creature with consciousness, like the dogs and the cats and the birds and the fish and the worms. And like all creatures, it is in connection, in communication with all other living beings on the planet. It is part of an ecological balance of life forms and can tell you many things about its own survival. It is set up to do just that, to give you constant messages and feedback about what the physical self needs in order to survive for the period of years that you are living in this life form.

It may surprise you to think that your body self has consciousness. Its basic equipment includes not only the sense organs and physical instincts, but also what you would call intuition: the ability to communicate telepathically. Those of you who have explored the complex capabilities of dolphins or bees or lions or wolves will recognize what we are referring to. It is a creature consciousness, geared both to preserve the sanctity of that life form and also to ensure a quality of individual existence.

The earth elemental self speaks to you through sensations, symptoms, imagery, direct knowing and your psychic abilities or intuitive receptors, and often speaks to you through events as well. A message from earth elemental self may register in your mind as a sense of guilt or shame: "I'm breaking some limit here, I shouldn't be doing this, I need something else right now." Or desire: "I really want to lie down and sleep." A craving: "Oh I'm so hungry, I think I'll eat some chocolate chip cookies."

How often, in rushing around, have you hurt your ankle or knee, requiring you to sit and do nothing for three days while the injury healed? That is an event created in part by your earth elemental self to get a message through to you in a way that you can't easily ignore.

In your culture you are not trained to work with your earth elemental self: to really speak her or his language fluently and to respond (or negotiate) in that language. As you are growing up, you see your parents, when they are tired, drink coffee to push the body further. You see people who have a need for love and physical contact ignoring it because they have work to get done. Then they don't really understand the sense of dissatisfaction that pervades their accomplishments. You see people who are sick—often a message of resistance on the part of the earth elemental—downing pills to suppress the symptoms so they can keep on working. That is like tying a gag over the mouth of a messenger, because you don't wish to hear the message.

The earth elemental lives mostly in time present; that is its strongest focus. But ironically, your earth elemental self is also the keeper of your memory. *It is from earth elemental self that you must request the images and ideas that you have stored.* Earth elemental is your anchor in this reality, not only the eyes and ears and hands and feet of your being, but also the self who determines ultimately how long you remain in this form, and with what quality of comfort, pleasure, and effectiveness.

Talking Self

Talking self is probably the "you" that you consider to be most fully your Self. It is the personality self that evolves in this lifetime. It says, "I'm this kind of person, but I'm not like that." It keeps making distinctions and setting up projects to express a personality forth into this life. Talking self communicates most frequently through language, through imagery, through thought forms, through talk. That's why we call it the talking self.

You do not come in as a fully formed talking self. But you do come in with certain predilections. It's as if you were an improvisational actor who has been given a few instructions. "Okay, you'll be female. You're going to be born in Nova Scotia, in a household where people argue a lot, you're going to be strongly attracted to everything that flies, and you'll meet up with the following five actors at key moments to have some important interactions." Your wiser self creates these givens as a scaffolding, from which your talking self can construct your life in all its rich detail and design.

Most conditions and appointments you set up before you come into this life can be changed. You can communicate telepathically (or directly) with the other person, re-negotiate with your wiser self, or just exercise your free will within moments of choice. But occasionally, attributes of this life are fixed as you are creating your committee of three.

For example, children born with one leg do not tend to grow a new one, no matter how much they pray for such a miracle. Instead, their creative talking self learns how to make that physical difference take on new meaning: a wholly different sort of miracle.

Talking self is the deciding self that manages and creates scenarios, enacts dramas in this life. Talking self dances through time and through different dimensions of reality, from the concrete to the dream. One moment you are focussed on tying your shoe, the next your talking self is engaged mentally in an adventure in Swaziland. One moment you are an adult, mentally and emotionally, and the next finds your talking self slipping back into childhood, with thoughts and feelings to match.

Wiser Self

The third part of your committee of three is your *wiser self*. We also refer to this self as your source self, your larger self, your soul self. It is the part of you that is an entity as we are entities, and knows what is healthy. It is the self that has created a plan for unfoldment, a purpose for your particular life, even as it convened the other two members of your committee. If the tree needs water and nutrients, it is the roots that send these to the trunk, leaves and branches.

Wiser self generally communicates with you through earth elemental self: through your body. Wiser self gives you feelings, images, sensations, insights, dreams, little events, and messages in a language that is both symbolic and often very concrete. Often what is coming through on the walkie-talkie is not clear language. It is a multi-dimensional set of impulses that can remind you of your truest values, deepest desires, greatest good and most resonant purpose. The messages and truth of your wiser self are like the dominant colors in a painting, they are easy to perceive when you take a moment and stand back to view your life. Wiser self stands outside of time.

Three Priorities

Given that you are each a committee of three, you are really carrying around three priorities.

You are carrying around the imperatives and needs of your earth elemental self. Now that isn't to say you can't have spiritual striving and work toward spiritual awareness, but to emphasize that you have work to do of the body. Work (or should we rather say celebration) to maintain the body. Work to cross-fertilize the body.

It is similar to the cross-fertilization of the flower. Although the nutrients come up to the blossom from the roots, the continuation of the flower is accomplished with the bees and the pollen and the wind and all the environmental forces that sustain and cross-pollinate the flower. By the same token, the physical activities you engage in, your movement of emotions, your cycles of rest, engagement and exchange all allow for the continuation of your earth elemental self.

Talking self is geared toward creating a life for you in this time, in this place, on this planet. Talking self makes a personality—actually a whole set of personalities—and is dedicated to evolving and defending those creations. She engages in dramas, forms relationships, gets jobs, initiates events in your life. She cares deeply about the symbolic significance of actions. While earth elemental self eats to feed physical hunger, talking self initiates activities to feed a craving for self-expression and stimulation.

The cultures that you create, the societies, the relationships, the symbols, the web of connection that you express in your dramas are the priority of your talking self and they feed your source self as well.

The agenda of wiser self is the fullest expression of your energetic nature. Its priority is to keep you connected. With a plant it is evident that if you sever a stalk from its root system or just pull the whole thing out of the ground, it will die, because a plant needs to be rooted. By the same token, you as a person, as an individual, need to be rooted in your larger or source self, because your energy comes from there.

Unifying Your Committee of Three

Your committee of three works together to create a unified Self. We compare it to making music. Your earth elemental self is your instrument and it needs care. If you leave an oboe out in the rain, you're not going to get very good music out of it the next day.

Talking self is the player or musician. She is the committee member who develops the skill on the instrument to play it expressively.

Your wiser self, your spirit, is the music. Without music to play, it would not matter how skillful your fingers were on the keys, nothing meaningful would come out of the instrument.

You truly need the contributions of each self. The experience of life on your earth requires this collaboration of three awarenesses.

Please note that we are talking about an equal collaboration. Your culture incorrectly sets up a hierarchy among your body, mind and spirit, promoting the spirit or soul as the most glorious, the mind as noble but a bit unruly,* and the body as the poor drudge or traitor who can never quite cooperate. This schema is not likely to inspire happy participation of the two so-called *lower selves*.

There is no rule that says talking self automatically knows how to get along with and work happily with earth elemental, nor that the two earth-focussed beings are in fruitful contact with the source self. Each self has free will and choice, within the parameters of its being, and a harmonious committee is for most people a learned skill. Sometimes you have internal tug-of-wars akin to sibling rivalry.

The committee is designed to work as follows:

Earth elemental, as we said, is your instrument. She is also your home base in this dimension of reality. Her job is to

---

* Some people would reverse this, demoting the soul, and seeing the mind as paramount.

embody, or manifest, the life force of all these selves. A certain amount of her time and energy is spent on just being a creature. She eats, digests and eliminates; she takes in energy, transforms it and sends it out again. She works with the forces of renewal and decay, within a limited physical context of time and space. It is her gift to the whole self, and it is necessary.

Her other job is to register, keep track of, and communicate the exchange of energies between the three committee members, and between you and others. What this means, in simple terms, is that both talking self and wiser self express themselves through this instrument. It is through the senses and mental capacities of earth elemental that you can know (in this life) your connections with other conscious beings.*

Earth elemental self is here in this earth reality full time; she is a creature of this reality.

Talking self, on the other hand, blinks in and out. Like Persephone in the Greek myth, she spends half of her hours here on earth, and half in other realms. While you are asleep, earth elemental self engages in the work of physical renewal and flow. Talking self takes off on adventures into other levels of consciousness, into dramas which are either practice for her later choices in this life or just dips into the ocean of possibility. She too engages in renewal and flow, but on her own terms.

Talking self visits the realm of wiser self more often than you might realize. Through flights of fancy, daydreams, moments of deeply centered listening, imaginative flashes, she experiences aspects of the wiser self reality. For that reality is created through perception and imagination, and exists most strongly on that level.

However, coded within the nature of talking self is a dependence on the physical manifest "reality" as a point of reference. She flies here and there, but has a strong need to return frequently to the earth elemental focus. If she doesn't, she soon experiences disintegration and what you call mental illness.

Talking self and earth elemental self have a crucial interdependence. Earth elemental provides the data, signals, and instruments of navigation; talking self interprets and tries to steer the ship.

How well do you hear the signals your body sends you? What kind of relationship does your mind enjoy

* All three selves use the mind and the intuitive senses, which are housed in the earth elemental instrument.

with your body? Many of our friends-in-body bombard
their earth elemental self with relentless contradictory
and critical messages: "I'm too fat, I want to eat, I'm
tired, I really want to go to that party...."
    Anxious to please, their earth elemental self careens
from one extreme to another, sending up louder and
louder messages of distress and confusion. Our friends
end up with exhausted bodies, disillusioned minds, and
lives that seem to be out of control.

Earth elemental is designed to be open to talking self's steering, but not totally dependent on it. She takes her ultimate guidance from wiser self, and also from protections (instincts) coded into her nature. Thus when talking self pursues a course that is dangerous to the body, earth elemental will send out frequent and increasingly insistent messages of warning. If you do not heed the warnings, then your ship founders, you lose power, or your wiser self activates energies to alter your course.

However, wiser self remembers that part of its purpose in creating you is to enable you to experience the struggle to coordinate these three frequencies of being. Thus it generally maintains a stance of noninterference. Your talking self and earth elemental selves are free to embroil themselves in any number of uncomfortable imbalances and impasses that cause emotional, mental or physical collapse. On the other hand, like a conductor with perfect pitch listening to an orchestra slipping out of tune, the wiser self will continue to sound the perfect note of your being again and again within you.

Each member of your committee possesses the ability to communicate, the desire to be in sync with the other two, and gifts and tools uniquely appropriate to make this collaboration thrive. We cannot tell you clearly and simply how to balance the needs and imperatives of these three beings. You must develop that skill yourself. However, the ideas we are presenting within this book may help you to recognize the workings (and shortcomings) of your particular committee.

In general we can tell you this: each committee member needs time and attention on a regular basis. Each day, each week, each month, each year, your body self needs time focussed on creature needs and creature comforts. She needs her rhythms recognized and honored. Your talking self needs time to explore and shift, to travel through the realms of possibility. She needs time for stimulation and release. And your wiser self needs time free of distraction to send its note resonating into your awareness. It requires time for contemplation, and for creative spiritual expression.

Three Densities

We do not wish to belabor this notion of three selves, but do you recognize the profound implications of your threefold nature? It means that "you" exist at three densities of reality. You exist not only as physical person, but as spirit (energy) and idea as well, and your yearnings will pull you in these three directions.

Imagine three zones, with abstract spirit at one end, and concrete reality at the other. Somewhere in between lies the zone of ideas and dreams. Your existence spans these three zones, and in fact your attention or consciousness continuously weaves from one to another. Picture the infinity symbol (a figure eight lying on its side) or a Möbius strip, spread along the three zones. This is a perfect glyph (symbolic representation) for the flow of your energy and your consciousness.

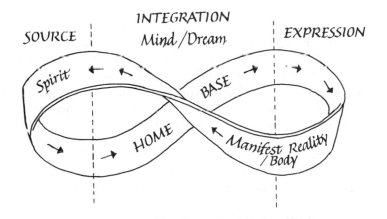

There you are. Something that has no beginning and has no end. As your consciousness dips down into the soul level, you bring up energy of your spirit. This energy enters your mind creating dreams, impulses, ideas and desires. These inspire projects in the manifest reality. Your experiences in your body nourish, ratify and enrich the powers of your mind, which then feeds this energy back to your source self in an ever-flowing cycle.

It is a rising up and falling back again, the rhythm and cycle of all life. So we want you to think of this, for a moment, and feel it. Feel this body that sits here as one of the dimensions of the infinity of yourself. Feel all those emotions and hopes and dreams and thoughts as crossroads, where the energy of your spirit is being clothed and fed, and where you are also giving meaning to the content of your material life. Feel at the other end of this continuous journey, the spirit pulsing at its own frequency.

Your travel along this Möbius strip is continuous, as we said; your life takes its meaning from this movement, this flow of energy. And the energy flows without your conscious guidance, just as the blood flows in your veins. So your task as a human being is not to get yourself moving but rather to become aware of the movement that exists, to recognize the ways you seek to block that flow, or hold on to one point or another in the journey.

You may feel more comfortable in one density or another. It is natural to have preferences. Where do you habitually park your awareness? You may prefer good solid hard fact, ethereal cosmic resonance, or the playful realm of imagination, as a kind of "home base" for your sense of self. Some athletes will center themselves in their physical density; some mystics may feel more alive in the realm of spirit; many people live most fully in their mind. We do not see this as a problem. Each of the individuals in your world will identify her or himself most fully at one of the points along this figure eight of wholeness. It may give you greater insight into the people you meet to try to recognize just what density of energy is their most comfortable home base.

Our reminder, though, is this: "reality" is the whole spectrum. Reality is the spirit, the idea, and the body, and, most important, reality is the flow of energy between these zones.

A scientifically demonstrable "fact" is not more real than a fervently held belief, or a deeply known personal truth. They are each real in their own realms, and gain power in their transformation from one to another.

Increase

When you are in the swimming pool, why is it harder to move quickly than when you are on dry land, but easier to float? Because of the nature of the element in which you find yourself. What is useful about understanding each of your selves is to understand the nature of their very different needs, priorities and desires, within the context of their very similar communications. When you feel hunger, is it your body, your mind or your spirit crying out for nourishment? Or all three?

When you understand these selves, then you are more effective as an integrated person. Each self offers you tools— the muscles, the will, the curiosity, the excitement and joy, the pure energy, the cultural and mental constructs—that allow you to move in your everyday reality. Together the three selves allow you to create what we call *increase*, which is the purpose of your being in body.

Increase is the alchemy that happens when you travel the Möbius strip of consciousness. The flow of energy from spirit to body and back again creates increase. Let us give you an analogy: in music, pure or ethereal sound may exist in some-one's mind, heard only by her, but there is something valuable in playing this music upon an instrument, making it heard in the world. In this life you are the music of your soul played upon an instrument. The playing of this instrument increases the value, the intensity, the expressiveness of your soul.

Two Kinds of Energy

☙

One of our dilemmas as teachers in your realm, is how to introduce highly abstract concepts in a way that will be of service to you in your everyday life. What we wish to do is to show you yourself, and the life you are living, through a kind of spectroscope. As you know, a color spectroscope takes light emanating from a single source and separates it into its diverse rays of color. Our purpose in singling out some of these individual concepts for you is to heighten your awareness that they exist. But it is also important to remember throughout the exercise that you are an integrated, complex being.

With that in mind, we wish to tell you this: you are working with two kinds of energy in this life. One is what we would call *source energy* or spirit energy. The other we call *renewable energy*.

Your source energy is basically your soul energy. You might refer to it as vitality. It's like a candle flame: you come in with a certain amount of wick available, you burn steadily forth, and when the essence is spent, your light goes out. Or, it is as if you were given a tune with a set amount of *resonance*. When you have used that resonance, whether or not you have finished the dramas created by your talking self, you fall silent.

If you think about the people you know, you will recognize their soul energy. It is basic to how someone is, regardless of the details of their life. You think, "Joan is just so alive. I don't know where she gets her vitality. Sandy on the other hand is kind of low key." Perceptive awareness of soul energy is part of your everyday vocabulary.

We have spoken earlier of the image of a gong sounding. Imagine that your birth into this life was the striking of a gong. The soul energy pulsing from you is the reverberation of this gong, and when it is silent, your life is spent. This resonance can be stifled, blocked or weakened far more easily than it can be strengthened. In fact what strengthens this type of sound best is to create stillness and silence around it, to provide an atmosphere in which it can resonate.

Your soul energy pulls you into self-expression. It impels

you to place yourself in certain situations which cause you to resonate and to seek like-spirited others whose reverberation somehow matches yours. The reverberation of a like-spirited other can act to strengthen the base note of your nature.

Soul energy burns whether you are doing one activity or five. It is supported not by quantity of living, but by quality of living. It requires a certain life pace and rhythm which varies from individual to individual. Many of you suffer because your basic soul pace is slower, or faster, than that encouraged in the community and society in which you are living. When the pace of your life style matches not some external imperative but the pace of your life-force energy, then you are most fulfilled, most expressive, and most alive.

You also have another kind of energy, what we call *renewable energy*. There's much talk now about renewable energy sources; it's about time the world has begun to pay attention to this concept. Renewable energy operates a little like money. You can deposit it in a bank account, save it, invest it, and spend it. This energy is created every time you take in nourishment. When you eat food, you are given energy from that food. When you receive loving from a friend, enjoy a beautiful sight, read a good book, play with ideas pleasing to the talking self, you can use that as fuel as well. The earth elemental self runs on the fuels of food and exercise and love. The talking self is fueled by mental and emotional stimulation of all sorts, by self-expression and recognition. And the wiser self is fueled by being heard, and by the fulfillment of talking and earth elemental selves.

Renewable energy is meant to be circulated. You can see what we mean most easily when you look at the use of food. You eat to provide your body with energy to burn and nutrients to maintain its functioning. When you have used that food, you must either eat again or dig into the reserves, the stored fat. If you overeat, then you store the extra. If you consistently take in more than you need, then you find yourself slowed down by excess fat, logy from blocked energy, and out of touch with the hunger signals that help to guide your circulation of energies. If you consistently undereat, you use up your stored fat and then start breaking down vital organs.

Thus you eat, sleep, move, rest, and continuously take in, transform, and expend energy. You do it on the physical, emotional, social, mental, and spiritual levels. The work of this life requires renewable energy to keep going. When you run out of it you tap into your soul energy to sustain you.

Soul energy is meant to be like the capital in your bank account. It gives you the wherewithal to get started in developing renewable resources. It is there as a safety net. You can call on it to finance some of your bigger, more important projects. Think of the person who dips into her inner reserves to finally leave a difficult relationship. Or the person who calls upon sheer willpower and force of character to finish a demanding task. These are occasions when it is appropriate to use some of your soul energy to fuel your everyday life.

But some of you have not yet learned to balance the ebb and flow of renewable energies. You have not learned to eat when you are hungry, sleep when you are tired, see people when you need companionship, isolate yourself when your being requires quiet. Some of you have not learned how to stop, or how to get yourself going without flooring the accelerator. And so you end up using and wasting your life force, your soul energy, to accomplish everyday transitions, to get through the business of everyday living. And by doing this you are shortening your life or impairing its quality.

Renewable energy is associated with hungers and satisfaction of the moment. Soul energy is associated with a deeper hunger, not so much for satisfaction of the moment, as for the correct placement, and configurations of work and relationships in your life.

Soul hunger is often satisfied by awareness. By meditation, a quiet walk in nature, the composition of a piece of music, the painting of a picture. You satisfy soul hunger when you return to the level of **being** *(and its expression). Renewable energy requires attention to your* **doing,** *it asks you to listen to the need of the moment (for food, rest, stimulation, interaction), and honor it.*

The two energies are designed to work together in you. Your soul energy is the metronome ticking out the rhythm that is truest to your being. It is the character emanating out of you. The renewable energy is the music that fills the measure. It is the breath that you take in to blow on the flute. With it you can syncopate and trill to your heart's content, within the context of the given rhythm. And when the breath is gone, another is required.

Someone might ask: "If I keep generating renewable energy can I live forever?" No, because a certain amount of basic soul energy resonates out of you, and expresses itself forth as the gong of your nature. The trick is not to work toward *quantity* of energy or life experience, but to recognize the healthiest *balance* for you in expressing your life force and nourishing yourself.

Juggling these two energies and the differing priorities of your three selves presents quite a challenge. You have lots of choices and decisions to make. But then that is your work in this life, exactly what you have come here to do.

Let us give you a view through our spectroscope at the beginning of a sample day, to show you the interplay of these three selves and two kinds of energies. At all moments there is integration, but one priority or another is highlighted.

As you lie in bed in the morning, hovering between sleep and waking, the mind is dreaming lightly. Your earth elemental self is renewing herself not only through rest, but also through the chemical action triggered by the dreams. These dreams serve in part to rebalance the earth elemental self. They are also, in part, an approximation—as best earth elemental mind can comprehend—of what talking self is off experiencing. For talking self is in the realm of the imagination, trying on identities, rehearsing probabilities, replaying scenes that have caught her fancy.*

The primary energy is the light flow of soul energy, moving in a quiet steady stream. Your body is also partly using renewable energy as it responds chemically to the dreams.

Then the alarm sounds, and with it your earth elemental self produces a burst of adrenaline to activate its awareness more fully. Talking self is hurtled back into her role in this life. She hits the ground running (on renewable resources), crowding the mind with all the plans and obligations of the day. But then earth elemental self catches her balance, and calms her racing pulses for a moment. The memory of the relaxation of sleep creeps in and, with it, awareness of the being that you are, of your soul energy emanating in quiet waves from you. There is a sense of well-being for the rest you have had and the time spent on soul fuel.

Then you are up and out of bed, your talking self renewing plans and practicing scenarios, your earth elemental trying to activate circulation in her limbs, perhaps the two of you

---

* Occasionally a dream is a wake up call from wiser self, but these dreams tend to carry a particular charged feeling to them—you *know* you have dreamed something significant.

negotiating over whether there will be morning exercises today. Talking self says, "I should do it, it's good for me," and earth elemental makes her resistance felt a bit: this pace is too quick for her. The quiet steady beat of soul energy is drowned out by the shifting and jostling of emotions, ideas and actions, all fueled by renewable resources.

Talking self embarks on the morning routine; earth elemental takes some inventory of her needs and seeks to announce them: more sleep, hunger, slower pace, quicker pace, sexual interaction, solitude, more stretching or exercise, cleansing from excesses imbibed the day before, thirst, and so on. Some earth elementals are skilled at communicating the entire range of needs. Others have been thwarted over the years in trying to make talking self understand. So the communication gets flattened and simplified to a binary code: hungry/not hungry; willing/resistant. The more difficulty earth elemental has in communicating her true needs, the more likely she is to dip into soul resources, to override the energetic buzz of talking self or just to soothe her own stress.

She may choose to overeat at breakfast, in order to stockpile energy she feels she might need later in her struggles with talking self. She may be unable to stomach food, though she technically needs it, because of jangled nerves. Then she is running on stored (renewable) energy, and eventually on force of will (the soul variety).

So finally, after a smooth or difficult interaction in which your committee of three selves has once again taken up the shifting and balancing of expression, and your body self has been either fortified by food and cooperation or tired by struggle and difficult communications, you are out the door and on your way to work.

Your day continues like this. There are moments of quiet and contemplation, when the gentle (or vigorous) emanation of soul energy is felt as a kind of centered well-being. There are also moments of disharmony, when the talking self has one idea of what ought to be done, and the earth elemental self has another need.

You find yourself pushing to finish a report before you take a break. You find your mind racing and unwilling to concentrate on the task at hand. You find your selves pulling you in two directions, perhaps your earth elemental self yearning for a walk in the park, while talking self strives to arrange a business luncheon.

Each of these moments draws first on renewable, stored resources, and then, as a back-up, on your deeper will and force of vitality. Most of you are balanced enough in your committee of three that the times of harmony occur frequently and renew you. Some of you are out of sync between your selves. You are so polarized from chronic lack of cooperation that your talking self insists that hard work is utterly necessary for survival, and your earth elemental stubbornly claims that nothing less than a full month of vacation will satisfy her.

Obviously this kind of standoff is best to avoid.

Your culture tends to demand of you more giving than receiving. Throughout the day, you are expected to expend energy intensely and with little pause. It is not a natural balance of energy for most of you to work two hours then rest five minutes. It is not natural for most of you to produce ideas, actions and interactions for nine hours a day, then hope to renew, replenish, and satisfy personal needs in the remaining four hours of waking time. Thus many of you operate under unnatural expectations and experience unnatural hungers because of them.

In response to this imbalance you may chronically overeat or undereat, smoke cigarettes, sleep too little or unrestfully, drink too many stimulants or depressants, use sugar to try to regulate your energy levels or assuage rough feelings. Do you see, as we shine our spectroscope on you, that the solution to the problems of excess (or deprivation) rests in rebalancing your three selves, and in learning to work more naturally with your energy resources and rhythms?

Your selves are all extremely flexible and capable of change. Your selves are also able to defer gratification, make bargains, take turns getting needs met, and are able to re-balance themselves, if left the space and permission to do so. Thus you may collapse when your vacation time arrives but then gradually, miraculously feel yourself being renewed.

Whenever the ebb and flow of renewable energies gets tangled in knots, we recommend that you fall back on your soul energy. Not to draw upon it, but simply to contact it. Return to that baseline, centered energy, and just listen to it for a time. Watch your breath moving in and out. That is the essence of much meditation practice. And it is your greatest source of renewal.

After a time of listening to your basic life vitality, you will be quietly but clearly guided to rebalance your renewable energy sources. You will hear within you the simple suggestions: Eat. Sleep. Read a good book. Go out into nature. Paint a picture. Write a poem. Call her up. Stay away from the phone today. Walk, don't drive. Skip work, just this once.

Your power in this life derives not from your ability to produce, but rather from your ability to balance the in-flow and out-flow of spirit. And at the root of this ability, your teacher, the breath, moves quietly in and out, automatically regulating and meeting your needs. Observe and listen to this teacher. It will lead you to great harmony.

The Web of Connection

When you look in a mirror what do you see? You probably see your body standing there, the clothes it is wearing, its posture. You may also be fortunate enough to see the spirit shining in your eyes, or in the glow of your skin, or in the organization of your features. Sometimes you may only see the so-called defects: the wrinkles, the love handles, the bulges and blemishes and irregularities.

But when we look at you we see something quite different: a multicolored, shimmering being. We see your many layers of expression, from the densest elements in your flesh, to the most ethereal essence of your spirit. We see constant continuous movement in the flow of your matter, vital fluids and body electricity, in the shifting pattern of your thoughts, dreams and perceptions, and in the booming pulsation of your basic nature.

You are not a solitary object standing there. Beautiful strands of energy, intention, ideas, love, emotion, expression, and life force emanate out of you in all directions, and lead into you as well. You are part of a vast shimmering web of connection that is always shifting, changing and exchanging forces. Every living being, every form of consciousness involved with the earth experience is part of this web.

Have you ever seen one of those marvelous paintings by Jackson Pollock, covered with paint that has been thrown, dribbled and spread willy-nilly across a huge canvas? This is a delightful representation of the web of connection, the webwork of energies. Out of its apparent randomness emerges something deeply ordered. It is not organized according to logic, but the longer you gaze the more your consciousness and perception will find or create order in it.

So when we look at you, we see a miraculous sight, irrespective of what you may have said to someone at the party yesterday, or whether you have paid your bills on time, or whether there are twenty pounds more or less encasing your belly. It is useful, we believe, for you to join us from time to time and see yourself in the mirror through *our* eyes.

You are connected, through no particular effort on your part, to the web of energy that flows between all life forms, and there is a constant communication travelling that web. You have within your make-up the ability to perceive what is happening anywhere within the web, and to process that information.

A lot of the processing that you do involves screening others out. Obviously if your conscious mind were taking in all the information from the energy web you would very quickly become overwhelmed and you would lose your sense of focus within yourself. Just as your ear sorts through thousands of sounds to select the voice of a person speaking to you, your screening device sorts through the energetic events on the planet and isolates those which are relevant to you.

So it is as if you have an energetic screening chamber around your body. Some of you have heard this referred to as a portion of the aura. We want to steer you away from what you might have read or understood about the aura, because it is far more fluid and complicated than the literature generally expresses.

In the outer area of your energetic field you have a screening matrix that actually picks up and screens energies from the life forms on the planet. It is what keeps you enmeshed with the life force; it is what keeps you a part of the whole.

The best image we can give you for how this works is a telephone wiring system. Although your house is wired for telephone, you are probably not being bothered by your telephone at this moment. But that doesn't mean that conversations are not being transmitted constantly on the telephone system as you sit there. They are. If you wanted to tune into those conversations, you could pick up your receiver, get the operator and say, "Hook me up to what's happening over there." The operator, if she had the permission (which in the cosmic sense she generally does), could hook you into conversations anywhere in the system.

The screening matrix allows the energies to flow where they need to flow, but does not bother you, the individual awareness, with every telephone call (or energetic exchange) that is happening. Thus you are connected, and you are protected.

If there is something happening that can affect you, or is not in your best interests, or is not within the plan of the wiser self, you might get a sudden emergency call saying pay attention. *You have probably heard stories of the sudden flash of intuition, the thought that seemed to come from nowhere, guiding someone to a safer path. Often that message is transmitted to your conscious mind from the protective matrix surrounding you.*

We have heard some concern among our spiritually-striving students about the effects of negative thoughts on others. If you are all connected through this energetic web, don't negative thoughts cause harm?

There is a filter in your matrix, with a certain kind of wisdom and compassion built into it, that protects both you and other people.

In order to send a message through the web of connection, you must first activate your intention. Otherwise, what goes out to others are your thought and feeling tones. Think about this for a moment. In most instances of negative thinking, you are actually just venting frustration, experiencing jealousy, reacting to your own anxiety. And what goes out toward others are the *feeling tones* of frustration, jealousy or anxiety, not the specific thought that is in your mind.

Occasionally, though, someone who is unbalanced in himself will consciously send negative thoughts and intentions through the web of awareness. In these cases, your screening matrix evaluates the energy and screens it for you. What you will receive depends on the danger involved. Usually, you will experience a slight discomfort, as a warning that there is some problem with the other person. You may find yourself thinking that the person "gives you the creeps." The creeps are in fact a message from your screening matrix.

You might think of this matrix as the place, energetically, where your wiser self encompasses you. You might find it useful to envision your screening matrix as a buffer zone between your personal energies and those which do not belong to you.

In addition to the intelligent screening this matrix provides you, it also acts as an overload buffer. When you are striving to gather too much information, or being bombarded with too much energy, it acts just like the circuit breaker on your electrical system. It interrupts the signals and temporarily shuts you down. You may experience this mentally as a kind of spaciness or blanking out, physically as either agitation or lethargy, emotionally as blockage, apathy or anger.

Your receiver for the energies of the web of connection is your earth elemental self. And that receiver must be kept in good condition. Have you ever experienced a telephone that scrambles sounds? Even if it is plugged into the wall, even if it is plugged into the network, the sounds it receives make no sense. It is similarly possible to have an earth elemental self who is so confused and sensually overloaded that she cannot tell which way is up.

We will refer repeatedly within this book to the care and feeding of your earth elemental self. It is a self which is infinitely adaptable: think of the contrasts between conditions for the earth elemental self of a stockbroker working in the Wall Street exchange, and the earth elemental self of a shepherd on the hills of Greece. The stresses and nourishment experienced by these two are vastly different. Earth elemental self is capable of surviving and thriving in both settings.

However, in any setting earth elemental self requires a *balance* of stimulation and expression. She or he needs a loving and positive relationship with talking self. She needs to be treated as something more than a storage tank or punching bag. She needs her communications affirmed by talking self and by others. As you may have guessed, earth elemental self receives and filters information in terms of her own safety and sanctity; only then can talking self interpret the messages for use in her projects and relationships.

We remind you that communications received by earth elemental self come mostly in the form of sensations and images. Imagine how overwhelming it can be for the earth elemental self who is bombarded in your culture by stimulation. Just as Pavlov's dog would salivate at the signal for food, your earth elemental responds to the sounds and pictures of danger, threat, challenge and cruelty flashed at you by your media. The resulting chemical and electrical impulses can jangle and

clog your perceptive pathways, unless they are cleared by exercise, sexual or emotional release, or artistic self-expression.

You might wish to take stock of how well your receiver is functioning. Is there static, muffling or scrambling going on?

Think for a moment about how your particular receiver developed in this life. In the first few years, your basic task was to develop the capacity of your instrument. You banged and bumped and tasted and threw everything you could get your hands on, and if all went well, thoroughly explored a large variety and range of sensations. You got used to feeling things through all the senses you possessed. You got used to using your emotions to move or communicate these sensations. And your budding talking self practiced naming and identifying your experience.

This is the ideal situation for the young earth elemental and talking selves. But some of you may have been restricted in getting your instrument going. You may have had your perceptions denied or negated:

"Mommy I'm hungry." "No you're not, go to sleep."

"Daddy I'm scared." "Be a little man."

Over time, the denial of perceptions causes earth elemental to do one of two things (or both). She either screams louder, with psychosomatic illnesses and feelings of constant threat or ill-being, or she shuts down, and produces yearnings for numbness and apathy. Neither of these reactions allows her to develop as an effective receiver (or sender).

Some of you developed a deeply sensitive ability to perceive energies and sensations, but the tensions in your environment were greater than the fledgling talking self was able to interpret. Thus the young earth elemental self carried and registered great stress, and the young talking self took responsibility for events she did not really cause or control. The interrelationship between your two selves was damaged and blocked.

This difficulty is most apparent in cases where there was overt violence, abuse or cruelty. But for some of you, your two earthbound selves suffered more subtle hindrances, which impair you today. An analogy might be: if you are by nature a "violin," and your parents were by nature "harmonicas," then they were probably not aware of all your needs as a violin. Thus they had much they could teach you about musicality, about performance, and about being an instrument in general, but you may have experienced great frustration in trying to be a harmonica like Mom and Dad, or in not having your "violin" nature recognized.

In the normal course of things, there is no harm in a person or energy choosing to enter your world through parents and a home setting which are vastly different from itself. In fact this can foster great compassion and understanding of differences. But there is a tendency in your culture to homogenize differences of temperament and nature, leading to a lack of awareness that each of you needs quite special and individualized education, appropriate to your gifts and truest nature. You can take over your education at this point, find other "violins" to help you grow clearer in both your perceptions and ability to express your unique selves.

We have traveled a bit afield in describing the web of connection. But in fact, your ability to benefit from your deepest membership and connections does rest squarely on the health of your receiver and the interpretations of your talking self. When you overload your receiver with substances that clog, dull or alter the senses, and when you tie up the talking self with restrictions, expectations or fixed ideas about how life should be, then neither is free to do her job clearly.

Thus the bottom line of a spiritual practice is your ability to allow a balance in the in-flow and out-flow of energies. It is not really a question of creating contact with your higher power or deeper connections. Within the web of connection, you are permanently and intrinsically in contact. But it is through balancing your energies that you are able to feel and benefit from your rootedness in this web.

Grounding

Grounding in the Web of Connection

Shut your eyes for a moment and picture yourself in the living room of an apartment. It's a large apartment building, so imagine apartments all around you. And imagine people in each of those apartments. Perhaps someone upstairs is diapering a baby. Someone three apartments over is looking at his record collection, trying to find just the right music to suit his mood. Perhaps you see him drumming with his hands because he's wanting something with a beat. There is someone over there, on the other side, sewing something. Someone else lies on the couch feeling very unhappy because she's overeaten and has a stomachache. Someone not far from them has invited her partner to go into the bedroom to have some fun.

There are people all around you. Some are worrying, some relaxed; some engaged in creative activities, some doing things they don't want to do; others are finally getting to do what they truly crave. Some of them are physically comfortable, some are in extreme distress. Feel all the different variations of being in this building and in the buildings around this one. Just feel what's there.

And then extend your awareness outward through the city. There's a whole city full of people doing almost everything you could imagine a person doing, and maybe even some things you can't quite imagine. They are thinking in hundreds of languages. Some are feeling and not working with words at all. And there are other life forms. There are animals, plants, and they are each expressing their being in unique ways.

There are repeats. There may be hundreds of people watching the same television show. But those people are each watching it somewhat differently, each interacting with the information, taking in different aspects of it, making different comments, enjoying different things.

Feel the diversity. Think about how each of those individuals out there is going to wake up tomorrow and do something very different from the person next to him or her. The people going to jobs are each going to different activities and moods. The children going to schools are each going to a different experience of school.

Now send your imagination farther, to picture the globe, as if you were an astronaut out in space, looking through a very powerful telescope, revealing millions of little people-dots all over the planet.

Think of each of those people-dots, each living lives. You can see movements, diverse activities, colors, intensities. Someone is out in the wilds herding cattle. Someone else is in an office building 127 stories high typing numbers into a computer. You see dots with different purposes, different goals, different activity levels, in different moments of living.

Know that each of those moments, each of those goals, each of those possibilities, each of those identities, is a choice for you. Or has been a choice in another life, or is accessible to you imaginatively, through your mind, or through art works. And know that each of those roles is shifting and changing in each moment, and that you can shift and change in and out of those patterns; you can make so many choices about where you want to fit in, and how you want to be. There's no single expectation. Let yourself bask for a while in the shimmering, moving exchange of energies, ideas, purposes and feelings you can imagine in this massive web of consciousness.

Your Multiple Nature

❧

You will not be surprised to hear that we believe in reincarnation. Our view of this phenomenon may differ somewhat from what you have read in some of the Eastern literature. In order to understand your multiple nature, your many lives, it is good to look at a plant, blossoming with leaves in many directions.

You have a wiser self that blossoms in many directions that are many lives, just like the leaves of that plant. Each life is an expression of the larger self. Each life draws nourishment into the whole Self, just as the leaves draw sunlight into the whole plant and feed its health. So you sitting right there are one life expression of your larger self.

Your larger self might be called an entity. As each life progresses on its own terms and with its own experiences, then the plant is enriched and grows and flourishes. Some plants grow to be very large bushes, and other plants are not designed for that; they only put out a few leaves and that is sufficient to their nature. So each of you does have multiple lives, or counterpart selves, whose experiences and energies can feed you just as the energies or experience of one leaf can feed another leaf through the connective tissues of the plant.

How does this work in terms of past or future lives? If you look at the plant, there are leaves growing consecutively up from the bottom to the top, but this is an arbitrary order

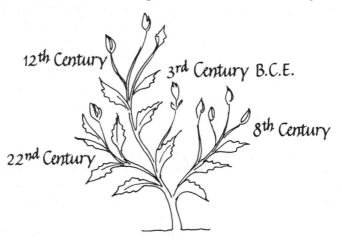

imposed by your perspective. The leaves in fact spring out in all directions. If you think of one leaf springing here, another there, and a third over there, then "here" might be the twelfth century, "there" might be the eighth century, and "over there" might be the third century, B.C.E. Although time is consecutive to you in your reality, from the point of view of the entity self, which is a multi-dimensional creature, time is an abstract location.

Consciousness is not consecutive in time. Yet when a plant unfurls, there is a certain order to the unfurling, and by the same token certain lives are *before* certain other lives in the energetic unfolding of the whole being. However, this "before" does not necessarily correlate with the time line. In other words, this life you are in now may actually, in terms of the unfoldment of the whole entity, be "earlier" than a life unfolding in the eighth century. We fear we are getting too abstract.

If you sit and meditate, try to look at a plant and understand its being; it might help you to understand the nature of multi-dimensionality in life forms. Your mind is so keyed into the notion of time, that it is very hard for many of you to step out of that framework.

Karma

We do not support the notion of spiritual evolution that says you improve from one life to the next, and therefore rich and happy people are somehow more evolved than poor and suffering ones. We also object to the notion that human beings are higher or more evolved than plants and animals. That is like saying a leaf is more evolved than a flower, which is somehow higher than a fruit or seed. Each life form is an expression of consciousness and serves its own purpose. You do not progress from one form to another; instead your being springs marvelously in all directions at once, encompassing a range and variety of life forms.

Just as you are one part of your entity self, there are other portions of the entity that are experiencing life as dogs, whales, insects, plants, rocks and even sub-atomic particles that make up what you think of as objects.

So where does that leave the theory of karma? There are two ways the law of karma operates. First is within a single life.

It is, simply stated, the law of cause and effect. If you plant cau-liflower seeds in your garden, then you are likely to get cauli-flower in the growing season. If you do something cruel to another human being, then that action will yield some kind of return. Perhaps the return will not come from the same indi-vidual, nor will it be an identical action. But whatever you put out returns to you threefold, it is the nature of energy travel-ing along the web of connection. If you put out an act of kind-ness, then the warmth of your intention will return to you threefold over time.

The second form of karma is what we would call the law of balance, or poetic justice. The entity self sends shoots out in many directions, that then spring forth with multiple leaves. Thus you might have a clump of lifetimes that deal with issues of loss and gain. Another clump of lifetimes might explore the realm of spirituality and religion. A third clump might be focussed on earth-bound experiences or mothering. Your enti-ty has many clumps of lifetimes, all of which are past or future lives. Some people prefer to think of the other leaves on the plant as counterpart selves, since *Self* for them is their identity in this life.

The law of Karma is the desire of the entity self to explore experience in its fullness. Thus if you have a lifetime where you experience great suffering, you can be certain that your entity has also created a life of comfort. If you have a lifetime where you are a saint, then the entity has also created a lifetime where you act dishonestly or hold slippery values. The balance is not always in terms of opposites, but rather spans a range of times and places and dramas in which your entity can explore the energies that interest it.

When you are feeling a need for strength, you can call for help from your past or counterpart selves. Since the talking selves all travel in and out of their particular reality, they are mostly capable of meeting with you in their (or your) dreams. Thus you have a bank of experience to draw on. The affirma-tion of self you do in this life will benefit your counterpart selves, as their affirmations benefit you. When you understand the law of Karma you can more easily develop humility: you are both criminal and cop, both parent and child, both liberal and conservative in some part of your being.

The law of Karma is the law of compassion. It teaches you consciousness of the effect of your actions, and that you are one with all of creation.

Past Lives

There is quite a bit of interest at this time in past life memories. The search to remember your past lives is the search for wholeness, for a greater familiarity with your entity self. So what you are looking for is not further credentials to put on your résumé ("I was once the Czar of Russia"), but rather insight into which energies your entity is exploring, and how those energies affect the dramas and aspirations you are creating in this life.

We are frequently asked questions pertaining to past lives: Does my interest in this person come from a past life? Are his feelings for me caused by something I did to him in a past life? In general, past life information is only useful as an illustration of energies that are here now, in this life. In other words, he doesn't hate you because of a past life. He hates you because he hates you, which is a theme you must both deal with in this life. But there may have been other lives where you and your friend have danced the dance of love and hatred in another configuration. Remembering that dance may give you insight into the dances you are dancing now. But the link is not causal, it is associative.

Soul Mates and Kindred Spirits

Your entity tends to travel in groups with other entities, like a touring improvisational troupe. Thus it is very likely that you have known most of the people you know in this life in other lives. It is from the multiplicity of roles and relationships that depth of experience is gained. It is from interacting again and again with the same beings that the tissue of your awareness is woven. You have known some of the people around you better than others. That is irrelevant. What is deeply relevant, is the interplay of energies in this life, and how they nourish you.

What is a soul mate? A soul mate is someone with whom you have a deep bond at the entity level. In other words, your entity and her entity are close friends, beloved. It is not merely a sexual bond, which you may or may not feel with the person; it is an energetic bond. But there is a misconception about soul mates. Some of our students have sought the mystical partner who is their *other half*, the one true love who will complete them. A soul mate is not your other half, she is someone who resonates deeply with you. You will have several soul mates incarnate on the planet during this lifetime, and chances are good you will encounter them; your wiser self tends to congregate with friends, even as you do.

The search for a soul mate is emblematic of a greater search you are engaged in, for kindred spirits. Like energy attracts like in the universe, and so you are drawn to and seek people who somehow have a similar sensibility, or outlook, or energy. This yearning is coded into your nature, which seeks unity with the whole, even as you are designed also to create a separate Self.

Imagine that your being resonates at a certain pitch on the musical scale, such as A-sharp. Then whenever you are around other people who resonate at that pitch, you are going to feel a certain strength and acceleration of your being. This can be a renewing and reaffirming experience. Here is someone who is truly a kindred spirit!

On the other hand, it can also be threatening to meet someone who resonates at the same pitch as you. Suddenly the sharp boundaries are no longer clear, the urge to be unique kicks in, and you may find yourself feeling hostile to this person who is so much like you. You may find yourself torn between attraction and repulsion.

If we extend the analogy of the musical note, then each individual resonates at her own pitch. And when you find yourself in close proximity with another person, you are going to be sensitive to the harmony or dissonance created by your two notes together. You may find some intervals desirable, others undesirable. It is a matter of personal preference. It is often the *basic note* of a person to which you are attracted first, before personality or ideas. Thus it is useful to recognize your habitual preferences.

It is also useful to recognize whether you are more drawn to harmony or dissonance. Some of you are natural harmonizers. You love to put things back where they belong, finish sentences, and make sure everyone is happy. You tend to be attracted to people who feel easy to know and get along with. On the other hand some of you are natural dis-harmonizers. You love to make (creative) messes, start new sentences, and make sure everyone is challenged or stimulated. You may well find yourself repeatedly in relationships with people who are difficult to get along with. This is not failure on your part; you thrive on the challenge of it.

We do not intend to split the world into two camps. Rather we suggest that you explore your own comfort point with harmony and dissonance. Play around on the piano to find the note that you feel instinctively represents your energy most clearly. See if you can hear the basic notes of your friends: what do the intervals sound like, when you play their note with yours on the piano?

Councils

❧

Since like energies attract each other in the universe, we entities form bonds and join together, just as you do with your friends. We call ourselves a council of entities, and describe ourselves as teachers and travelers: a metaphoric description of our basic energy.

When you look at fire, you can see yellow flame, blue flame, green, orange, red and other-hued flames, each burning at a different heat or magnitude. Entities, being energetic beings, "live" at different magnitudes of energy, like the flames. Thus you might describe one council as a "blue flame council," another as a "red flame council," and so on.

However, we find it is more useful to describe the various councils through metaphors, because *metaphors are the closest your minds have come to imaging the energetic universe.* There are councils of "web weavers," those who come most alive when they are making connections and weaving webs of connection. There are "tenders of the garden," entities who love to nurture growing things. There are "planters of the seed," who are different from the tenders of the garden. They are beings interested in initiating projects or ideas. There are the "turners of the page," interested in the unfolding of events and issues of historical consistency. There are the "pure math," "pure music," and "pure sound" councils drawn very much to work on levels you consider abstract. There are the "jokers," the "dancers," the "healers," and the "astronomers." We could go on and on: there are as many councils as there are metaphors.

Ellen's entity self belongs to three different councils. Your entity, too, will belong to anywhere from one to seven councils (more than five is rare). Each entity member of a council belongs to other councils as well, according to its deepest interests and energy. Thus a network of energetic exploration is created that underlies your reality.

Think for a moment about your networks of connection. You have your family, circle of friends, work colleagues, and other affiliations. Those individuals each have their connections, some overlapping, and others quite unique. But a web of acquaintance, friendship and exchange is created that is quite amazing.

Did you ever hear of the psychological study that was done quite some time ago, in which a letter addressed to a person on the west coast of America was handed to someone on the east coast who didn't know the addressee? They were instructed to "send this to someone who might know this person." In several cases it took only three or four people for the letter to find its way home.

Your networks of connection are reflective of the ways in which we organize ourselves.

One of the advantages of this organization is that your wiser self has access to support and resources beyond its own individual flowerings. Not only do you benefit from your past and counterpart lives, but you also have a number of soul mates in the universe, whose interests closely resemble yours. While your councils serve as guides to you, we must also emphasize that you are a member of your councils, not a supplicant. And your council has its council of deeper resonance helping to guide its unfoldment.

This arrangement is not a hierarchy of dominance or rulership; it is a description of *locations* of beings and entities within the divine energetic whole.

Recognizing your councils and naming their energies is a matter of tuning into the strands of energy that feed you most strongly. You can ask your councils to send you images representing their (and your) nature. Your council energies will be those expressions of life force that occupy you most fully.

Are you a teacher, a healer, a singer, a poet, a seamstress, a nurturer, an initiator, a completer, a support person, a bridge builder, a leader, a questioner, a challenger, a celebrator, a mourner, a visionary, a wanderer, a pragmatist, a delver, a surface skimmer? Make a list of as many nouns and adjectives you can think of to describe your energy and sensibility. Those that ring most clearly and strongly are probably clues to your council energy.

You are all multidimensional creatures, as are we. We are not suggesting that you limit yourself or that you are limited to the energies you identify as truest for you. We just say that it is useful to know what fibers you are made up of. What are your primary colors? What is it that is most awakened, or most awakens you? Knowing these things will help you to make life choices that are truer to your nature.

Many years ago a fellow came to us, saying he was very unhappy because he didn't know what he wanted to do with his life. He had tried over forty different jobs and had many more ideas he could try, but he wanted to know what was "most correct" for him. He said, "Tell me what I am supposed to do when I grow up." He was about 45 years old at the time.

Of course we recognized him. His entity was part of a council that we had met before, called the "troubleshooters," because they are beautiful wandering spirits who step in when needed with a little bit of extra help, love, or energy. They participate in projects as they come up, according to their interests of the moment.

Another metaphor to describe this fellow's energy is "tinkerer." He is happiest and most fulfilled when he is doing a little of this and a little of that. Forty years of steady work at the post office might kill him. His whole purpose is to change and dabble and explore opportunities, troubleshooting as he goes.

When we explained to this fellow that he was a tinkerer and had been on his path the whole time, and that he was doing a splendid job, his entire being lit up. He said triumphantly, "Then my mother's wrong!" His mother wanted him to get a Ph.D. and a steady career, because he was so bright. Not able to recognize the value in his nature and celebrate it, he was tearing himself apart trying to be something he wasn't.

He eventually found a job for himself as a jack-of-all trades, where his agreement with his employers included continuous changes. He held that job longer than any other job in his life, because he was able to truly express his nature.

Your councils have multiple projects in the universe, mostly having to do with the energies at their core. We have the project to teach you, to train individuals like Ellen, and to plant the seeds of our understanding within your conscious minds. We have many other projects as well. We invite you to appreciate that your council, too, is busy making multiple contributions, and that you are a valued part of that energy expressing itself across many dimensions.

Life Purpose

ৡ

The most frequent questions we are asked by people have to do with life purpose: "What is my purpose?" "What am I doing here on the planet?" "What is my mission?" We have a short answer and a long answer to that. Our short answer is: your purpose is to be alive. To be as fully alive, as fully expressive of your inner resonance as possible. And if you complete that achievement, if you write that book, if you build that organization, if you make that social change, it's really wonderful that you're able to put out that leaf and that branch. But even if you don't, you are still vibrating your life force, you are still part of what sustains the planet.

Your contribution is there whether you see the external manifestations of it or not. You are part of the energetic web of *being*, which means that your contribution, at its root, is through your very nature. The *doings* are meant to be extensions or expression of that being.

Thus our short answer is: you breathe, you are, you exist. Come back to what is simple and basic. You each came here to be here: on the planet, in this time frame, in this body, with these cultural tools and potentials. Because you are here as a being, you can make choices about doing.

Our long answer has to do with the follow-up questions we get.

"But didn't you say we each have an energetic truth that relates to our purpose in life?"

Yes you do. If you imagine the web of connection as being woven of many different strands, multicolored and multitextured, then of course you came here with a purpose that relates to the kind of energy you are.

Some of you came in to be messengers, some of you came in to increase the aesthetic beauty on the planet, others of you came to make connections, to fertilize the planet with children, to organize the shared reality of forms, to work with abstract thought forms…. You all came with your own energetic truth and will find yourself drawn to certain activities or goals.

But we wish to differentiate a bit between mission and purpose. When we say you have a purpose, it is an inner need to realize your energy in some way. You can realize your inner need to teach, for example, by showing a child how to bake cookies, or by working at a school for international relations. You can realize your purpose in a million small ways as well as through a single grandiose project.

A mission is an external goal. "My mission is to save the ecology of the planet." This easily becomes focussed on outcomes and achievements: "I can only fulfill my mission if I get an advanced degree, develop political pull, and learn to manipulate large corporations." What gets lost in the formulation of mission is your personal human needs, your multidimensional self. If you are here to work with ecology and balance, then this goal is something to explore and pursue on many levels, not to use as a whip with which to beat yourself, or as a test of your worthiness and value.

But the best way to avoid that self-flagellation is to not push yourself to find a life mission, or even a life purpose. Keep it simple: think in terms of expressing your values and listening to your predilections.

"How do we find our purpose and not get confused by a momentary wish or something that the socialized mind throws up as an answer to that question?"

When you listen to your needs of the moment, when you listen to your energy and are true to that, you will automatically be living your purpose. You will automatically be guided to follow the path that is truest to express yourself. You will have achieved that purpose because you are drawn to the things that you need; you automatically put out the energy that is true for you and call in similar energies.

But it is true that your mind is strongly socialized. You have a whole internalized list of things that a good person should do and be. It starts with how a good person should look and act. This expectation does a lot of damage to most of you as you are growing up. Think of how children learn to taunt those who are different, to reject those who are slower or faster in school, fatter or thinner than the norm.

Yet each of you is designed to be different. It would be a very boring world that specified that all trees must look a certain way, and have certain dimensions. It would be a sad world that did not accept as good those trees that did not fall into narrow guidelines. You would not do that to a house plant or an animal. You would not go to the zoo and look at a polar bear and say "Why isn't that polar bear the same size as a snake?" Because a polar bear is a polar bear and a snake is a snake and you accept that. So within your culture, there are lots of pressures to conform, to be uniform, the same. But in fact you are all wonderfully diverse, wonderfully different.

You are special, and you get to do that thing, or those things which are most special to your nature. But you need to start small, with doing what you need and want within one moment. If you are waiting for someone to come along and give you permission to fulfill your life dream, then you miss those individual moments that are a part of that dream. You miss the small moments of fulfillment that add up to a fulfilling whole. And while some of you may be handed permissions to do what you truly want to do, many of you will need to give yourself permission, because only you can decide what has value to you as a pursuit, only you can honor your own potentials.

If you think in terms of your values, and living according to them, then you can ask yourself, "What can I do today that expresses my values?" Your baseline values are to be creative, to be alive as a creature, to recognize and celebrate your connections with other people, to enjoy your selves, to be as expressive as you can. These are values coded into your nature, whatever personality or life story you have developed. If you listen to them, you have splendid criteria for planning your days and weeks.

So we are recommending that you seek out and live experiences that feel right for you in the moment. And periodically, especially when you are older, or on your deathbed, you can look back and say: "What was the pattern I created by doing that?" That will give you clarity on your larger purpose.

We encourage you to be daring and creative. If your truth for now is a desire to go into the woods and be alone for a year, then we suggest you find a way to honor that desire, if only in a small way. Too often we see you trapped in the *whole package* of your life. You get so caught up in the obligations to other people, fulfilling prerequisites, living a certain lifestyle, and sustaining consistency in your career, that there is no room to listen to your needs and desires of the moment. But it is through these needs and desires that you are given the next guidance on your path by your larger self.

As you strive to identify goals for living, there is always a need for balance between the abstract and the concrete, the large scale and the immediate, between the practical and the ideal.

"If we know we have the instrument, and we are the musician, why should events come along, seemingly outside of ourselves, that frustrate us and keep us from playing the music we want to play?"

You have been taught a misconception that plagues you, which is that the Self is a noun, and you are creating a work of art that is somehow an object. But you are not an object. You are a set of energies interacting, and life is a dance. As you get into the rhythm of it, it is not hard at all. When you are out of the rhythm, it becomes very difficult.

When you are dancing and you hurt your ankle, then you need to stop and rest that ankle, or you will dance with great discomfort. If you are thinking you are in one dance, but in fact are in another, then you will be dancing out of step. So often what seems like blockage is because one of your selves, usually your talking self, is interpreting the events or inner need incorrectly and is trying to do the wrong dance to the music.

Most of the true difficulty in life comes from being out of sync or out of balance.

It is really a splendid endeavor, this being human. And it takes a lot of skill and practice. You are not just doing it in order to gain expertise however; you are also doing it for enjoyment. That has to be one of your regular criteria, so that at any given moment you can say, "I'm really here to live. I don't care what my résumé says when I die, but I do care that I feel alive in any given moment."

Then you can start to free yourself from some of the social pressures that hem you in. You can start to see the events that come to you as little dramas, and you can be like the actor who throws herself into a play and says, "Now I am this role and I will play it, but when the play is done I will come back to myself, to my own identity."

The more flexibility you have to go into a moment or an experience on its own terms, the less difficult it becomes. Most events do offer many options for dropping out, for resting, for doing things a different way, for changing your goals or expectations so that the event becomes very manageable.

"It is funny you chose that analogy of being a dancer, because that is precisely what I always wanted to

be in life. A dancer. But every time I got an opportunity
to dance, I had to quit and earn money. I couldn't get
free to be who I wanted to be."

We do not wish to minimize the pressures many of you
face because of money. Your culture pays wages more readily
for some activities than others. However, the opportunities to
realize your inner truth in some way are there for you. What
most often blocks you is one of three things: an all-or-nothing
attitude, obligations to support and take care of other people,
or fear.

The all-or-nothing attitude takes many forms. You can get
stuck because although you are a dancer, you are not getting
famous quickly enough. Or you can dance several hours each
day, but your pride is hurt by having to teach others. You can
feel that it is not enough to enjoy the activity, you must have
recognition from others in order to feel valid as a dancer. You
may not enjoy dance at all; it may be the *idea* of dancing which
pleases you, and so you continually find reasons why the
opportunity to dance isn't good enough.

Your obligations to others may throw you chronically out
of balance, so that you cannot really achieve your heart's
desire. You may be raising children, caring for needy relatives
or friends. You may be hooked into a partner's demands of you,
or someone else's crises that drain and exhaust you. You may
be so busy helping others with favors and good samaritan acts
that you are just too tired to put on the music and dance.

There is a fine distinction between obligation and responsibility. Obligation is what you owe someone. In truth, your
only obligation is to take care of your health and spiritual well-
being, so you have something to share with others. It is helpful to no one if you allow others to devour your time and energy, or if you devour theirs with your needs. Even children,
except for their first few months, do not require your full time
and energy.

So if you find yourself unable to preserve even half an
hour a day to try activities you would like to try, then your life
is tied up in a knot which needs to be untied. It is generally useful to seek professional help in untying such tangles.

True responsibility is not obligation. It is the ability to
respond genuinely and from the heart to people and situations.
Thus true responsibility comes out of personal balance and fulfillment.

If at the very least you dance for half an hour a day, and start to let in the joy that you have craved, then that enriches your whole life. You no longer carry the resentment and bitterness that, "I was not allowed to be a dancer." Anger, resentment and bitterness block up energy that could be used to celebrate what is.

We will address fear later in this book, because it is a large topic. Let us just say here that fear is almost always a reaction to your expectations. The looser you are in setting up expectations of yourself, the less likely you are to be blocked by fear. There will be room to feel it, work with it, and pass on through.

If you want to dance, put on some music and dance. Put on some music and let your body move. If that activity feeds you—not the idea of being a dancer, but the activity of moving—then you will be guided to a next step. You may be drawn to say, "This makes me feel great. I feel able to do it again tomorrow." And tomorrow, if and when you feel that urge, you dance again. As you dance, you become the dancer. You build the muscles, the interest, the momentum to dance.

Since your culture only pays money for certain activities at certain levels, you may or may not become a professional dancer. So if you hold on to that as the only true expression of your desire to dance, then you may suffer disappointment and feel thwarted. But we remind you, your profession is not necessarily the sum total of your spirit's work. We also remind you that the essence of your love for movement and dance may be expressed in a variety of ways.

You may find paid work that embodies some aspect of your desire: you may get a job that is physical, allowing you the joy of using your body all day long. You may find work that enables you to teach others to move and awaken to the dance within them. You may use your technical knowledge of the body to heal people. You may choose to take up something like flying or driving for a living, to express your love of movement.

It is never too late to do something you wish, if you can recognize the essence of your desire. If you pursue the essence, then the forms will eventually fall into place.

"You talk about purpose in terms of inner unfoldment. Do we ever reach nirvana, or is it an eternal process of evolution?"

Nirvana is a state of utter attunement and resonance to your being. You can reach nirvana at every stage of the process. There is nirvana in the moment of tasting the peach, and there is also nirvana in the moment of recognition of an abstract concept that sets your spirit resonating. So it is not an evolution toward an arrival where you will be a certain kind of being. You flash in and out of nirvana, throughout this and all your lifetimes.

What we suggest to you is that you practice nirvana in a second, because a second of achieving this liberation is a lot easier than a continuous state of nirvana. Yes it is possible to experience nirvana in every second. What is not possible is to achieve liberation by denying the present. You can never experience nirvana if you cannot be present in the moment, for the moment is the doorway to nirvana. The present sensation is the doorway to all knowing and all awareness.

The Dance of Self

Grounding

Making Contact with your Infant Self

Shut your eyes and get comfortable wherever you are sitting. Feel free to squirm around until you find the best position for yourself. Shift and re-shift your weight as you would like. And take a deep breath. As you release it, let go of tension. Often if you make a sound with your out-breath it helps release stress. Wait before you take the new breath in. Then take a new breath. Hold that breath for just a second, then release again and rest emp-ty. When you feel the need to bring the breath back in, start your in-breath.

Your breathing is such a wonderful key to what your mind is doing, where and how your energy is moving within your body. You might find yourself holding your breath, barely breathing at all, or panting with no pause between breaths. Perhaps you take a lot in and don't let it all out.

Without trying to control your breathing any further, just let it settle into a normal pattern, whatever normal is for you right now. You may find that you need a lot less air than you think you do, or that you need more than you generally take. When you sit and observe your breathing, without trying to control it, it gives your mind something to do that is right here present and immediate. It quiets the mind.

Now we would like you to imagine that someone has just handed you an infant and you are holding her or him in your arms. Take a moment to explore how you feel holding this child. In your mind's eye examine this bundle. What is she like? What is she doing? Notice your own reactions. You do not have to judge them; just notice if you are comfortable. If you feel anger, delight, longing, notice your response. Continue to hold the infant.

And now, imagine that this infant is actually yourself as an infant. You do not need to change her to fit your memories or the stories your parents have told you about your early days. Just imagine that you are holding your young self there. What would you like to give to this small being? What are your feelings toward her?

What would you like for this child when she grows up? If you can feel love for her, take a moment to love her. If you don't feel love, just notice what your feeling is, and continue to hold the infant, even if it is not an entirely comfortable experience for you.

If you wish, call in an imaginary childcare helper. Call in some expert who will protect this child and provide for all its needs. Ask the helper to stay with the child as she grows, to guide her, to hold her when she is hurt or needy.

Then, placing the infant in a cuddlepack against your breast, if that is comfortable, or gently setting her in a cradle in your mind's eye, return your awareness to your room and open your eyes.

The Dance of Self

ℰ

Imagine you are on a balcony, looking down upon a wonderful old-fashioned dance hall. Hundreds of colorfully dressed people weave in and out, forming lines, circles, squares, all moving in time to the music. Individual dancers come together and move apart again to the underlying beat of the bass notes and the thump of shoes on the floor. The joy, enthusiasm and energy of the dancers rise to draw you in.

The web of life all about you pulls you in with its colors, rhythms and patterns. Each of you has a different response to this celebration. Some of you wade right in, dancing energetically until you drop. Others try to control the dance, sending constant signals to the band and your fellow dancers in an effort to alter the pace. We know that some of you get stuck on the balcony, agonizing about your inadequacies and insecurities. Sometimes you fear you will be a perpetual outsider, looking in on the moving kaleidoscope of celebration that is your reality. But this is not true, for you are a splendid dancer, with the opportunity to contribute to the larger pattern in all that you do.

However, if you wish to enjoy this dance, it is useful to understand the dancer. When you are conscious of your three selves, and of the unified Self they are creating, you have more basis for choosing your steps and working within the rhythms of co-creation.

The Dancer

If all life forms are connected, in what ways are you separate? What is a Self? The most discreet sense of *me* you will feel is in your body. This package of flesh, filled with circulating fluids, bones, and miles of electrical nerve circuitry, is somehow different from the body of the chair you sit on, the substance of air around you, the Self of the dog that lies snoring at your feet.

Yet when you examine that package with microscopic vision, you see that you are composed of moving atoms, like the dog and the chair. There is a constant exchange of energy particles between you and that supposedly separate environment. You see the air which gives you life moving in and out of other life forms as well. You see the interplay of chemicals, of energetic waves, of consciousness between the *you* and *not you*.

But even if the borders are fuzzy, you still have a discrete physical sense of Self which you must maintain in order to stay healthy and alive. If you ignore those physical limits you will soon find yourself crashing into walls. Your earth elemental self has an immune system to protect its sanctity. If your immune system fails to distinguish between *you* and *not you*, your body quickly succumbs to illness and decay.

You probably recognize that your body is not really the only container for *you*, even though it is your instrument of expression. You also exist in the thoughts and perceptions of other people. You are also able to communicate your personality and emotions through other instruments, like the telephone or the written word. You are a composite, a film comprising millions of frames of experience and perception. You are a bundle of understandings and feelings.

Even though these abstract aspects of you are shifting and changing, your talking self also maintains a fuzzy but discrete sense of self, and distinguishes it from the not-self. We have appropriated the term "ego" from your common language to refer to this miraculous mechanism: your ego is your instrument for creating a distinct Self.

Talking self has its own form of immune system, a mechanism which we call the gatekeeper. Your gatekeeper helps you mediate between your Self and your environment. It gives you constant messages of attraction, aversion and alarm, to help you evaluate the energies you encounter. Without a gatekeeper your talking self would have no protection: you would experience the emotional or mental equivalent of an allergic reaction.

Thus the dancer is a creation of your three selves, held together by the ego, protected by the gatekeeper. Using the ego and gatekeeper, your three selves organize all the history, sensation, perception and living which you experience in this life into a somewhat unified identity.

The Dance

In this human dance the themes of separation and connection underlie all that you do.

You come into the earth reality and you separate somewhat from your wiser self, from your focus within the divine. You put blinders on your understanding which keep you focussed here in time and space. You may have blinders set at a wider angle, so you have great curiosity about your past lives and larger connections. You may, on the other hand, have tighter blinders designed to limit your perceptions and interests to the here and now of this life.

You will feel within you oppositional pulls: to connect with others and to realize a separate Self. To explore and attend to the events and activities of your world, and to return your awareness to your own integration with the source of life.

As you strive outward to connect with others, you form an energetic root system—air roots—with them. The love, interactions, exchange of ideas, shared creation of events, and sense of membership you have with other people and creatures nourish you.

But that nourishment isn't enough. You also require insights, renewal, and self-love. You require a regular connection inward to your center, paying attention to the integration of your three selves.

Consider the implications of what we are saying. Finding satisfaction in your life is like trying to hit a moving target. One moment your goal and need may be to make love with another, but not long after that the need and impulse will shift so that you crave your separateness and individuality again. One moment you may be engrossed in solving an intriguing problem at work, and yet some time later work will fail to satisfy you, you will need contemplation and quiet down-time.

We are giving you a key to use in exploring the question: "How do I find fulfillment in this life?" You find it not by seeking or having the perfect relationship, the perfect job, the perfect home, enough money, a certain identity. You find fulfillment by learning to dance, by recognizing which direction you are being pulled, and by honoring that in some immediate way. Happiness rests in your ability to move in time to the music.

When you learn to experience greater connection, with yourself and with others, and when you learn to work with the energies available to you, you are living most authentically. Each authentic moment awakens you to your larger potential. You remember more of your spirit connection; your blinders open wider to let in more light.

It is a lifetime practice to learn to nurture your separateness and your power to make satisfying connections. The more you dance this dance, the more insight, energy, and compassion you will feel for yourself and others. You will recognize those practices that disconnect you from yourself, cut one person off from another, prevent exchange in groups or communities, and clog the perceptions and perpetuate pain. You will see ways to heal yourself and others.

It is a profound gift to the planet each time you make an authentic connection and recognize it. It is a profound gift to humanity each time you perform the dance of Self with awareness and care.

Ego

The ego has a bad reputation among some spiritual seekers. They say a good person should strive to get rid of her ego, judging ego concerns to be less important than spiritual concerns. But we believe your ego is absolutely necessary and is one of your great gifts. It is an amazing mechanism which unifies your three selves into a composite self-awareness. Ego concerns are spiritual concerns too.

Imagine yourself for a moment surrounded by a large membrane or sack, like a fetal chick is surrounded by the egg. But this ego membrane is not rigid and fixed like egg shell. It is more like a balloon. It holds the air of your spirit, giving it shape and definition, yet it is pliable and responsive to inner and outer energies.

A healthy ego is flexible yet strong. It gathers up all the energies of your three selves into an integrated sense of Self, and holds steady through all the mutations and fluctuations of your consciousness. When your talking self is blinking in and out of this reality, the ego holds its identity, blind in a way to your temporary absences. The ego integrates past, present and future for you, blending your actual physical reality with your imagined potential and hopes.

When you awaken each morning, your ego is there, retaining the memory of who you are and how you are, sustaining all that your three selves have decided are part of the "I" you are creating. When you are sick, or unable to function, the ego holds onto your larger reality, so you don't get lost in present circumstances.

The healthy ego operates a little like a hot air balloon. It is responsive to the flame of your being. When that flame flares forth with expressive energy, the ego expands with natural pride and courage, allowing you to soar up into the realms of new experience and expression. When the flame of self is receding, through lack of nourishment, then the ego contracts, cools its ardor, and brings you gently closer to the earth and your grounding in physical reality.

In its healthy state, the ego establishes the boundaries of self that are guarded and protected by your gatekeeper. It helps you to balance consistency with change.

How does it do this? Your ego is a mechanism rather than a consciousness. It is designed to be responsive both to your three conscious selves and to atmospheric conditions. It is designed to expand and contract gently and subtly in response to need, both inner and outer. Thus if your inner flame of desire flares forth to say, "I want to learn to paint," your sense of Self gently expands to include that possibility: "I can do that. I am someone who can learn to paint." Your gatekeeper then opens the gates to experiences which support that attitude.

But if one of your selves flares forth with a desire that will somehow threaten another of your selves—for example, "I want to have two full-time jobs because I need the money."—the ego gently reflects the limits it has been programmed to keep: "No, that is probably beyond my ability at this time; I can't handle such stress."

Using hope and doubt, the ego helps your three selves regulate their diverse needs and desires. Using the parameters of can do/ can't do, in character/ out of character, healthy/ not healthy, enjoyable/ not enjoyable, productive/ unproductive, and realistic/ not realistic, the ego protects a composite you.

The ego doesn't just arbitrarily set these limits. Your three selves all work together to create and program it. Wiser self programs into the ego a sense of pride-of-self, courage, hope and confidence. Natural pride is an echo of deep memory: you are part of the divine; you are special and valuable; you have certain energetic potentials that you know intuitively and sub-consciously, which you feel impelled to explore and express. Natural pride is not something to deflate or get rid of; it is recognition of and gratitude for your particular gifts. The ego will clamor for experiences and opportunities that match your inner sense of potential.

Talking self programs the ego to hold a set of identities which are its creation in this lifetime. She uses information from her own sense of who she would like to be, and blends it with perceptions of her self reflected back to her by parents, teachers, friends, siblings, peers, and so on. If she is helped to program the ego correctly, she teaches it to hold all data flexibly, subject to change. She is helped to teach her ego the stance that, "this is who and how I am for now, but I can grow and change and try new ways of being as well." She also programs in certain limits based on her predilections and goals.

We remind you that we are describing the establishment of the healthy ego.

Earth elemental self programs into the ego a body image and a set of attitudes, expectations and fears designed to help maintain that imaged body. She uses information from her own perceptions and experiences, and the interpretations of talking self to establish habits and limits within the ego. "I need lots of sleep in order to function well;" "I love/hate exercise;" "I am healthy/sickly." The ego uses these instructions to create a feedback system to the three selves. Thus even if you are renewed occasionally after four hours of sleep, the ego will send up doubts: "I need more sleep than this in order to function well."

The body image held by your ego provides a reference point for the earth elemental self when talking self is focussed elsewhere or gives too many conflicting instructions. Through storing a consistent body image, your ego also allows earth elemental self to maintain itself in health while its message pathways are being used for communications between the other two selves.

Your ego is your created Self, representing you to the outside world. Unless it is extremely flexible and responsive to your fluctuating inner truths, you may experience your ego as a barrier between you and your greatest potential, or between you and other people. The very features designed to protect and maintain you can be frustrating.

Your ego remains blind to present truth in the interests of "steady-state" truths. This allows you to be a fairly consistent person through all the shifts and fluctuations of energy and awareness which are actually taking place within you. However, when you want to change some aspect of your character quickly or radically, you may find your ego clinging to the old ways of acting and feeling. Your ego requires time, some new experiences, and consistent redirection to change its sense of Self.

Your ego blends both realistic and imagined information about you. You have a baseline self-concept which combines truths about your character which have been proven by experience and a sense of yourself which you know intuitively. This allows your Self to expand and fulfill potential. But you may find yourself regularly bumping up against the inconsistencies between who you know yourself to be, and who you can show yourself to be. The ego ability to tolerate discrepancies between real capacity and desired skill allows you to learn and grow.

Your ego creates a natural expansion and contraction of confidence. It responds to inner yearnings and outer limitations, to the needs and expectations of your three selves, acting as a regulator of your identity. Some days you will believe that you can accomplish anything. Other days, your ego will feel tentative and constrained, and you will doubt your abilities or choose a more conservative path. This allows you to move forward and take risks, but also gives you opportunities to step back and evaluate your choices. Like all regulators, your ego can feel like a limiter. Those days when you have grand ideas about what you would like to achieve but feel shaky in your confidence, it is difficult to accept the value of this ego mechanism.

Ego qualities are both gifts and liabilities.

What happens when the ego is unhealthy? In general, it becomes rigid. It may get stuck in an over-inflated state, giving you grandiose messages about what you should and can accomplish, or it may stay fixed in an under-inflated state, whispering constant messages of doubt and failure. It may, like the astigmatic eye, be distended in some realms, and contracted in others, giving you alternating flashes of egotism and self-deprecation.

The unhealthy ego may be programmed with attitudes that prevent you from celebrating and expressing your spirit and goals in this life. Some children are given such strong messages about who and how they are, that they can't develop a sense of self which reflects their inner truths. They are constantly struggling to live up to ideals which don't ultimately fulfill them. Some children are so neglected that they create untenable expectations and an identity based on their lacks and failures rather than their gifts.

When your ego is unhealthy or unbalanced, then you won't feel comfortable, no matter how many of your dreams and expectations are fulfilled. Your achievements will feel hollow and false. If your ego is not reflective of your inner truths, then others will be uncomfortable with you, distrusting you without knowing why. You may find yourself fluctuating between elation and depression which don't necessarily correlate with external events and stimuli.

How can you tell if your ego is an adequate representation of your inner truth? By your level of comfort and security, by your level of satisfaction, and by the sense of authenticity when you do something. If you feel hollow, as if your accomplishments weren't really yours, or as if no one can really know you, then chances are your ego is ailing and needs some work.

In general a healthy ego has the following characteristics:

You know your limits and know how to say no—and yes.

This means that you can make a choice based on inner desire rather than on a sense of obligation. It means that you are not afraid to define yourself, your preferences and choices.

Your inner voice balances praise and criticism.

The evaluation going on in your head contains recognition of successes and failure, of pleasures and discomfort. It is neither too rosy to allow you to learn from mistakes, nor too negative to allow you to accept partial successes and the Self-in-progress.

Your inner critic is kind, constructive and compassionate.

The inner critic needs to respond to specific events and experiences, without generalizing to blanket condemnation. "I feel bad about how I reacted to my friend," is healthy ego. "I am rude and inconsiderate," is not.

You can differentiate between your role and your essence.

If you think of yourself in terms of the qualities you embody, then you can experiment with expressing those qualities in many ways. But if you think of yourself primarily in terms of roles: "I am a doctor, and church deacon, and mother," then there is a good chance you are dependent on those roles to give you a sense of Self. When that happens, the ego becomes invested in making sure it has the right scripts and forgets to stay open to change.

You are involved, but not the victim of your life circumstances.

Do you feel you could pick up and start over after a flood, fire or job termination? The healthy ego cares about the dramas you engage in, but is able to re-group after crisis, emerging strong and still flexible. The healthy ego is able to take responsibility for painful events without blame and shame. It says, "I participated in this event," rather than, "I am bad and that's why this happened to me."

You know how to initiate and live with change in your life.

There is an art to seeing things through to conclusion and

an art to changing when a behavior or activity has served its purpose. The healthy ego knows how to read your truest rhythms, and to find a balance between consistency and change that is healthy and satisfying for all three of your selves.

You don't need to show yourself; you can allow yourself to be seen.

The ego does not need to become your agent, promoting its latest discoveries. The healthy ego knows how to disclose the Self to others, without needing to convince those others of its validity.

Gatekeeper

&

All of you who suffer from hay fever, who sneeze uncontrollably around cats, or who swell up like a puff-adder when bitten by an insect may have cause to wonder just what kind of gift your immune system gives you. What harm can a few specks of pollen, some cat dandruff, or a small amount of insect saliva really cause? Yet those of you who have witnessed or experienced the breakdown of that immune system, through AIDS, cancer, or other diseases, know that it is crucial to your survival and well-being.

Your immune system is your physical identity-keeper and gatekeeper. It says: "This substance belongs; this is an invader."

Your immune system sets limits for you. When you are worn down, you often experience congestion or come down with a virus, a message that it is time to rest, to flush, purge and clear out your system.

But the immune system does more than reject invaders and messengers, it also regulates good health. It activates powers of cell generation to heal wounded tissue. It provides for the assimilation of nutrients through the production of co-enzymes. It is instrumental in the chemical chain of messages which lets you know that something more is needed: nutrients, physical exercise, even medicine.

If you have struggled with illness or allergy you may feel that your immune system has a mind of its own. You may feel more imprisoned than protected by this physical gatekeeper. But it is only a mechanism, programmed *chemically* by your heredity (genes), nutritional habits, and physical environment, and programmed *energetically* (using nerve messages which activate chemicals) by your mind, your talking self, and your energetic environment.

Your immune system is the physical part of your gatekeeper. You also have an energetic, mental gatekeeper.

The gatekeeper is a mechanism in your mind which guards the gates of your Self, regulating what comes in and goes out.

Like the immune system, the energetic gatekeeper is an identity keeper, distinguishing what is you from what is not you. It, too, helps you to regulate good health: mental, emotional, and energetic.

Most of the emotions you feel are actually gatekeeper messages alerting you to energy trying to come in or needing to go out. Many of the strange reactions you find yourself having to situations are actually gatekeeper reactions. When you run into someone who looks like your ex-lover, the panic you feel is a message from your gatekeeper saying, "Based on past experience, this person could spell trouble!" When you find yourself gravitating to someone appealing at a party, it is your gatekeeper saying, "Here's someone whose energy I like."

Your gatekeeper is not some little homunculus sitting in your mind opening and closing gates and making decisions. It is a feature or mechanism of your mind. It is a kind of automatic pilot, mediating between your Self and the energies out there around you. It allows you to function and interact with your environment even when your attention is not focussed on perceiving energies or evaluating situations.

Your gatekeeper performs a triage on the energies coming in or going out of you, sorting, assessing, identifying them based on your past experience. It follows the blueprint of your ego identity and the decisions you have made in the past, just as your immune system follows the blueprint of your genes and the resources you have provided for your body.

When it is working correctly, the gatekeeper activates your attention and provides information, so that your three selves can make conscious choices about how to respond. When it is not working correctly, you may feel that you are at the mercy of your past experiences and your emotions. You may feel that your emotional reactions are akin to sneezing or hives.

Perhaps it would be helpful if we gave you an image to play with. Imagine your gatekeeper as a corps of tiny robots, constantly patrolling the periphery of your ego. It is something like a complex security system. Each robot has been programmed to give you messages about energies trying to come in or go out. And each robot is on the watch for something special. Just as your antibodies are keyed to react to certain cells, each gatekeeper robot will react to a certain kind of energy, attitude, situation, or state.

For example, while growing up, you may have suffered humiliation and embarrassment as a sister or brother teased you. Your gatekeeper mechanism set up a robot, sensitive to teasing and sarcasm. It coded into its memory banks the feelings and sensations associated with your experience, as well as any decisions or thoughts you had on the subject.

You may have decided in your seven-year-old wisdom that your tormentor was "just stupid." Now you have a sensitized little robot patrolling the borders of your ego, ready to set off an alarm if it encounters teasing. And so when a colleague pops into your office with a breezy sarcastic comment, your gatekeeper alarm goes off. You may feel anger or fear, similar to what you experienced as a child. You may find yourself thinking, "What a stupid jerk!" This thought and the feelings that come up are a gatekeeper message. It says, here's some energy you need to pay attention to.

But it is only an alarm, not really a conscious conclusion on your part. You will need to reflect whether this person is truly someone you fear or hate. You may need to evaluate whether he is in fact a stupid jerk, or whether you need to rethink your response to teasing.

Not all gatekeeper messages are negative. Imagine that you had a loving family situation while growing up, and experienced teasing as an affectionate form of acknowledgement. Your response to a colleague's flip comment might be to experience a flood of warmth and well-being. You might find yourself thinking, "What a witty guy, he really likes me." This response, while more comfortable, also requires some evaluation. It may or may not be appropriate to the situation.

In many cases, gatekeeper messages are general alarms, suggesting you pay attention. If your experience of teasing was mixed in your early encounters with it, you might find that your colleague's comment sets off mixed messages in your mind. You might think, "did I do something wrong?" and at the same time, feel an overwhelming urge to please this person. You might experience a generalized depression, noticing you feel unattractive or have suddenly started worrying again about some chronic lack in your life (symptoms of general unease and insecurity), without understanding the connection between these feelings and the event which triggered them.

It is extremely useful for you to know that you have such an alarm mechanism. It gives you a way to understand your emotional reactions and the many conflicting messages that can jam your conscious mind. As you learn to work with your gatekeeper and respond in a healthy way to the information it provides, you will see that you are increasingly conscious and present, less at the mercy of your feelings, your reactions and your pain from the past.

The gatekeeper's primary task is to maintain the sanctity of your Self. It keeps the gates so that you are separate and whole. Its secondary task is to provide you with information about what will help you to connect better with others; what will meet your needs, and what might overload your system.

Your gatekeeper sends you constant messages about your inner or outer state, and then releases (or contains) energy in response to the situation as it has perceived it.

This is easy enough to recognize with something you fear. A man who is badly dressed and unshaven approaches you on the sidewalk. Your gatekeeper picks up his energy and sets off a mental and emotional message within you. The contents and intensity of this message will depend on your experiences with such strangers in the past. For many people, trained by their parents to avoid poorly dressed, unkempt individuals, the gatekeeper alarm will sound apprehension, fear. That particular gatekeeper robot will bring up thoughts: "What does he want from me? Is he drunk? Is he dangerous?"

Then before your conscious talking self can decide whether he is dangerous, your gatekeeper will fund the energy to deal with danger. You will experience a rush of adrenaline, blood pumping faster, breath speeding up. You will feel your muscles tensing, as if for action. You may experience weakness if your gatekeeper has learned from past experience that you are vulnerable or unable to protect yourself in response to ill will.

This all happens without your conscious volition. It is your alarm mechanism, your emotional/ energetic immune system getting triggered and behaving the way it is designed to behave.

When the gatekeeper alarm goes off in you, you may experience the fear and the physical rush, but you do not need to rely on your gatekeeper's interpretation of the situation. It has called your attention to the man. Now it is up to you to consciously assess who is approaching you and how to respond. It may be that when the man draws closer, you recognize him as a familiar figure, or can see that he is drunk but not dangerous, or you perceive he is in fact a threat. At that point you can choose an appropriate response to the situation.

We have suggested that you see your gatekeeper as a corps of protective robots, all programmed to respond to a certain energy, situation or state. Some of these robots were programmed yesterday, or last week or last year, and many were established when you were a child. The thoughts, feelings, and intensity of these gatekeeper messages often reflect your maturity and understanding at the time the particular robot was established. That is why you will find yourself reacting childishly to someone, or having a feeling that is out of proportion to the situation that triggered it.

You aren't stuck with these reactions for the rest of your life. The gatekeeper is a shifting, flexible mechanism which you can re-educate to reflect your shifting, present understandings and values. But in order to re-educate it, you need to first understand that it is a mechanism. When you feel a hit of fear, desire, excitement or caution, or notice your mind filling with unbidden thoughts, judgments and conclusions, then it is useful to say to yourself: "One of my gatekeeper robots just went off. What is really happening in this moment?"

When you pause to recognize the alarm, and acknowledge to your gatekeeper that the message has been received, it will quiet down. Then you can spend some time investigating the situation further, truly assessing what is happening and making conscious choices about how you would like to respond.

Your gatekeeper gives you a way to monitor and regulate the energies coming in and going out of you. It helps to reference and cross-reference experience in your mind. It allows you great latitude of consciousness, because it stays on duty, patrolling your borders and alerting you to situations which need your attention.

But it is not a decision-maker. Its perceptions and conclusions are often inaccurate, based on situations you have encountered in the past that may or may not turn out to be similar to the present situation. When a gate-keeper alarm goes off, what you feel, think and hear in that moment is your automatic pilot reaction to the event. It is a signal that you need to consciously assess and respond.

If you learn to recognize the language of your particular gatekeeper, you will be able to work with it better. Some gatekeepers use a broad lexicon of feelings and thoughts to keep you safe, others are quite limited and repetitious, even obsessional.

In general, your gatekeeper gives three kinds of messages: *aversion, attraction,* and *general alarm*.

Aversion messages are a suggestion from the gatekeeper that it has picked up energy (outside or inside of you) which may not be good for you. The messages register differently from one person to another, depending on your temperament, and on how that particular robot was originally coded. Typically, aversion messages register as anger, disgust, contempt, scorn, hatred, dislike, fear, sadness, abusiveness, withdrawal, manic laughter, restlessness, tears, physical illness, or sneezing and other allergic symptoms.

Attraction messages signal that one of your robots has perceived energy that is good for you. Attraction signals tend to register as cravings, love, excitement, happiness, interest, willingness, desire, stimulation, authenticity, sexual arousal, greed, acceptance, serenity, enthusiasm, physical well-being, approval, or need.

General alarm messages signal that the robot in question is not comfortable with the energy it perceives and wants to call your attention to it. General alarms are also set off when the robots have been coded with mixed messages, or when your mind has received too many robot alarms at once. Common forms of general alarm include depression, fear, guilt, boredom, overwhelm, discomfort, jealousy, addictive and compulsive behaviors, love-hate or push-pull feelings, obligation, self-hatred, hurt, feelings of victimization or confusion.

As you find yourself asking, "Why am I so angry?" or "Why do I feel so confused?", we suggest you respond to that angry, confused Self by saying: "The gatekeeper alarm has gone off again. For some reason I feel unsafe. Energy is out of balance, either inside of me, in my understanding or in my environment. I've been put on alert." Take some time to comfort yourself in response to the feelings. Then set about to investigate with your conscious adult understanding what has been triggered for you and how you might make yourself secure in this moment so your gatekeeper can calm down.

Over time, as you respond to the gatekeeper this way, with compassionate awareness, it becomes a more accurate protective mechanism. It allows you to enact the plans and desires of your three selves in a healthy and ever-evolving way. It allows you to develop emotional maturity and wisdom. It allows you to embrace and experience the changes in your life with greater serenity and comfort.

Energy, Power, and Placement

ॐ

There is an illusion in your culture that power has to do with how much influence you wield, how much money you have, or how physically strong you are. But true power comes from within: it is a question of how well you harness your soul energy and how aptly you work with renewable energies to enact your dreams, visions and ideas.

Your power comes from how clearly you play the music of your particular instrument. And while a trumpet may play louder than a harp, or a piano may have more notes than a recorder, there is nothing intrinsically superior in playing louder or having more notes. Thus your power is not relative to other people, nor does it have anything to do with status in the hierarchies of your culture. It has to do with *integrity*, your ability to know your Self, be true to that Self, and place yourself in situations which allow the full expression of your spirit.

The word integrity is related to the verb "to integrate." As you integrate your three selves and their particular gifts, as you strive to love, work, and move through the world in an integrated way, you are learning to play your instrument as beautifully as it can be played.

Your ego and gatekeeper help you achieve integrity, for they are the tools which allow you to harness the potentials and gifts of your three selves. Your ego allows you to create an integrated blueprint for the personalities and composite Self you are creating. Your gatekeeper enables you to recognize and regulate the in-flow and out-flow of energy required to realize these designs.

Let us give you an example of how they work together. Imagine you had success doing math problems as a child. They made sense to you, because you had good experiences with counting and sorting beads and buttons, and you were praised by your parents for being clever with your counting. Over time, then, an identity of being good with math built up in your ego. You looked forward to the math lessons at school because they were a chance to shine, feel competent, and receive praise.

The difficult problems didn't faze you, because you knew you were generally good at math, so you had the patience to struggle with challenges. You also had the energy to struggle with those challenges. Your gatekeeper, enacting the blueprint in your ego, opened the gates to math experiences. You felt drawn to exploring and learning, and you felt energized whenever the topic of math came up.

Another child probably experienced math quite differently. She may have been more naturally drawn to language or interactions, and so in her play she didn't get as much chance to feel confident with counting and figuring. When she encountered math in school, it was too abstract or perplexing for her in that moment. So her ego blueprint contained an identity of being *bad with math*.

Responding to that attitude, she set up a gatekeeper robot with the judgment that "math is a bore" and her gatekeeper closed the gates somewhat to math experiences. She felt aversion whenever a task called for calculating, and felt less interest and energy when the topic of discussion was math. You can see how the ego blueprint for this child could get reinforced over time. Responding to her low energy and inability to focus clearly, the other children and teachers probably helped reaffirm her belief that she was not good at math.

The fact is, your brain is capable of understanding all the math and language and science and history and human emotions that you will encounter in this lifetime. But what your mind is willing to embrace is another question. Your willingness to explore, learn and develop abilities is dependent on the ego you have constructed. If your ego belief is that you can handle almost anything, and that most subjects can be interesting at the right time and place, your gatekeeper will open the gates to experiences which prove and reinforce that attitude.

Thus the key to your energy, interest and power lies in the workings of your ego and gatekeeper! You may have a natural talent for music, which in the beginning will draw you to musical experiences. But if you are criticized, judged and strictly tested, ridiculed or overly controlled in your explorations of music, then your ego will create a negative attitude toward music, and your gatekeeper will block your energy whenever you try to make music.

You may have little inherent gift for cooking, but if early experiences with it are praised and supported, your ego attitude will be positive, and your gatekeeper will signal interest and release energy whenever you are given the opportunity to cook. And of course with increased opportunity, you will generally increase your skills.

Your ego attitudes develop in response both to inner inclinations and gifts, and to outer experience and reinforcement. You can see then how important it is to give children plenty of opportunity to discover what their inner inclinations are, and also to support them sensitively, so that their ego judgments and attitudes reflect an open stance.

Unless you had unusually sensitive parents and were fortunate enough to be in sync with the curricula presented to you in school, your ego beliefs about what you can and can't do are probably inaccurate. You are capable of far more than you think you are. And your power is probably far greater than you are able to express in your life and projects.

Knowing Your Power

When you have been taught and tested and compared to others all your life, it is difficult to break the habit of seeing your power in terms of other people. How do you compare to them? What are you able to do better than others? How do other people see you? We suggest you work to break this habit of thinking; it is one of the quickest ways to block your energy and limit your powers.

Your power comes from living your life in a way that does justice to your dreams, your spirit, and your nature. Your power comes from being able to be present in the individual moments of your life, and value what is happening in terms of its impact on you. True power is often quiet. It is a sense of quiet achievement, when something you have worked to finish is finally completed. It is a recognition that you are in the right place at the right time and can feel a certain hum of contentment in that knowledge.

We encourage you to work with your powers on these terms. Too often our students describe the incredibly powerful experience, guru or group they have encountered, and yet apart from the rush of impressive energy they felt, there is little true effect of this power. When you hear yourself saying "Everyone is impressed by...," or "Most people believe that she is...," stop for a moment and think for yourself. Are you impressed? Is this person, idea or power appropriate to you in this moment, in the particular circumstances you are living right now?

If you meet a powerful teacher, then ask yourself how you might integrate and use the gifts of that teacher in your day-to-day life. Are you swept away by the teacher as a charismatic role model, or are you using the teachings themselves to benefit you? If you encounter a powerful idea or group, ask yourself what that encounter empowers you to do. Are you excited by the impact of this group on others and flattered at the prospect of membership, or are you inspired to strengthen your own habits of thought and action? A teacher, a love, an idea, a movement, a situation can only be powerful to you in specific and direct ways.

The search to know your power is a search to open up your interest, listen to inner inclinations, and learn to work effectively with your own energy. A secondary aspect of power is the effort to work effectively and respectfully with other people's ideas, actions and energy.

We are not suggesting a selfish "me only" attitude. We are saying that your power needs to be grounded in your own needs, your own life, your own particulars, or else it easily becomes unbalanced, abusive or overpowering. If you see your power as *motive force*—as the fueling of your own life on its own terms—then you are more likely to avoid the many ways that power can be abused and misused.

Ironically, the key to your power lies in your ability to be vulnerable: to allow yourself to experience new sensations, to allow others to teach you, to let yourself be comfortable with transition and with the insecurity which is a natural part of growing and changing.

You are more likely to discover your own powers when you are able to become a beginner again, to allow yourself to explore, make mistakes, and be unskilled. You are more likely to develop greater power if you can suspend your ideas of yourself and let your identity shift and grow.

You increase your power through positive experiences, healthy support and willingness to learn. You help your ego to expand and your gatekeeper to open to new experiences by admitting your fears and resistances and being patient with yourself, suspending judgments and condemnation.

When you shift your attention from outside results to

your own intuitive guidance and desire, you can over time develop the power to express your nature and potential more fully.

Working With Energy

You are an amazing transformer of energies. Stop and think for a moment about your body. Every time you wish to do something, your body activates the energies that fuel it. If you want to walk to the store, your body transforms the food it has eaten into calories that fire the muscles. If you wish to make decisions about work, then mental energy is released in you.

Your body contains every kind of power generation known. It contains chemical, electrical and magnetic energies. It uses water pressure—blood in this case—like the pressure created with steam. It uses wind power; think about your lungs bringing the air in and out. There is nuclear power, the atomic energy of the sub-particles exchanging charges, splitting and shifting. There is hydraulic power in the pumping of fluids throughout your body. These all interact and are transformed within the human body. So what your human body is and what you are, is a transformer of energy.

Energy is the life force moving. It comes into you, you use it and transform it, and then express it outward again. This is true not only on the physical level: your whole being acts in this way. You transform ideas into actions, feelings into expressions, physical energy into motions, inner vision into outer reality.

You transform inward also. You turn the experience of seeing beautiful art work into a feeling that then fuels your willingness to try a new project. Everything you take in gets put through the mill of your being and comes out in another form that is useful to someone else or to yourself in another setting. And everything that you put out transforms those things around you.

All the systems that you know and live in interact and exchange, allowing your spirit to move, just as the chemical, the electrical, the magnetic, the circulatory, the kinetic, the hydraulic and the atomic all interact to allow the body to move.

Thus your work and play of this life is the transformation of energy. You create social structures, which are then animated by the life force. You create an idea and give it life with your enthusiasm and expression. You create a relationship and fuel it with your loving exchanges. You create a job and fuel it with your actions.

You do not need to control all this energy, any more than you need to control your breathing. Instead you need to understand it and move with it, the way a sailor works with the winds. When you understand your energy and how you participate in this massive circulation of the life force, you have a key to your personal powers.

But some of you never get to do much sailing in life. You suffer because you never learned how to care for your body or to recognize its individual and special ways of circulating and transforming energy. Some of you suffer because you misunderstand the nature of your particular fuel and what it is best suited to. Some of you are like machines that are only partway plugged into the wall socket: your access to the flow of forces is clogged, and you find yourself at the mercy of painful physical, mental and emotional fluctuations.

If you wish to harness your powers, then you need to maintain the equipment, be sensitive to the forces you are using and transforming, and keep your access to those forces clear. In practical terms, it means learning to take care of your body so it is a vehicle for you, developing your mind and personality so that they work effectively for you, and learning to tune in to your spirit and allow it to guide you.

Fortunately, like a well-equipped boat, you have several gauges and instruments which allow you to do this.

Your emotions, imagination, sensations, physical activity level, thoughts, intuitive sense, and desires can all give you clues as to how your energy is moving and why. The psychic skill of "reading energies" involves working intimately with each of these gauges.

You can learn to create an imaginary instrument panel in your mind that will help you to read your gauges. Reading energies is really fairly simple. It is a matter of posing a question, "What is going on in me?" (or in another person, or situation), and creating a vocabulary through which you can understand your earth elemental responses.

Your **emotions** signal energy which is in motion (or trapped) in you. Remember that we said energy is the life force moving. Your emotions register that movement. When you are happy, you are feeling the life force expanding and moving freely at a comfortable pace. When you are sad or depressed, you are feeling the life force condensed and compacted.

Your gatekeeper frequently uses the vocabulary of emotions to signal the inflow and outflow of energies. Since energy is always in flux, you always have some emotional sensation present, even if it is a neutral state that feels pretty unemotional and still. Shifts in your physical energy, your social environment, your talking self dramas, or even your telepathic connections with others can all register in your emotions.

Women who have felt emotional ups and downs in relation to their monthly cycles will know what we mean when we say physical shifts register in the emotions. When you are tired, too, many of you will register a sense of sadness, defeat, aversion, or anger. The particular emotion that is activated in you by each energy state depends on how you learned to recognize and name your emotions as you were growing up.

Your social environment is full of energetic "checks and balances." You give, receive, and exchange with others continuously, and when these exchanges fall out of balance in some way, you will probably experience an emotional reaction. If a friend doesn't call you when expected, if you are overloaded or understimulated by the people around you, the energy imbalances of these situations will all trigger feelings in you.

Talking self also activates the emotions as she shifts and changes her identities. Some of you will experience your energy shifts as a roller coaster of emotional states and feelings; others of you will find you have a quieter and less active emotional gauge.

When you are feeling an emotion, it is easy to be engulfed by it, and swept up in all the thoughts your mind produces in response. But it is also possible, with some practice, to step back from an emotion and observe or investigate how the feelings express themselves in your body. Where do you feel sensation? Where are you tense or loose? The emotions register energy in motion (or blocked) in you. Can you feel what your energy is doing? Is it moving at a comfortable pace without obstruction? Are you tensing to contain it, and resisting release?

***Where in the body are the sensations strongest? With
time, this exercise can help you to feel and work with
your emotions more effectively.***

Take some time to interpret the energetic message being
expressed by your emotions. Recognize whether the energy
movement or blockage being signaled is in the physical, emotional, mental, spiritual or interactional realms. One way to
do this is to create an "emotionometer" in your imagination.
Picturing the emotionometer, ask yourself where you are
blocked, and watch the imaginary needle swing to one of the
realms.

We remind you that energy can transform within a
moment and you can help it to transform. So rather than taking any particular mood as a prison sentence, see it as a temporary gauge of where the energies are in the body, life and
spirit, and ask: "How can I work with the movement of these
energies? What are my tools available to get them moving?"

For example, anger is energy that needs to release. While
you may choose to express your anger by confronting someone, you can also use it to fuel an angry session of house-clean-
ing or an angry walk, which will not only help to dissipate the
pent up energy, but can also shift your physical, mental and
emotional equilibrium. You are not controlling your emotions
when you do this. Instead, you are learning to honor and work
with them; you are learning to hoist the sail that can best use
that particular wind.

Your **imagination** is also a powerful gauge that can tell

you what is happening to you energetically. Often the little mental soap operas you create, complete with imaginary conversations, give you clear insight into what you are needing, wanting, fearing. In other words, your imagination supplies dramas to explain your gatekeeper signals of aversion, attraction and alarm.

Can you remember sitting around feeling very tired, dull, bored, uninspired, when suddenly you imagined that you have won the lottery or have been offered a fabulous job? Your energy can be transformed by this news. You can use this drama to read your energetic needs, and then respond creatively. You may not be able to manifest the winning lottery ticket in that moment, but you can certainly honor the need for adventure, or security, or surprise expressed by your imaginative drama.

Some of your mental fantasies are attempts by the earth elemental self to rebalance energy or create movement. You imagine your beloved walking through the door and embracing you tightly. In that moment, the tension of feeling disconnected falls away, your breathing shifts and adjusts, and you find yourself just a bit more open, relaxed or secure. Mental dramas can get your energy flowing again and remind you of needs you may have been neglecting.

Your imagination offers you a wonderful gauge to your energy state. Do I feel like a crab that is about to be cracked? Do I feel like a ball being bounced? What is the image about your life that comes to mind for you in this moment? Your imagination can supply an image, and in working with the image, you can also help to move the energies related to it.

Say you are experiencing difficulties with a couple of people at work. Ask your mind to supply an image. You might say, "I feel like a ball that is being bounced back and forth between two people." When you have that image, you can work with it directly. Imagine yourself, the ball, being scooped up by a loving hand and gently moved elsewhere. Or imagine the ball sprouting arms and legs and walking away from the situation. Or perhaps imagine the tenor of the game changing, so that the two people are handing the ball back and forth in a most friendly manner.

Transform it. Melt the rubber down, play with your imagination and your ability to create images. Like the game of *inner tennis**, the imaginative work you do will activate your energies and catalyze changes in your situation.

Your **sensations** are the physical vocabulary your gate-keeper can activate in signaling energy shifts. Your sight, hearing, smell, taste and feeling are always active, but what they register consciously is a message to you about needs and activity.

Can you remember a time when you were feeling vulnerable or weak and at the same time found yourself shivering with cold? This is an instance of your physical sensations being used as a gauge, signaling aversion or alarm.

You have a wide and varied vocabulary of physical sensations that signal not only physical states, but also mental, emotional and spiritual states. When you are needing food, then the physical sensation of hunger is clear. But you also have physical ways to signal mental, emotional or spiritual hunger. It might be a hunger sensation in the head or throat, it might register as shortness of breath or uneven breathing, it might register as jaw tension, or a tightening in the groin.

The better you have balanced your physical energies (taking in, using, and releasing), the more clearly and accurately this gauge can register the movement of all energies. If you are tired, inebriated, buzzed on coffee, sluggish from lack of exercise or blurry from too much concentration, then the signals of this gauge may be displaced or distorted. Indeed, the knot in your stomach may turn out to signal happiness.

Since your sensation is easily befuddled, it is important to keep it regularly tuned and balanced. If you have not been affectionately touched in a while, then this gauge can go out of balance and distort your perceptions about what is happening within and around you. If you have overeaten or undereaten, your emotions may be seesawing and activating all kinds of mental and emotional messages that are not much more than alarms signaling imbalance.

Like all the gauges, your physical sensations can be used to shift and move energy. Take a nice warm bath at the end of a busy day and you will see clearly what we mean. When you have been working too hard, then you can move your energy by taking five minutes to gaze at green grass and leaves. Sounds

---

* An approach to tennis in which you visualize yourself playing tennis, stroke by stroke, and the mental exercise helps you to improve your physical game.

and music can move or shift your energy state as well, soothing (or activating) the savage beasts in you.

Your **physical activity level** is a related gauge, offering you clues to what is happening energetically in and around you. We're sure you are familiar with this gauge. You are sitting in a waiting room and notice that your toe is tapping or you are rocking back and forth. It gives you a message that there is energy inside you needing release. It also gives you a hint to look into what might be happening with some of the other gauges. What are the emotions registering at that moment?

Are you feeling sluggish, active, tight, loose, busy, comatose? All of these are within the scale of the "activity-ome-ter" and can give you information not only about how things are moving (or not), but also about what kinds of instructions your gatekeeper is getting from your ego about the opening and shutting of gates. When everything is working properly, then energy is released to fuel your projects and activities. When the energy released doesn't match the situation—when your body is nervous and overactive in a waiting room, or sluggish and slow-moving at work—then you are getting a message about imbalance among your three selves.

Your **thoughts** are the gauge that translates information from the other instruments for the use of talking self. Talking self likes thoughts, verbal interpretations, mental constructs. When your blood starts racing and you experience shortness of breath, talking self will try to interpret, telling herself that she is scared or anxious.

Take stock of how accurately your thoughts match a situation. Many of our in-body friends have quite a gap between their energetic truth and the message in their mind. They feel their energy flag and think, "I will never get this job done." They pick up a sensation of aversion in someone else and think, "He's angry at me, he hates me." They experience a hormonal shift and think, "I'm depressed, something is wrong with my life."

Talking self is quite creative and often flamboyant in interpreting energetic states, especially internal ones. Because it is her job to create dramas, she can easily over-interpret the feelings, emotions and energy moving through you or around you. With some practice you can learn to "translate" your interpretations to less inflammatory forms. When you hear the thought, "I will never get this job done," you can insert the compassionate observation, "I must be feeling tired and frustrated." When you hear the thought, "he's angry at me, he must hate me," you can translate it to, "he must be having a difficult day. It probably has little to do with me." When your talking self starts to scare herself with: "there must be something wrong with my life," you can remind her, "this despair is hormones talking. I need to hunker down and console myself for a while."

Your thoughts will tell you that some gauge has been activated, and is picking up energy. They will reflect the activities of your gatekeeper and can give you information about whether you are experiencing aversion, attraction or just general alarm. The more accurately your talking self learns to name sensations, feelings and energy states, the more effectively you will be able to use them as gauges.

Sometimes a thought will pop into your mind *before* you feel anything energetically. You will think, "I need a vacation." Only after you have examined your sensations more closely do you realize that you are tired, or perhaps even hungry. Do you see that we are encouraging you to listen to your thoughts, but also to take them with a grain of salt? Talking self uses plenty of poetic license in interpreting perceptions and energetic states.

Your thoughts are also, like the imagination, a powerful tool in moving energy. When you think over and over, "I am tired," it can be an interpretation that energy is flagging or it can act as an instruction to your earth elemental self, who then signals "tired" in physical symptoms.

The thought gauge tends to be overused in your culture. That is why many spiritual teachers work to help you retrain your mind and attitudes. They teach you new precepts, mantras or prayers to focus or quiet the mind, so that it can be re-tuned as a gauge.

Your **intuitive sense** is the gauge which uses your subtle or inner vision, hearing, feeling, scent and touch. When energy is moving in or out of you, you have subtle sensors to register the energy as suggestions in the mind or imagination, or as physical sensation.

Often an intuitive message comes as a flash of direct knowing. You see yourself signing papers, and realize intellectually that you are moving toward the choice of buying a house. You experience yourself suddenly as an enthusiastic small child, and interpret from that that you are needing more play and creativity.

Since you are enmeshed in the energetic web, you have constant intuitive information coming into you. How well you listen to it has to do with how much practice you have had reading the instrument.

You get lots of instruction as a child on using most of your other gauges and connecting them to events. But some of you have had little encouragement to use your intuitive gauge, and may have been discouraged from doing so. We want to encourage you to play with it. It won't harm you: it is a source of information which your conscious selves can use as they make decisions and choices.

Like the other gauges, your subtle senses can be used to affect the energy flow. You must have felt this phenomenon. If someone you love is suffering, even in a different city, you can send them love and support through your powers of telepathy. When there is hostility in a room, you can help to ground the energy by breathing deeply and calming yourself. Through a form of telepathic osmosis, this can affect the others in the room.

We are not suggesting that you can control hostility or suffering with your intuitive instrument. But you can certainly use your love and intention to help move that situation into a more balanced or healing state.

The last gauge we wish to describe to you is your **desire.** Desire is partly emotion, partly sensation and partly thought. But it is useful to read your desires as a gauge. They will provide a clue to your motivations and beliefs.

You have a natural desire for wholeness and fulfillment. You have a natural desire that pulls you toward what you think you need. Thus when you want something, it is either an indication of what you need, or what you think you need.

The natural desires are to sleep, to be active, to eat, to drink water, to integrate or assimilate or process, to release, to create, to connect, to separate and to be stimulated. When the selves are working in harmony, there is a nice rhythm that shifts through these desires, just as the plants move through the seasons of their growth and decay. But when the rhythm gets disturbed for some reason, or thwarted, then more than one desire will be signaled at a time.

When your gatekeeper signals multiple needs and desires, it is because the rhythm of being and doing is off. Or there is blockage in your flow and transformation of energy. Sometimes your sense of past, present and future gets confused, so that in addition to signals about what is needed right now, you are also getting signals about unmet needs from yesterday and tomorrow.

In working with this gauge, the first task is to listen to it. To hear the contents and essence of your desires. If you find yourself, for example, craving food, money and fame, it may be a signal that there is some emptiness at the center: you are clogged at your roots, and thus crave the security of recognition and wherewithal from outside yourself.

If you are overwhelmed with desires, then it can cause your energy to become bottlenecked. You can probably recall a moment of frustration when you desired to sleep, eat, take off a hot jacket, run to the bathroom, and finish your conversation all at one time. If your desires have been chronically ignored or stifled, it may be hard to hear what it is you want. You may have to begin by listening to what you don't want.

Listening to your desires is like using a windsock to give you information about which way the winds are blowing. It doesn't mean that you will turn and head in that direction exclusively. You may tack from one sub-goal to the next. But it does give you information about where you wish to be headed, and how you can best motivate yourself.

Power and Placement: Soul Energy

If you want to harness the power of a stream, you build a water wheel. But if you want to use the power of gasoline, you build a combustion engine. Your power in this life comes from two things: constructing an identity to fit the nature of your energy, and placing yourself in situations where you can be an effective energy transformer.

It will do you no good to try to wangle a job as a high-powered executive if you are by nature a dreamer and visionary. Similarly, if your natural gift is to process numbers and figures, then you will be frustrated if you try to force yourself to work extensively with people. If you are a nurturer, then your work and play in this life is strongest in situations where you are able to nurture.

We do not wish to cast you in a mold or limit your possibilities. But it is true that the mill of your being is particularly
suited to certain kinds of energy work. Your natural energy has
a certain tone or resonance to it.

*You would laugh at us if we suggested you throw a
coal burner up in the air to catch the wind, or dip a car
engine into the stream to make it go. Yet many of you
find yourself listening seriously when family, friends and
your internal judges pressure you to set goals that are
just as unrealistic to your nature, and persuade you to
ignore or underrate activities that truly give you power.*

Power is transformable but not interchangeable. What
makes you powerful may have no meaning to someone else.
What gives them power may feel shallow or valueless to you.
Since the web of activities on your planet is designed to reflect
all different energies and natures, this is understandable.

Your power comes from creating a fulfilling and conscious life. The challenge is that you are each asked to determine what will fulfill your particular nature, and decide where
to best place yourself. Do you want to be a big engine and place
yourself in the big engine room and run the big ship that's
going on the big ocean? Or do you want to be a little engine,
put yourself on a little putt-putt motor boat, on a tiny peaceful
lake, and go that way? Where do you place yourself, and what
kind of engine do you need in that placement? What are you
striving for?

It is very difficult for someone living in your culture with
its hierarchical values to believe that those two choices are
equal. From the point of view of the soul, the big ship on the
ocean is no more valuable than the little boat on the lake. It is
a matter of your natural preference and your natural sense of
comfort. When you listen to your desires and experience, they
will reflect how well your identity is serving you. When you
listen to your inner guidance, the diverse signals you are given
will reflect the placement which is best for you.

Authentic Living

ॐ

You are here on the planet to celebrate your spirit and its potentials. You are here to play, to make messes, to try ideas and situations on for size. You are here to write your own biography as you go, playing a variety of characters and scenes. Your contributions happen in a million ways; when you die, you will see that the meaning of this life derived not from your particular job, position, consistency, accomplishments or purchases, but from the satisfaction and verve with which you lived your moments.

Many of you create unnecessary suffering for yourself by getting mired in feelings about success and failure. You have been taught to strive in this life toward greater accomplishment, or status, or even toward something like sainthood. We recommend that if you strive at all, you strive for authenticity.

Authenticity is an inner sense of rightness. It is a buzz or hum you feel, a resonance, when your event-of-the-moment matches your sense of truth, desire, or need-of-the-moment. It is the feeling you have when you are doing something you are truly in the mood for, something that is your clear choice. And what is authentic for you may be quite different from what is authentic for another person.

For someone whose deep affiliations have to do with justice and truth and social engagement, becoming a lawyer might be an authentic choice. But if you become a lawyer because it is a family tradition, without feeling your inner truth activated, you will be wasting your time, no matter how successful a lawyer you are. There is no true security in a choice which rings hollow emotionally, no matter how much the money or status seem to compensate you. The unbalancing effect of doing work that doesn't really nourish you can, over time, damage your health, relationships, and self-esteem.

Authenticity starts with individual moments and how you live them. Each time you consult your inner sense of truth and make choices that reflect that, you feel more alive. Each time you honor your life force in its rhythms and patterns, you feel more alive. The more you live the moment, the more your life means in ultimate terms.

It takes a great leap of faith to believe this. So many of your belief systems revolve around achievement and professional accomplishment, and the idea that if you sacrifice now, you will be enabled to do what you want later. You are asked to pay your dues when young, and protect the rigors of your profession when older. This is so foreign to our perspective on your life. From our perspective, each moment can be meaningful on its own terms. You are each a member of many delightful groupings, and your membership is assured by your nature.

From our perspective, your challenge comes from integrating the needs and desires of your three selves, and finding a satisfying rhythm in your dance of separating and connecting. Each time you share a real moment of connection with another human being, it should go on your résumé as a great accomplishment. Each time you listen inward, hear the desires of your three selves, and find ways to enact those desires, you are "achieving," because this is where your life draws its greatest meaning and resonance.

There is all the difference in the world between an authentic experience that truly fulfills you, and a hypothetical choice that fulfills some idea of what might be good. If you are hungry, and crave a tangerine, then eating that tangerine is the most authentic choice for that moment. If you are not hungry, but eat a tangerine anyway, then there is less resonance to the action and less nourishment on the spiritual, emotional and even physical levels. If you crave sleep, but force yourself to go to a concert instead, you may be glad that you didn't miss it, but in fact, you were not fully present either.

What we are suggesting as a goal is to strive to be focussed in the present in your life. As you cultivate a deep appreciation of the infinity of experience that exists within each moment, then you will find you no longer need to waste energy with resistance, self-doubts, or trying to control outcomes. You will find that you have more to give, the more you allow yourself to truly *receive* within your experience.

Your power is greatest in the present. If you are tired, sleep. If you are curious, explore. If you need to create, get yourself some tools and start creating. If you need stimulation, stop and take some in. Work with the energies as they come and go in you, relinquishing the fixed ideas of what you must get done today. Stay open to guidance and inspiration and felicitous accident. If you push and push and force yourself through, you will end up feeling jaded, clogged, unconnected or worn down. And if this is the outcome, what was the point of your effort?

Even in the busiest life, there are ways to be authentic within individual moments. We know that many of you work full time and have loaded yourself down with commitments. We also wish to acknowledge the constraints imposed by poverty and obligations to others. But even within such constraints, it is possible to locate your authentic motivations and find ways of expressing and satisfying aspects of your nature.

You can remember to give yourself breathing space. Take five minutes to just sit down and rest in between activities. Let yourself center on the next task facing you and locate within yourself the heart of your desire which will motivate you to participate. If you need to go grocery shopping, for example, you can rush into the task grudgingly, or you can stop for a moment and find a way for the experience to feel more rich or meaningful: enjoy the visual stimulation of the packages, play with creative decisions about what to eat, make an emotional connection to the gift this food offers you and to all the work that has gone into making it available to you.

There are nourishing ways to work with the energies that come through you to accomplish ten times more than you accomplish when you push and force your way through. But it takes a leap of faith and some perseverance to turn your mind and life around, living your natural rhythms. It might require you to rethink your obligations and commitments and let go of those which consistently drain you.

It takes some real courage to begin living for the moment rather than for achievement, security or future fulfillment. It is hard to trust that your needs will be met as you address them one by one, and those achievements that are true to your nature will come naturally.

But we assure you this is so.

Internal vs. External Authority

What happens to deflect you from authentic rhythms and choices? You are taught from a young age to defer to external authority. To eat on schedules, to learn certain topics, to be polite and well-socialized. Some of you even learn to feel most happy when pleasing others, short-circuiting an awareness of what might be right or true to your own creative talking self and to your other two selves as well.

The word authentic is closely related to the words author and authority. They all contain the concept of "determining what is right." An author puts forth views and opinions, and an authority pronounces which views and opinions are correct ones, based on knowledge and experience. Thus if something is to feel authentic to you, then it must develop out of your inner authority, and your willingness to be the author of your own life story.

We do not wish to pretend you live in a vacuum, or suggest that you think only of yourself. Part of what fulfills you and feels authentic is interacting with others. You choose parents, teachers, friends, lovers, colleagues, mentors and even rivals whose influence is important to your growth and thinking. However, there is a difference between letting yourself be inspired, taught and supported by others, and letting others' ideas determine (and limit) your choices.

Right from the start your talking self develops through interactions with other people: they teach you language, help you to understand shared social practices, set limits and contexts for you as you are growing up, and let you know both subtly and overtly what they expect of you. You need this help from others to develop a talking self. This guidance is supposed to keep you safe while your ego and gatekeeper get established, and provide you with criteria for your actions and ideas.

There is great motivation on the part of your family and society to socialize you to fit in. In terms of your safety and effectiveness in this world, they are doing you a great service. But most of you have been greatly over-socialized. The identity and expectations your family put on you while growing were meant to be a loan. They are meant to provide structure which you then replace with your own structures, identity and expectations as you mature.

But in your culture, the emphasis on conformity is strong. The emphasis on obligation, and security, and responsibility to others is strong. There is a lot of insistence on external measures of success, happiness and achievement, in which you are asked to listen to external authority and overlook your own perceptions of reality. These things are not bad in and of themselves, but they can cause you great distraction or distress as you try to find your inner authority and truth.

Consider some common values in your culture:

There is a strong work ethic that says hard work is noble, service to others is better than "selfish" activity, and public work is more important than "personal life."

This creates great conflict and self-condemnation in those spirits whose life purpose revolves around personal evolution, or whose natural rhythms appear lazy because they are slower than the norm.

You are encouraged to cultivate "objectivity." A subjective view is considered less reliable or accurate.

We do not believe objectivity is possible. There is always a subject doing the perceiving, choosing and evaluating. Even the so-called objective tests are designed according to subjective value-laden criteria. Your power rests in being able to acknowledge your subjective reality and take responsibility for your perceptions, observations and experience. Objectivity is used as a stance in your culture by individuals in power, who tend to discount individual perception and experience. They consider objectivity to be superior as a perspective because it rises above passion. Yet your passion is your life force resonating; why try to divorce yourself from it?

"A job finished is a job well done."

Each of you has a different relationship to concrete accomplishment. You may be well satisfied with ideas and first steps. The end result is only one portion of an experience, and the quality of your process is (in most cases) more important than completion.

You can supply other sayings or beliefs that have been drummed into you. Some of them you may have truly embraced. Others cause you to curb your behaviors and feel guilt and pressures that keep you from listening to what you really want. In this environment, even when your inner truth causes you to rebel, it is difficult to differentiate between the desire for freedom from these strictures, and your authentic choices. As long as you are reacting against parents, friends, or society, your natural rhythms and desires will be skewed.

It is a challenge indeed to develop a strong sense of inner authority in your culture. How can you know what you want when you are bombarded with stimulation, pressured by financial obligations, and strongly trained to think in ways which may or may not fit your natural patterns of thinking and feeling?

One of the single most destructive concepts we have encountered in your shared reality is *status*. Even those of you who do not participate in the race for the fanciest home or fastest car or most attractive partner are still affected profoundly by this concept. You have been taught to feel good when achieving something, but bad about wasting time. You have been taught that it is better to help another person than to sit around doodling on a note pad. You have been taught that it is more valuable to meditate or think about spiritual matters than to play golf.

We wish to encourage you to rethink your ideas about status. No activity has inherent status. *It is valuable to do what is authentic for you in the moment.* As long as you have a mental hierarchy of high and low status activities, you are robbing yourself of meaning. Each activity finds its value in the context of your life and unfoldment, and serves you in response to your needs. Only you can really know and feel what those needs are.

Authentic Rhythms

We are great believers in balance. Since your life force is expressed in repeating movements of in-breath and out-breath, your lifestyle is healthiest when it embraces the complementary energies of being and doing, feeling and expressing, stimulation and peace.

Your culture tends to emphasize the active principle, encouraging you to define yourself by what you have done and expressed, encouraging you to spend your free time seeking stimulation. This means that most of you suffer from a lack of down-time, where nothing is required of you, where you can be peaceful, integrate your experiences, feel their effects on you, and know yourself directly, through the hum of your being.

When there is too much emphasis on doing, some individuals become over-doers, trying to make up for their sense of imbalance by initiating even more projects, growing even more gregarious, and striving even harder for fulfillment. Some individuals, when they have passed their balance point, experience resistance, blockage, emotional shutdown, or increased moodiness.

If you look at your day today, how much time did you

spend just being? How often did you allow yourself to space out, to rest your body, to sit down after an encounter and just feel the sensations and emotions it evoked in you? How much serenity did you feel, not only in between your key events, but during them as well?

When you are *on the points* of your nature, meaning *within the balance of your being and doing,* then all action and rest feels right. Even the difficult interactions and challenging tasks are somehow right. You no longer feel driven to accomplish things, because you are taking the time to be truly fulfilled by those actions you are taking. You may do less, but you accomplish more.

When your self-esteem is nourished through both your being and doing, then you are more free to listen to your inner rhythms and authority; you have more direct access to your wiser self and its guidance. Wiser self communicates more clearly during times of quiet reflection, when the pathways of your nervous system are not filled with the messages required by the active mind and body.

Many of your problems and blockages are caused simply by being out of balance in your being and doing. You contribute to needing to collapse for longer periods by not resting well, not breathing well, not listening well. You contribute to the bad luck, conflicts, failures, illness and accidents in your life by not taking those pauses to internalize, to bring yourself back home, to feel, to resonate, to just be.

People come and ask us, "What can I do about this problem in my relationship? What can I do about this money problem? What can I do about x, y or z?" Our answer is sometimes very hard to take. There's no doing involved. There's being. You're out of balance: you've done, done, done, and your self needs to just be for a while. The more balance you have in your life, the more these problems will either start to evaporate, or resolve themselves with time. Or you will be able to hear inner guidance and have the emotional resources built up to do what you need to do, and let go of what you need to release.

Doing does not address a need for being. So step back for a moment to look not at your problems, but at your life rhythm and balance. Are you balanced *on the points* of your nature?

We have observed that many of you suffer primarily because you are out of sync with your surroundings and out of touch with your inner guidance. And you have not yet given yourself permission to be different. Think for a moment about the pace of life in the city or town where you live. Is it too quick or too slow for you? Think about the frequency of tasks during your day. Would you rather take more time with each activity? Do you berate yourself for being too slow, too unfocused, too intense, too lazy? All of these judgments reflect a mismatch between your energy and the expectations of your environment.

Some of you have never really had the freedom to set your own context and find your own rhythms, but you each have an attention span that is most authentic to your nature. You may work in short spurts of ten to twenty minutes, then need a shift in focus. You may need to juggle three activities at once to feel authentic in your actions. You may need to move slower or faster than the norm in your society. You may need more or less privacy than is standard. You may be at your best around six p.m., when others are just quitting their active work for the day.

If you are one of the lucky few who have managed to find your natural rhythms and live them, then there is probably a deep sense of rightness in you, and confidence that you can hear your own inner authority. Being in sync with your truest rhythms allows your talking and earth elemental selves to operate most fully together, and to communicate the tones of wiser self.

Finding Inner Truth

If you held your hand up in the air for thirty years, it would feel strange, and perhaps painful, when you tried to pull it down again. If you have been adapted to the pace of life around you and to the expectations of others most of your life, then it may be similarly difficult to feel comfortable when making a shift to find your natural rhythms. Even when the unnatural rhythms have caused problems and been uncomfortable, they are at least familiar. The new ones may not feel any better, at first.

The best way to find your larger sense of authenticity is to practice finding it in a single moment, on a basic level. Your earth elemental self is constructed to let you know immediate needs. For one week, take notes on the desires and inclinations you feel, and what you do in response. Do you eat when you are hungry, or according to schedule? Do you sleep when tired, or only when other obligations are fulfilled? Do you play when you feel like playing, and work at tasks which really attract you?

If you have lived your life according to the expectations and desires of others, or in a state of regular deprivation of your natural rhythms, then striving toward authenticity will require a time of re-balance and compensation. If you have spent years adjusting your sleep patterns to the requirements of your job, then when you finally make time and space to sleep naturally, there will be a period of transition in which you sleep too much, or fitfully, or too soundly.

If you have spent your life dieting and restricting your choices to food plans, then permission to eat won't at first release your natural hungers. It will release all the cravings and fears you have stored about food over the years. Only after a time of lifting restrictions, and shifting your criteria for what you eat when, will you discover the healthy patterns and desires of your earth elemental self.

Authentic living is not a question of total freedom, formlessness, or following all your cravings at any moment. It is a question of establishing patterns and structures that reflect your inner sense of truth. It means realigning your goals and activities with your inner values.

Authentic living does not mean that you would never work, or never be responsible to others. It means that your patterns of work and responsibility to others shift. You work when you feel you can focus on it productively, and shift your attention to something else when you can't. You learn to rotate the crops of your attention so that you are working with your natural rhythms, rather than against them. You don't pretend to work just to please others. Your responsibility and gifts to others come out of an overflowing and fulfilled heart, and not out of a sense of obligation or need.

It is a large task to strive toward authenticity. The first step is to give yourself permission to rethink your obligations, and make time in your schedule for the being, reflecting and feeling that will rebalance you. It may take you a long time of sleeping more frequently, or letting go of your mental work on a problem and just sitting with feelings, before you are able to get accurate signals from wiser self.

The second step is to practice listening to internal authority within a moment. If you feel sleepy, shut your eyes for five minutes to honor that truth. If you feel jangled, turn off the radio or tv and let quiet seep into you. If you are not hungry, wait to eat, perhaps allowing the people around you to go ahead and eat without you if they are hungry. The more clearly you recognize your energy of the moment, and communicate it to others, the more you clear the way for change.

We are not suggesting you consult only your own inclinations, disregarding other people. We are suggesting you focus honestly and more specifically on your needs, and make time to meet them. We are suggesting you work to get *on the points* in your life. Twenty times a day, forty times a day, a thousand times. When you do this, you will find you have plenty of energy to cooperate with others too.

You have the potential to see and hear your own needs, resources, direction and best possible paths and choices. But internal authority isn't just a right-answer oracle speaking in your head. It is a state of balance in your overall rhythms. It is a *practice* of authentic living. It's your three selves working together, all having the permission and clear communication channels to let you know how to make the most creative, productive, fulfilling and rewarding choice at each juncture of your life.

Getting your own house in order and developing inner authority is a prerequisite to authentically and cleanly helping others.

When you achieve this kind of balance, then you develop the power to be a visionary and healer for the planet and for the shared cultures as well. Once you have clear access to your own root system, you have greater access to the interconnected root system that links all people. Once you have great familiarity with all your energies then you have some good experience, insight, and wisdom to help make decisions for the good of the whole. Your life becomes a dance, with even the most mundane moments allowing you to express your spirit and exchange with others.

Waking Reality

Grounding

Water Grounding

Draw in a clean sweet breath. Feel it and let it go again. And when you are ready, draw in another.

Imagine you are sitting beside a warm, welcoming bath. Steam rises from the water, enveloping you in an inviting swirl. Perhaps there is music playing softly in the background. You are all alone.

The water in this tub is no ordinary liquid. It is the water of all resolution and it has the power to dissolve all your cares, your worries, your rough edges.

As you sit there beside the bath, feel what aspects of your life and mind you would wish the waters to cleanse. Perhaps it is a difficult or stubborn thought pattern. Perhaps you are burdened by too many obligations. Perhaps you feel jaded from difficult interactions with others.

Let yourself dwell for just a moment on all that encumbers you. Then when you are ready, let yourself step down into the waiting waters.

Feel the warm liquid envelop you and hold you. Let yourself get comfortable, sitting or floating, and imagine the heat and the moisture sinking deep into your being, gently melting all rigid resistance and concern.

You may wish to ask the waters to return you to a neutral state, no longer over-committed and over-involved in the details of your particular dramas. Feel yourself being purified and restored back to your essence.

When you feel clear and released, climb out of the bath and allow yourself to be wrapped in a large comforting towel, swaddled in its soft folds. Know that this towel is a protection for you, and that this bath can be a haven, to return to whenever you need to be held and renewed.

Waking Reality

ॐ

What do you awaken to each day? You awaken to the opportunity to be human, in all its dimensions. You awaken to the shared illusions of your culture and its dramas, you awaken to the challenge of trying to create an effective Self in this dense medium of concrete expression. You awaken to spirit, expressing itself in a myriad of ways.

Think of a scene in nature, bristling with life. Dawn brings a stirring of winds across moist grasses. Insects scurry from place to place in search of food. Leaves rustle in the trees, soaking in the early morning sunlight, beginning the process of photosynthesis. Small mammals are stirring, the young pushing up to their mothers for food; the older ones set out to forage. Each life form has its activities and focus, unfolding again and again.

You too awaken to a bristling of life, to a need for activity and nourishment. When the life that you unfold is indeed nourishing to you, when you are deeply satisfied with your days, when you awaken happy to be alive and to be participating in the life you have built, then there is no need for you to view your life through a spectroscope of special awareness. When your heart is open and you have deep compassion and kindness for yourself and others, there is no need to penetrate the illusion of your waking reality and examine its workings.

But if you wake up in pain or confusion, if you spend your efforts struggling to change or mold your waking reality so that it is more to your liking, if you find yourself hurting or unable to cope with others, then it is indeed useful to understand your mind in a deep intimate way. It is useful to investigate your mental containers, interpretations, reactions. It is useful to penetrate the illusion with your larger awareness.

What is your waking reality? It is the arrangements of events and experiences within your mind. It is the plot of your particular dream of Self unfolding. It is the terms you bring to life.

Mind

ॐ

Your mind is an amazing and versatile instrument. It creates the links between your creature self and the realms of spirit, allowing you to skip through imaginative realities one moment and to focus on a concrete task the next. It is the instrument your talking self uses to create and shape her waking reality.

Much of what you consider your experience takes place in your mind. Let us give you an example.

Imagine that we call together everyone in your neighborhood, telling each person we have some news for her. Then we split everyone into three groups. We put group one into a plain room and ask them to wait for an hour. We say, "We have some very good news for you, but we can't tell you for another hour what it is. Just wait here and we will be back to tell you." You can imagine what this group might experience during that hour.

Now we take the second group and put them in another room, and we say, "We have some bad news for you, but we can't tell you quite yet. If you could just wait here, we'll be back in one hour." The experience of that group is probably going to be quite different from the first group. Both groups will be sitting in a plain room, both will have the same resources available to them. But one group is sitting there with their minds saying "good news, good news," and the other group hears "bad news, bad news."

Then we take the third group and we put them in a plain room saying, "We have some news for you, but we aren't quite ready to tell you. Please wait here for an hour, then we'll come and get you." There's another set of reactions. Within each group the experience will differ from individual to individual. How would you respond to being in each of those rooms?

In the bad news room, one person might be struck with anxiety, worried that the IRS has found some problems with his tax return. Another poor soul might tie herself in knots, imagining disaster scenarios involving members of her family. Another kind of person might respond with anger and restlessness, chain-smoking, while someone else leafs through a Bible, trying to focus her mind on her faith.

The people in the good news room will also vary. One may

be sitting there smiling, certain she has won that lottery she entered last month. A less optimistic person might grow anxious, asking, "What good news? What's the catch?". Someone else might be annoyed at wasting so much time on what she suspects to be a sales gimmick. Others just speculate together on what good news they would like to hear.

Then there are the people in the neutral news room. A busy student opens her backpack and pulls out her books saying, "Great, I needed an hour off. I don't know why I'm here, but I can sure use this time." Another type of person might question the whole setup, asking, "Who gave them the authority to put me in this room and make me wait?" Someone else would get restless, another might grow bored.

You each experience events in your own individual way, and you each shape your reality by what you do with your mind. The quality of your experience often has more to do with your habits and patterns of mind than with the actual events. The experience is sitting in a room. The experience is one hour of time. You have a wide latitude of choice in how you use it, what you do with it mentally.

We suggest you make an assessment of what you do with your mind. Many of you carry a habitual expectation that whispers "bad news, bad news" in your ear, and you react accordingly. Some of you are so anxious to maintain control that even good news or neutral news is suspect. If you have had charged or difficult interactions in the past, that is going to color your present experience. If your life has been secure and open, that too will shape your expectation.

This is part of the work of a spiritual practice. How do you use your mind to anticipate and alter your experience? How can you use your mind to creatively shape and support your experience? How can you learn to be present in an experience, and if you do choose to enhance it with fantasy, how can you enhance it skillfully?

How Your Mind Works

We are often amused when we overhear someone telling another person, "It's all in your mind. Face reality." As if there were a "reality" outside yourself, separate from what you create or structure with your mind. For in fact your mind is the place where your portion of the shared reality is created. It is the place where your experience is designed, perceived and given meaning. It is the workshop of your talking self.

How you organize your workshop is going to profoundly affect your ability to create your talking-self reality. If things are stored haphazardly, you may spend much of your time looking for what you want and getting sidetracked by what you find in your searches. On the other hand, if things are stored too neatly, it will be difficult for you to feel free to putter and make a mess.

When your workshop is too cluttered with past experiences and unfinished projects, it becomes a difficult place to work. Every time you enter it, this unfinished business is going to call out to you, begging for attention or overwhelming you with a sense of too much to do. But you have at least two helpers in your mind who aid you in keeping things organized, putting information away, and finding it when you need it. They are on twenty-four hour duty. One is your logical ability, the other is your intuitive ability.

By nature your intuitive brain is your creative artist. It chooses the context, general contents and focus for your experience. The intuitive side of your mind holds the receivers which pick up the communications of your various instruments and selves.

Your logical helper is a lot like a librarian. It loves to organize, categorize and file. It loves to create systems for efficiently managing the details and data, and for making structures which can support the goals of the intuitive mind. So when intuitive mind imagines an experience or reality, logical mind organizes the resources and calls up the necessary supports to enact it.

Both sides of your mind have a lot of autonomy, but by nature they are meant to be interdependent.

The intuitive mind is supposed to steer the ship and make choices about the nature and quality of the voyage. The logical mind is designed to take care of the mechanics, keeping the crew organized and checking the maps to make sure your thoughts are running on course.

Unfortunately, there is an over-emphasis in your culture on logical mind and many of you have been encouraged repeatedly to be logical in your choices, to detach from your intuitive hunches and focus on proof, data, and rational structures for making decisions. This is directly backward from how your mind is designed to work. Whenever you use your logical mind to make decisions and choices, or your intuitive mind to organize details, you are going to run into trouble. You will quickly find yourself off course and in great danger of running aground.

If you read about the mental processes of your great thinkers and inventors, you will find that what fueled their genius was the ability to use these two parts of their mind as they were designed to be used. They were able to listen to their dreams, imagination and intuitive hunches to guide them in the right direction, and to use their wonderful logical abilities to work out the details and proofs which demonstrated what they knew intuitively to be true.

Although your brain is the physical center of your mental activity, in fact your mind is an extended instrument. When you talk about your heart in terms of being a center of emotional exchange, or your gut as relating to courage and instinct, you are recognizing some of the branch offices of your mind. *Your mind permeates your entire energetic field.*

We are belaboring this notion so that we can emphasize that you "think" with your whole being. Thought (logical, rational thought) and feeling (intuitive, energetic processing) are both necessary tools of talking self in using the mind and intelligence wisely.

Active and Passive Thinking

Each of your conscious selves has the gift of *attention*. Your talking self can focus her attention on whatever she chooses; it is like a spotlight of consciousness. But her activity is not limited to where that attention is focussed. Talking self carries on lots of work outside the spotlight of attention: planning, doing, interpreting, integrating, assimilating, even decision-making.

This phenomenon of attention is perhaps clearer when you look at your earth elemental self. When you are walking, you may pay general attention to the movement of the creature self: that activity is in the spotlight of your awareness. But at the same time, your heart is beating, the blood is pumping,

your ears are filtering sounds, your sense organs are all oper-
ating, the cells are fully active, the gastrointestinal system is
digesting. And you are fortunate that you don't have to consciously attend to all these events at once.

We call this ability to create a focus of attention *active
thinking*. We call the mental activity outside the spotlight *passive thinking*.

You have a mirror of active and passive thinking in your
vision. Your ability to focus clearly on an object at the center of
your field of vision is like active thinking. Your ability to pick
up shape, motion, depth, and other information from your
peripheral vision is like passive thinking. If something enters
your peripheral field, you must turn your head and center it in
your vision in order to see it clearly. The two kinds of vision
work together to give you clarity and breadth of perception.
The two kinds of thinking work together to give you clarity
and breadth of thought.

Your eye is designed to see one thing clearly at a time.
Everything else is peripheral and blurry. In order to take in
more than one point of vision, the eye moves constantly,
sweeping across the view it wishes to take in, and pulling
together a composite, clear image in your mind.

Your mind, too, is designed to focus only one spotlight of
awareness at a time. This spotlight shifts and moves across a
field of ideas and thoughts, which then come together in a
composite awareness in your mind. So if you wish to create a
mental state that is healthy, clear and in focus, you need to take
a look at where and how you are shining your spotlight.

When you chronically try to attend to three things at once,
none of your experience is clear; your awareness grows blurry.
When you chronically focus your attention primarily on logical calculations and thoughts, then the intuitive information
gets squeezed out of the picture you are building in your mind.

**To allow the greatest possible sweep of
consciousness and clearest possible picture, you need to
regularly shift your spotlights from one self to another,
from your physical focus, to your mental center of
activity, to your spiritual pull, and back again.**

In order to keep your eyes healthy, you frequently blink
them, temporarily shutting down the focus and letting them
rest. The eye rests when the lids are shut. If you stare into space

with the vision parked unconsciously, you can actually damage and blur your vision.

In order to keep your mind healthy, you similarly shut off your spotlight of active thinking, and rest in the passive realms of activity. Like shutting your eyelids, there is a mental closing you do that signals the active thinking to shut off. If you do not do this, for example if you go to sleep without choosing to let go mentally for a time, you will wake up tired and mentally blurry.

Turning on your spotlight is a matter of turning your attention to something. Turning it off is a matter of letting go.

You do not have to consciously tell your heart to beat, and yet it does so splendidly. Nor do you have to tell your blood where to go. It knows where to flow. Similarly you do not have to control the workings and activities of your mind. It automatically brings in information and processes it; your talking self continuously makes creative decisions and choices in response, whether or not you are conscious of these choices.

The job of your active mind is to shape your conscious awareness so you can create the composite experience, the life that you wish to live. You need to learn to recognize the information being presented by the passive mind as well, and learn how to use it wisely. Those vague hunches, hits of intuition, and thoughts that whisper in the background of your mind are all evidence that your passive mind is working on something significant.

When you keep your active mind flexible, then it is not difficult to pause in your everyday concerns for a moment and let your mental scanner drift into the murkier realms of your mind, allowing it to highlight and bring to your awareness perceptions and thoughts which will enrich your understanding, even when they don't yet fit your logical frameworks.

With all your mental activity it is easy to get lost or inundated with thoughts. If you want to use your mind more effectively, notice where you regularly shine your attention. Do you know how to let go and rest? Make room for variety in your attention: listen to all three of your selves, to both your logical and intuitive minds. Observe (with patience and compassion) where your mind (or your experience, or your perception) is getting stuck.

Your creative, splendid mind rises from a place deep within you and extends beyond your conscious awareness. Your mind is the arena where you create your own portion of the larger dream. Learn to watch it. Learn to work within its rhythms. Learn to set things in motion, then get out of the way, trusting your intuitive capacity to direct and steer your choices, and your logical ability to evaluate and make adjustments to your course.

Containers

ৼ

What makes you different from a cat or dog is that you are striving for meaning in life. You want your efforts and endeavors to add up to something, to have larger significance. This is a natural function of your mind. Therefore, much of what you choose to do with your waking reality is to set up events and projects calculated to add meaning to the whole drama of self you are creating. In order to give you meaning, your mind creates containers of perception and expectation, which you then industriously set about filling.

A container is the frame that you put on your life. It is the shape that you give to your experience. It is a goal that you set for yourself, or the criteria you use in evaluating experience. Every time you say, "This week I want to get the garage cleaned out," you create a container which affects your choices and actions for that week and sets criteria for how satisfied you will feel.

If you have cleaned your garage by the end of the week there will be a sense of closure, of satisfaction: a container has been created and filled. If on the other hand you find the weekend rolling around and you have made no progress toward your goal, there is a sense of unfinished business that hangs over you, making it difficult to feel at peace and relaxed.

Your containers come in various sizes. When you say, "This person is family to me," you are creating a large container to give significance to a whole range of exchanges. When you say, "In the next hour I would like to sleep," that is a small container, a temporary focus that guides and determines your choices for only a short amount of time.

The framework you place on an action, the context you place it in, the expectation or goal that you set determines its value and impact upon your consciousness. Much of your power to feel satisfied in this life rests with your skill in creating containers that work for you.

If someone you think is poor and homeless hands you a dollar for a charity you support, it will seem like a great gift. But if you believe that same person is a millionaire, the dollar will seem petty and small. If you are in a mood to stay in bed and read, then a rainy day will feel wonderful. But if your container, your plan in this case, was to go on a picnic, the same rainy day is a disappointment.

Your power and your satisfaction are always relative to the goals you set or accept. When your job calls for sharp intelligence and constant alertness, it will only be satisfying if these are energies you wish to express. Otherwise, you will find yourself feeling angry and frustrated that your job is so demanding and limiting. It is a container which does not fit your nature, energy or needs.

There is nothing intrinsically valuable about a particular container. There are only those which work for you now, which allow you to explore and express your energies, and those which don't work for you because they are too small, too large, stultifying, overly stimulating, and so on.

Remember that old advertisement from the Peace Corps that asked: "Is this glass half empty or half full?" Your attitude greatly affects your perception. Your happiness is much more dependent on how you receive and frame your experience than on what events happen to you. Your joy is facilitated not so much by getting everything you want and need but by your ability to allow the meaning and value of your experience to satisfy you.

If you wish to be fulfilled, then you need to set and accept containers that can in fact be filled. You may also need to reject those containers (expectations, goals, settings) which you are not in a position to fill.

When you have a deadline hanging over you which you can't possibly meet, it can invalidate or sour the work you can accomplish. When you decide that this year you will finish your degree, obstacles to that goal can make you feel as if you are wasting time. A shift in containers can make those same experiences feel acceptable or comfortable. You can decide the deadline is unreasonable and instead strive to do your best within the time given. You can let go of trying to finish your degree so quickly, instead focussing on learning from the lessons and challenges of the present moment. These shifts of attitude give you a new container in which to work.

Think about the relationship in which your partner wishes to change you. How frustrating to be straining to fill a container of expectation and field all the judgments

that naturally arise when you cannot perform as
expected. Think about the job which calls for skills you
haven't developed, and has no room for those skills you
do possess; how demoralizing it is. Containers which do
not fit can create misery for all concerned, and seriously
damage your self-esteem.

You develop self-esteem by creating containers that express and represent your selves accurately. You need a balance of large containers and small ones, of temporary containers and permanent ones. You may create a container that is a belief, such as "I am a good person." Implicit in the word "good" are all kinds of expectations, such as being helpful to others. At the same time, you may need to set up another container that is a privacy container: "One day each week, I will put my needs ahead of others, so I can rest and be renewed."

If you regularly set containers that are too big for you— you have to find true love, make perfect relationships, do perfect work, use your leisure time productively, be constantly attaining spiritual insight, produce prolifically and creatively— you will live in a state of frustration.

If you regularly set containers that are too small for you— you only try things you know how to do, you adhere to a set and rigid routine, you focus only on small tasks and drift without larger goals—you will find your self-esteem sinking and boredom or dissatisfaction eating at you.

The art of creating containers involves learning to plan your time wisely and flexibly. It means learning to locate and use resources. It means learning to make your own goals, listen to your own values and your own interpretations of events. If you consult your inner sense of what is right for you, you will get desires and inclinations about what you want. Your talking self then needs to create a framework for honoring that desire.

When talking self is good at creating containers, you will experience regular success and regular challenge. You will feel confident of your ability to do most things you set out to do, but will also know that occasionally you bite off more than you can chew and need to rethink projects, goals, and expectations.

How often do you let your problems create the containment you need in your life? Your day is dominated by the stress that came from a misunderstanding. Your week is hemmed in by pressures because you couldn't say no to friends who wanted favors. Your year passes by in an unsatisfactory way because you have ping-ponged back and forth between overscheduling and exhaustion. Your life seems miserable because of neighbors who play music too loudly, family members who make you feel guilt and obligation, partners or colleagues who seem to need rescuing.

Problems can certainly serve as containers, and you may feel good or strong when you have resolved them, but we would remind you that you can also create other containers that are more joyous, that are not so painful. And you can learn to avoid those problem containers. There is nothing that says your life should be an ongoing process of overcoming adversity. If you let others (and their problems) create your containers, you will almost certainly find yourself in constant struggle, caught in inappropriate containers.

How do you solve your problems? By rethinking your commitments. By creating containers that truly make sense for you, that are natural small goals, that are attainable, that honor the three levels of your being and your three selves. Sometimes the most profound spiritual practice you can have is to practice making good arrangements of time, resources and energy. Practice reframing your expectations and perceptions. The more you do that, the more those things that seem like problems out there get resolved or go away.

When you have a difficult relationship with someone, it is often the container that is wrong: there is too much or not enough commitment and expectation; there is a differing understanding about what each of you will do for the other; there is a boundary threat, the sense that one or both of you will somehow violate the needs or safety of the other. Even when your bond with someone is deep and strong, it needs an adequate container. It is frustrating to be contained too closely with someone you don't feel bonded to, and equally frustrating to have no adequate container for a bond you do feel with someone.

Take some time to examine your containers. The identity you carry is one large container in your life. Your ideas about where and with whom you belong create a container for how you will interact with others. The commitments you make to people and activities, the attitudes you have about how much you need to get done

within a day, a week, a year, create containers of
expectation. Do you see that any way your mind shapes
energy and experience is a container?

Most of you will have containers that conflict. You want
to be alone, spend lots of time with friends, work long hours
and go on frequent vacations too. Your life will only have room
for so many containers at any one time. You cannot contribute
to every pot, be part of every group, act on every interest fully,
carry several personalities and lifestyles effectively. While you
are an amazingly complex and flexible creature, you are limited by the constraints of time, space, physical energy, and mental attention. These limits are there to enable you to create
meaning, not to rob you of your potential.

Your talking self brings meaning to your whole being by
learning to make conscious and responsible choices. To what
extent do you want interactions with others? When and how do
you set them up? To what extent do you open yourself to ideas?
Which ideas are going to inform your world-view? What commitments will you take on? Which people are your kin? Which
circles are you going to participate in? You cannot physically
be part of every circle, even though in your wiser self you are
part of the whole. What values are your values, and what goals
are truly your own goals?

Many of the containers which give shape to your experience are implicit. They are the rules and expectations of your
society. They are the financial shifts that affect how you choose
to spend your time. They are the fears or guilt or responsibility that hem you in. They are the accidental containment of
being thrown together with neighbors, colleagues, strangers.
The more conscious you are of these containers, and the more
you are able to make them explicit in your mind, the better you
can choose to re-frame them to serve you.

You may not be able to control how your work situation is
organized, but you can choose your mental container that
guides your participation in it. You have some choice over how
you let it affect you. For example, if your work is dull and repet-
itive, you may be able to sing while working or create small
incentives and challenges for yourself or continuously shift
your focus from one aspect of the task to another. You may
see ways to re-negotiate parts of the container if you are aware
of how it limits you and how it serves you.

If you do not want life to limit you, if you do not want

your work situation, other people, failures and problems to define you, then set your own limits and keep shifting and changing them as your needs and desires shift. And you will find that very rarely do you need to be limited and contained by other people. You will be so clear on what your container is, that those things like jobs falling apart or relationships ending (which we do not mean to trivialize), will seem right because you will have finished what you need for that container anyway and you will be ready to let go.

You are free to set up whatever expectations of yourself you would like, within the limits of your own health, social milieu, physical constraints, sanctity of self and sanctity of others. What allows you this power is your ability to communicate your containers to others. If you have created a relationship with someone and there are expectations flowing between you, you can't necessarily stay in the relationship to avoid hurting the other person. But you can take responsibility by working to change that shared container, or by communicating clearly the ways that container is no longer working for you.

Many of you feel pressure to hold onto a particular container at all cost. Keep the house, even if it requires too much work to pay for it. Keep the relationship, even when it has long since failed to meet any needs. Keep the job, the identity, the behaviors and beliefs which have become outmoded containers for you. There is great sadness for many of you and even a sense of failure when a container has been filled or no longer serves you. You can diminish some of this pain by shifting your attitude toward containers.

They are all temporary, and will require regular amendment and re-structuring. They will serve you for a time, but then as a matter of course will be replaced by other containers. That does not mean you must cast away your relationships every few years. It means instead that you must reconstruct your relationships periodically, so they can serve as vital and healthy containers. If you wish to stay at the same job for thirty years, then your responsibility is to shift your understanding, attitude and approach to the work as needed over time, letting it satisfy you in different ways.

There is no universal rule that says a long term container is more valuable than a short term one. You are not necessarily striving to create containers that will last you a lifetime. The universal rule says that you

*create containers to serve you, and then create new ones
when the old ones are no longer right.*

We recommend that you set yourself some larger visions
and dreams to sail by. Perhaps you will want to open to greater
awareness, to love your fellow creatures better, to be more
awake to who you are. Then we suggest you keep your visions
at the back of your mind, as touchstones, and you create some
little containers, just temporary ones, which reflect the spirit of
those dreams or aspirations. Can you this week pay attention to
small acts of kindness? Can you focus for a day on the sense
of touch, so you understand it more deeply? Can you try, for
one month, to express your needs verbally, so your partner has
clearer cues and information about what it is you are wanting?

If you focus on containers that reflect the essence of
things, you will be able to be more flexible about structures. If
at your job you can see your contribution in terms of the types
of service you provide—connection, or support, or guidance, or
production of goods—you will be less wedded to the job title,
status and protocol of the container. In other words, we are
suggesting that you consciously shift your sense of fulfillment
from the details of a container to its essence. A slight at work
will have less power over you if you can be clearer about the
essence of what gives your life meaning.

The creation and maintenance of containers is the primary work of your talking self. Thus it is a lifetime practice and
project. Your talking self is just naturally drawn to new challenges, new relationships and new ways to organize your life
and thinking. Within these new challenges and events she creates, the meaning comes from talking self's ability to assign
and perceive significance and satisfaction.

*Meaning is a gift of the talking self, as she sets
containers for the Self. It is not something you are
assigned or can be given by others.*

Mental Stance:
Arrangements of Mind

ॐ

Imagine life as a vast embroidered tapestry which you are helping to stitch. It has been divided into sections, and you are working collaboratively with a few thousand other artists on your particular section. Within that, you have been given your own small portion of empty canvas to fill.

You have selected the needles and beautifully colored threads you wish to use, and have decided, together with your partners, on some general themes for your subsection of the tapestry and now you are free to proceed with your task.

Step back for a moment, and watch your fellow artists at work. Over there in that corner, you see someone with his nose buried in his work, busily stitching away. He never looks up, barely pauses, and seems to have no need to stop and think about what he is doing. It is the bulldozer approach to embroidery.

And over there, to the left, there is another artist sitting with hand poised, as if to sew, but she has a book hidden in her sewing basket, and she is clearly far more interested in reading than in stitching her portion of the canvas. Every once in a while, she looks up guiltily, puts in a stitch or two, and then goes back to her reading.

And the person next to you has an interesting approach. She stitches in a portion of her design, stands back for a few minutes scowling, then rushes forward to tear it out again. After that she fumes and weeps for a while, then picks up her needle and starts the process all over again. Her canvas is torn and stretched from so much action; there is little embroidery remaining there.

A fellow down the way has quickly stitched his section in geometrical rows of cross stitches, and is now wandering back and forth in his area, giving free advice to whoever will listen. There is someone near him stealthily copying the section above her, and the person next to her is surrounded by a mound of papers which are obviously rejected designs. There are a myriad of pencil lines darkening his canvas.

Someone down the way is clearly an artist. You watch her for a longer time, because she seems to be able to figure out what she wants and execute it. But even as you watch, for some reason, she puts away her things and wanders off. Perhaps she feels satisfied and is done for the day. Perhaps she doesn't really feel challenged. Still, you can't help admiring her lovely designs....

There are as many approaches to this task as there are artists. What is yours? It is useful to step back from your life from time to time, and look at how you are organizing it, how you are approaching it. There are cycles to your energy, patterns in your changes, and you also have what we would call a fairly consistent *problem set*.

You are an artist, creating your life as you go, and it will help you create more effectively if you understand your mental stance: how you arrange the furniture of your mind.

Cycles

First of all, look at your cycles of energy, because it is energy that fuels your mind. On a daily basis, there will be certain times when you are at your strongest and most alert, and other times when you require rest or withdrawal. Beyond being aware of whether you are a morning person or a night person, you can pay attention to how your energy ebbs and flows characteristically throughout your day. You can use these tides of energy in arranging your work and play. You would not try to sail in the ocean without paying attention to the tides, yet many of you sail through life oblivious to these very strong energetic shifts in you.

The food you eat and your nutritional choices can be coordinated with your natural energetic patterns. You can find which kinds of foods your body receives most fully at which times of day. There are some nutritionists doing work in this direction, but unfortunately their ideas tend to be put forth as prescriptions for everyone. Each of you has particular physical tides that relate to your inner energetic resonance and your response to the physical and emotional environment in which you live. So you are free to design the diet that nourishes you most fully.

Your life is not a formless meander. It has patterns and themes which organize it or, to be more precise, your mind organizes your life into patterns and themes and cycles. Some of you have chapters of your life which last about three years. Others of you experience five, six, seven, nine and even eleven-year cycles. (And every number in between.)

It is useful to know this. If you want to quit your job, is it because you are blocked and running away, or is it because, in fact, you have reached the end of a natural cycle and need to make a major change? If your relationship is boring and stale, is it because you are in the boring and stale phase of its natural pattern, or have you in fact finished a cycle and neglected to consciously and actively start a new one?

Many of our students have sought out psychic or astrological readings to gain insight into these issues. They ask: What are the larger themes and patterns affecting my life right now? What is the larger context in which I am trying to make my decision? It can be useful to get this type of insight from a skilled practitioner, but it is also something you can become more aware of yourself.

Write out a timeline on a piece of paper, and then jot down major events, turning points, and significant memories that seem to have meaning for you. Are there patterns to these events? How many relationships have you had, and how long were the intervals between major involvement with other people? How long did your friendships tend to last? How frequently have you had fertile and fallow periods in your life?

The goal of this exercise is not to make your life conform to some kind of mystical mathematics, but rather to see if you can recognize patterns to your energies, attention span and aspirations. If you notice, for example, that every time you reached a fallow period in your personal relationship, you were also conducting a job search, or also suffered health problems, then you have some information which can be useful to you next time you experience that particular configuration of themes.

We suggest that you develop a kind of personal astrology, relying not so much on what the stars and cosmos have to say predictively about your life, but using the major events and emotional moments of your life as stars and cosmos to navigate by.

Personal Style

You are allowed to develop a personal style. You are free to hide a book in your work basket, free to work and re-work the same two inches of canvas, and free to take breaks and examine what others are doing. Your only obligations are to respect the sanctity of other people's portion of canvas—their right to determine their own life—and to satisfy some inner sense of truth or rightness.

For some of you, the bulldozer approach to life is immensely satisfying. It arises as a pattern deep within you, and makes you feel most alive and fulfilled. Others of you have learned to bulldoze, but that mode doesn't satisfy you.

There are three strong influences on you as you develop your mental stance. One is your inner sense of rightness, a second is what you are taught by family and teachers, and a third is the peer pressure from the fellow artists in your section of the canvas. But when all is said and done, the only influence which is really significant to you is the first. When you die, you leave your portion of the canvas behind, but you take with you, as soul nourishment, whatever fulfillment you have been able to get from the task as you conceived it.

Remember that old game which asks: if you were an animal, what kind of animal would you be? Would you be a beaver, busily building a dam? Would you be a friendly beagle, constantly hovering over your loved ones? Would you be a butterfly, going through distinct and wildly different life phases? The kind of animal you would be reflects some of the aspects of your personal style.

Your personal style is the way you approach the task of filling your portion of canvas, of living your life. It includes where you focus your energies, what containers you create, where you fall in the range between active and passive, what aspects of life fulfill you, how you proceed with something you have chosen to do.

Do you attack life's challenges with a vengeance, let things flow as they will, struggle your way from one crisis to the next, soar for a time, then rest for a time? Do you run through life, hop, skip, swim, drag your feet, or spend your energies trying to hitch rides?

It is perhaps easier to answer some of these questions about your friends. You can more easily stand back and get perspective on someone else's life. It is easier to see, for example, when your best friend is complaining that no one loves him, that in fact he has a pattern of growing intensely close to people, then backing off suddenly and feeling unloved. But what are those patterns in your own style of being?

Your personal style sets the context in which you can interpret individual actions. For example, if you are someone with high energy who tackles life with enthusiasm, then a few months of boredom and alienation are going to be far more significant than if you were someone who tends to rush into involvement then crash. If you tend to be low-key and unruffled, then a conflict at work has far more significance for you than for someone who thrives on regular struggle and conflict.

It is useful to recognize your personal style and come to terms with it. Events in your life are not just free-floating happenings. They are scenarios in an on-going drama of Self, and if you can realize what character you are striving to portray and what your approach is, you have a way to refine your actions so that they are more effective.

So many of our friends in body spend time berating themselves for aspects of their character which we find charming. They say they are too feisty. They call themselves pushy. They accuse themselves of being too loyal, or too intense, or not serious enough. They don't allow themselves the scope and leeway they would to the animals around them. They can appreciate the ostrich for its quirks and traits, but carry on a constant inner tirade against their own tendencies.

We suggest instead that you learn to know and accept your tendencies. Develop an appreciation for how you proceed in this life, what is valuable in your style, and how well your style serves you in achieving your goals.

Not everyone has identical goals. In fact, it is a delightful exercise to look around you and recognize some of the weird and interesting projects people set for themselves: a woman in Arkansas is trying to grow the longest fingernails ever measured; a man in Wisconsin wants to build his own seaplane and fly to the West Indies; a twelve-year old in Idaho has decided to collect every type of insect on the planet.

Many of our students believe that everyone is striving for the same things, and they too should strive for these vaguely-defined goals. But this is a myth. You are splendidly designed to be someone unique, living in a style best suited to you.

Problem Set

Many of your goals and challenges for this life were established as you encountered difficulties while growing up. This was not entirely accidental.

Your spirit chose a landscape for you to travel as a child which provided opportunities to develop certain *muscles* and also encounter certain challenges. If you grew up in a family where money was plentiful and not emotionally charged, you tend to have good money muscles, a good sense of how to work in that medium.

But the same family may have been bad with fighting: fights were hidden from the children and denied. So throughout your adult years you will be plagued with difficulties relating to conflict.

Each of you has certain muscles and certain areas of weakness. Your areas of weakness are what we call your problem set. It comprises those issues which occur and reoccur in your life, sometimes changing form or context slightly, but remaining essentially similar. These familiar challenges seem to follow you from place to place, from relationship to relationship, but in fact you tend to be drawn to relationships and settings in which you can work on them.

For example, you may find yourself, once again, in a relationship with someone who is too busy. Even though you left the last relationship because your partner was a compulsive worker, you thought this person would be different and you wake up one day to find that the two relationships are very similar. There is no need to kick yourself and think you are stupid. It is an old friend, this issue, and something about it is attractive to you. It is part of your problem set. It belongs to you.

Your problem set shifts somewhat, as you grow and evolve in this life, but it also contains recurring issues which seem frighteningly persistent. These charged issues are the areas where one of your selves has decided to do some extensive development, some insight-building, some more exploration. That is why you find yourself in parallel situations over and over again.

Many of the New Age books are misleading on this topic. They say, "you create your own reality" and the implication is that you are somehow to blame for the struggles or problems you encounter. We would describe your role in creating your reality differently.

Each of your selves has goals and predilections which affect your choices. Just as you will crave ice cream because of some combination of hunger, nutritional need and plain old-fashioned opportunity (the ice cream parlor is there in front of you), you call forth and choose experiences through a combination of energetic truth and felicitous opportunity.

The problems, disasters and conflicts that beset you are not something that you secretly choose in order to test your spiritual mettle. They are, in some ways, the side effect of your choices. For example, you may be attracted to people who are ambitious and very energetic. There are certain problems and difficulties that come with the territory of this choice of partner. The energetic people you consistently choose may also be consistently over-extended, or difficult to get close to, or unable to receive gifts very well.

Thus there is no purpose in blaming yourself for having chosen the problems, or in suggesting you created them. Instead, recognize that it is a landscape you chose to try to enter, for reasons of your own. In crossing the landscape, you may have wanted to strengthen the particular muscles required by that setting. On the other hand, you may have forgotten or been unaware that those problems might arise within the choice you were making. Some painful experiences happen to you because your radar is not tuned to intercept them. Others happen because your choices have led you to be in the wrong place at the wrong time.

We encourage you to avoid the facile explanations that describe problems as soul choices. Because you are a committee of three, your choices arise from all three domains. Some of the mistakes, painful misunderstandings and crises you experience *are* selected at a deep level in order to open you to greater awareness. But many are due to blind spots or limited understanding on the part of your talking or earth elemental self (and on the part of the talking and earth elemental selves of your friends, family and colleagues).

Your problems offer you a chance to shift or refine your personality self and your mental understandings of life. Relax and celebrate these challenges. They offer you opportunities to work on building better skills and stronger muscles on behalf of your multiple Self.

Your problems may reflect lacks in your understanding,

but do not define lacks in you. If love chronically goes wrong in your life, it means you have not yet developed the appropriate skills and radar to love comfortably. It does not mean you are somehow karmically doomed to fail at love in this life. If love is in your problem set, it indicates a need for more teaching, better role models, and the patience to let yourself learn new skills.

Every one has a problem set. You may struggle with love issues, but feel fine with issues of work and professional identity. You may struggle with work, but feel comfortable in your social milieu or your body. It is useful to identify which issues are not problematic for you, and which are truly alive and charged for you.

Threshold of Functioning

If you sit there reading this and think, "But I have problems in all of these realms!", then most likely your primary problem area is self-esteem or security. The only people who regularly suffer from problems in all realms are those who tend to be chronically stuck below what we call a *threshold of functioning*.

There is a certain emotional, social and physical threshold below which everything seems problematic, and above which the same problems seem insignificant. It is easy to recognize this concept when you look at your body. If you have been sick for several months, so that you haven't used your muscles, then going up a flight of stairs can feel like climbing a mountain. What an ordeal!

Yet after a couple of weeks of exercise, building up your strength, you will find yourself able to run up the steps without even thinking about the effort it takes. The exercise has put you above a certain threshold of functioning, where simple tasks are simple to do, and you have the resources necessary for your most frequent challenges.

There is a threshold of functioning in your emotional and social skills as well. When you are too lonely, too tired, too isolated, too critical, too perfectionistic, too dependent on others, your self-esteem may drop, your ego may swell in exaggerated self-protection, and you sink below a threshold of functioning. At that point, things go haywire in your life. Money problems, love problems, work and housing problems may seem to materialize for no reason.

The reason is there, however. You are disconnected from

your roots or chronically out of balance. You are binding your muscles and not allowing them to strengthen. You are stuck below a threshold of functioning. When you are below the threshold, everything feels impossible—and in some ways it is. We are sure you are familiar with this feeling; think about when you are very tired and trying to force yourself to work.

If your problems seem to be endless, the antidote is to look for ways to raise your threshold. Back off from a focus on your problems, as best you can, and focus instead on activities which will rebalance you.

Get enough sleep, neither too much nor too little. Get your body moving to increase your circulation. Make opportunities to be around other people (not too much, not too little), and stimulate a healthy social circulation. Eat well, neither too little nor too much, and avoid stimulants or depressants.

Ignore the voices in your head for a time or take them with a grain of salt. Your gatekeeper robots have a tendency to go haywire when you fall below the threshold of functioning. They will suggest all kinds of reasons for your discomfort, when at root you are not comfortable because you do not have a basic balance and circulation.

Find some small activities that you can do for the sake of doing them, balance them with rest, suspend your larger expectations of yourself for a time, and strive as best you can to get things circulating again.

Policy Beliefs

You carry a mental identity and image of yourself, which you store in your ego, and which you use as a kind of index to truth, no matter what the truth-of-the-moment might be. For example, you might think of yourself as a liberal. You tend to use that as a criterion in your choice of attitudes and causes. Yet in a specific situation, you may find yourself reacting with outrage to someone's liberal behavior. Instead of revising your view of yourself, it is more likely that you will either be unaware of your inconsistency or else see this particular reaction as an exception.

Policy beliefs can be useful in maintaining your mental patterns and self-esteem. For example, say someone has always believed she had beautiful hair. She carries a policy belief that her hair is beautiful. Then she goes out in the wind for a day and her hair gets blown into a tangled, knotted, dry mess. That person goes home afterward and sees the mess of her hair as merely a temporary situation. It may take a few days for her hair to get back to normal, but she doesn't admit the temporary messy state as real or as truth, because she carries a *policy truth* that allows her to maintain her self-esteem even in the face of deflating evidence.

That is how policy truths can serve you.

But policy truths are also often used in harmful ways. You codify past failures into truth about yourself, and ignore evidence to the contrary. For example, you may say, "I am bad with children." This kind of policy truth, while based on experience, tends to shape your future experience in this direction. Because you think you are bad with children, you act embarrassed and awkward around them. They in turn do not respond to you, and the belief gets reinforced. If you happen to run into a child who seems to like you, you say, "What an unusual child!"

It is easy enough to recognize your policy beliefs. You tend to whisper them to yourself as mantras. You tend to offer them up to strangers as you tell them about yourself. You tend to use them as apologies and brags and rationalizations. They tend to come to mind as explanations for your actions, disappointments, successes. And often they act to rob you of authentic experience and the power of the moment.

How many times have you brushed aside compliments using a policy belief? Someone says to you, "That presentation went really well, you must have worked hard on it." And you dismiss your efforts: "Public speaking comes naturally to me, it runs in the family." This is more than just modesty, it is a form of mental blockage created by your policy beliefs.

The positive use of a policy belief is in creating a strong self-image and helping you to keep some of your goals and aspirations in mind. If you say, "I'm a fun-loving and adventuresome person," this is part truth, part wishful thinking, but it carries you through those moments when you feel neither fun-loving nor adventuresome.

The policy truth can counteract your tendency to register failure or negative experience more strongly than positive experience. Suppose you cross a road ten thousand times with no mishaps, but once while crossing you are sideswiped by a truck. You learn to think of road-crossing as a dangerous activity indeed. But if you carry a policy belief that says "I am generally safe crossing roads if I pay attention," then your experience with being sideswiped gets stored in a different mental category: that of *unusual occurrences*. Instead of reacting to future road crossings with fear, you are able to respond with greater caution. Your policy belief has instructed your gatekeeper how to interpret the experience correctly.

Do you see the dilemma with policy truths? On the one hand, you want to be realistic and safe in your beliefs, and on the other hand you want to carry policy beliefs that enable you to grow.

Activity

Take stock of your policy beliefs and truths. Write a little character sketch of yourself, as if you were introducing yourself to a potential lover. Free associate a web of adjectives and phrases that describe who and how you are. Listen in to what you are telling yourself (and other people) about yourself.

Then make up some policy beliefs that can help you change and grow. Let your wishful thinking point the way. Do you yearn to love your body, respect your mind, believe in your potentials, trust you will be loved?

"I am an intelligent and creative human being and I can learn."

"I can change, I am multifaceted."

"The more you know me, the more of me there is to know."

"I am capable, and I enjoy being a beginner and learning new things."

"I will receive what I need. There is plenty of time."

Introduce some of these policy beliefs into your mind. Try them on for a day, and practice carrying them. Treat them as seeds you are planting in your garden. Put them in your mind, water them with playfulness and hope, and trust them to grow in their season.

Talking Self Dramas

We have been giving you a guided tour of the many dimensions of mind which affect your waking reality. By now we are sure some of you are thinking, "Yes, I know that my mental interpretations affect the quality of my experience. But things happen to me as well. That car crash last year was not just painful in my mind. It also hurt physically, and wreaked havoc with my finances. And this dead-end job I am in is not exclusively a question of *my* attitude. There are some aspects of it that I can neither control nor see a way to appreciate."

Your life has plot. It has drama. It takes place in various settings which do affect and sometimes constrain you. We would be doing you a great disservice if we implied, from our comfortable disembodied state, that living successfully in body is just a matter of working with your mind. If that were the case, you wouldn't have bothered to include the earth elemental dimension in your existence.

Living successfully in your waking reality requires you to develop skill as both a plot-maker and an actor. You write a portion of the drama you live, co-authoring it with others, and then you get out there on the stage and enact your life, again coordinating with others.

Those two dimensions, creating and enacting, together form your waking reality.

When you pick up the phone and invite a friend to dinner you are creating plot in your life. You are setting up a drama in which you will later participate. When you choose to accept one job or not to apply for another, you are also setting up a dramatic framework. These frameworks, like your mental containers, will greatly affect the life you are able to live.

Some of you have learned great skill in setting up satisfying dramas. You are able to communicate with your fellow actors and make clear decisions for the most part about what to do and when to do it. Others of you struggle with the plot of your life. You feel you are rarely in the right place at the right time. You set up too much plot and find yourself overwhelmed by the physical and emotional demands of all that drama. You fear plot and hold back from making choices, letting your life path be determined solely by fortuitous accident and other people's decisions for you.

Take a moment to look at this aspect of your life. What do you create? What do you agree to? What are you able to enact and follow through on? Which aspects of your life seem to fail because you are not yet able to do what you plan or commit to?

We have suggested earlier that you can greatly increase your sense of satisfaction if you adjust your mental expectations and interpretations of events. We would add the suggestion that you can also greatly increase the quality of your experience if you work on your skills of enactment: choosing reasonable dramatic frameworks for yourself, knowing how to respond to the dramas you find yourself in, learning to communicate clearly, and using your earth elemental instrument with skill and sensitivity.

This is a tall order. A first step is to allow yourself to make mistakes. If there is no room for trial and error, for rehearsals in this physical existence of yours, then every moment becomes too charged and fraught with meaning. If you cannot allow yourself the time and space to do things badly, to be a beginner and a learner, then you will never develop new skills and you will be limited to those actions you already do well.

A second step is to learn to tolerate discomfort. If you are not willing to be uncomfortable physically or emotionally for a time, you will be unable to make a plan and carry it out. Most new effort includes some discomfort, because most new effort includes unfamiliar feelings, sensations and perceptions. You have a good model for this in your body. There is discomfort in exercising new muscles in new ways, but if you can tolerate it, while working respectfully with your body, the discomfort soon passes, and you find yourself stronger from the effort.

But do you see that some pain is also a warning to back off? If you pause to investigate the pain, to listen to it and find its roots in your mind or body, you have the discernment (and inner guidance) to tell whether it is resistance or serious warning.

We recognize that this might be hard to do. When you are feeling pain, stop, shut your eyes and just feel it. Let it pulse, or pull, or sting, or pressure you as you lie still and feel it. Examine where it is located in your body. Watch how it moves or shifts as you breathe. Does it have a limit to it? Is it constant, or does it come in waves or in response to movements or tensions on your part? What is your mind whispering in this moment? Are you stoking the flame of your pain with fearful thoughts and images, accusing voices and guilt?

Try to clear your mind and focus on your breathing. See if you can feel the pain as nerve sensations, and receive these sensations calmly. The more you understand your pain and the way it is behaving, the more able you will be to move through it and respond to it appropriately.

A third step is to allow the plot of your life to evolve and grow. If you have sketched out an entire plan for your life, with expectations and pressures to achieve, then there is not much room for the everyday creating your talking self craves. If you perceive the events of your life as so interconnected that each thing you do will make or break your identity, then you have mis-plotted your drama. You are first and foremost a creature, enjoying a creature existence. You are secondarily a social being, enjoying social roles and expressions.

It is important to find a balance between caring so deeply about the turns in your plot that every moment seems of dire importance, and detaching from the talking self dimension by saying, "An event is just an event."

Let the events of your life have meaning on their own terms, apart from what you chose to do yesterday or might choose tomorrow. Leave room to discover who you are and can be, rather than expecting yourself to somehow control this act of creation you are engaged in. Keep in mind that although your choices and actions have results, there is also a space for other people, fate, your own wiser self to play a role and turn the drama in quite unexpected directions.

Let yourself try new activities just for the enjoyment of them. Let yourself have unplanned unscheduled time, so there is room for felicitous adventures. Make sure that you take time each day to listen in to your inclinations and desires, examine your fears and constraints, and let go of your judgments or dissatisfaction with your life. Choose at least one activity each day that you do just for the sake of doing it, for the pleasure, the interest, the experience of it.

A fourth step is to learn to back off temporarily from the dramas in your life and remind yourself of basic values. Use your sense of humor to enjoy the turns of plot and the great diversity of conflicts that can arise. Use your sense of compassion to recognize that each life includes a whole range of experiences, from the tragic to the celebratory, and that each of these dimensions adds depth and richness to your lived experience that goes far beyond your mental tendency to see events as good or bad.

How dramatic is your talking self? It will be useful for you to know this. Some of you chronically struggle, not because your life is harder than other people's, but because your character feels most alive when engaged in passion and struggle. Others of you encounter difficult dramas, but experience deep and quiet sensations of meaning that carry you through situations that might vanquish another kind of person.

Events are not in and of themselves tragic or felicitous. They take their meaning from the context you create for them within your mind and emotions. It is helpful to recognize your manner of proceeding and your relationship to drama in your life. It will help you to evaluate whether the level of activity and engagement you experience is appropriate for your inner sense of spirit and purpose.

A student asked us recently: "When do I design my own reality and structures, and when should I await the will of my higher power?" This is a good question. If you remind yourself that you are a committee of three, then you can see that the will of your wiser self is like the bass note setting the rhythms. It is only part of the music you are creating here. The other two parts are your talking self creations, and your earth elemental enactment.

It is a great coordinating act to bring these three dimensions together. Sometimes action is called for and you are required to act first and evaluate that choice later. Sometimes it makes more sense to listen in to the wiser self, and then choose a path of action. The more attuned you are to your intuition and your basic values, the more likely you are to choose wisely, even when pushed to act quickly.

Living is like hiking. Think about how you hike through unfamiliar territory. First you make a decision that you will go on this hike. Sometimes you hike for entertainment and sometimes you hike to get somewhere. If your hike is born of need (your car has broken down and you must find some help), then your mood and fears will greatly affect the quality of your experience. If your hike is based on a positive choice, you will probably set out on the same journey with very different feelings.

In either case you are hiking through territory, putting one foot in front of the other. If you sit at the beginning of the path paralyzed, then there will be no hike. And if you push your way blindly into the territory, without consideration and attention, you will greatly increase your risk.

As you hike along there will be moments when you stop to scan the ground ahead, choosing what looks like a plausible and safe path. There will be times when you mis-calculate and must retrace some of your steps. There will be times when you discover a shortcut or meet other hikers who can point out the way. There will be moments when you are energized and moving easily, and others when every step feels like a chore.

This is all part of the visceral and mental experience of hiking. And the fact is that no matter where you are heading as a destination, your experience of getting there is primary and demands your attention. The more you can cultivate an attitude of enjoyment, a respect for the challenges and risks and a willingness to engage with this landscape while not being engulfed by it, the more likely you are to experience it in a healthy and balanced way.

Your role as a creator is only one aspect of your experience. There are also other actors on the stage, there are other authors of plot interacting with you. Therefore, it is important for you to cultivate a flexible outlook on life. If you expect yourself to create a perfect masterpiece of living events, achieving great things and loving others skillfully and cleanly, then you are setting yourself up for disappointment. The physical and emotional dimensions of your existence are designed to be occasionally messy.

You are neither the sole creator of your experience nor its victim. You are a co-creator, with great latitude of choice and input, but also with vulnerability to the actions and decisions of others. When you climb in your car to drive, you are interdependent with the car itself and with the others on the road. There is a massive amount of decision-making and communication that goes into your drama of driving.

On a conscious level, you assess your skills and alertness. Do I feel capable of driving? You use your intelligence and experience to choose a route and set a reasonable speed. You use your familiarity with the machine to recognize whether it is in good working order. You use the turn signal, brakes, accelerator and other features of the machine to carry out your plan. You use the rules of the road and your own sense of safety to guide your driving. You use your eyes and ears and intuitive radar to scan the road you are on. You use your hands and feet to steer, brake, shift or accelerate as needed. And much of the time, this combination of skills and attention carries you to your destination safely.

Occasionally, though, there are accidents. You may be slammed into by a drunk driver who appears out of nowhere. You may crash into another driver because you have miscalculated or lagged in your attention. You may just be at the wrong place doing the wrong thing at the wrong time.

There are many spiritual seekers who have seen that there is a deeper level of significance to events, and who believe that there are no accidents. They ask, "Why did this happen to me? For what cosmic reason did I need to have this accident?"

We would suggest that indeed there are accidents. It is a beautiful and exciting dimension of your reality that events and objects dance and occasionally collide. Are the accidents in your life based on some soul choice, designed to teach you a spiritual lesson? Sometimes, but not usually. Usually, you crash your car because you were not paying attention, or because another driver was negligent, or because the many factors you needed to coordinate smoothly did not come together correctly.

The *fault* may be mechanical, physical, mental, emotional, spiritually yours, someone else's, or just one of those things that happen. The *lesson* is whatever benefit, understanding and learning you are able to derive from the experience.

This is very important. Your car crash may bring you great hardship, disabling you in some way, altering the path of your entire life. It may also bring you some gifts, such as time off from work or insurance money that enables you to change your living circumstances. But it would be overly simplistic to say you subconsciously chose to have an accident so that you could be disabled or enriched. Your soul choices interact with your personality choices, your intuitive awareness interacts with your intellectual awareness, and the plot of your life unfolds with twists and turns which are both planned *and* accidental.

There is a larger movement of themes and energies in your co-created universe. When population grows beyond the bounds of the earth's resources, your collective intelligence does co-create the epidemics and natural disasters to prune it back. When you see many individuals around you struggling with similar problems, responding to similar goals, there is an element of wiser self collaboration going on. But if you believe that nothing is accidental, and thus everything should be within your control, you do not allow for the give and take of co-creation and of energy moving and shifting forms.

Rather than agonizing over why you would choose the traumas and sorrows, ask yourself how you contributed to their formation, and what benefit or gifts you can gain. Let yourself mourn the losses; talking self does not like to be deprived of something she feels she wants or needs and earth elemental self does not enjoy being damaged or hurt. Then allow yourself to also remember that you live only temporarily within the conditions of this earth reality. Whatever has been lost or gained brings with it new conditions you will need to address and work with. If you can address these changes with compassion and work with them on the physical, mental, emotional and spiritual levels, each event and experience will add meaning and value to your evolving drama of self.

Gratification

✿

Some of our friends in body carry goals around like sandbags. They say: I won't feel good until I get that new job. I won't feel good until I finish this chapter. I won't feel good until I've lost ten pounds. They defer gratification, feeling they don't deserve it until they have accomplished something.

But goals are not meant to be heavy weights on your spirit; they are stars to navigate by. And gratification is not a prize to win at the end of a long struggle. It is something to experience as you inhabit each moment.

Gratification is the ability to take experience in, to **receive** *sensation, experience, nourishment. It is the ability to pay attention to the conditions of the present and to participate in the present on its own terms.*

If you need to sneeze, then sneezing can be a gratifying experience. If you are hungry, then food can gratify you. If you are receptive, then your friend's love will gratify you. It is this simple, and yet so many of our friends in body do not feel gratified very often. They send their mind and expectations ranging toward the future, thinking about how good they will feel when they accomplish x,y, or z, and without realizing it, cut off much of their own power.

It is not self-indulgent to gratify yourself; it is necessary. Your mind hungers for experience, sensations, participation in life; gratification is your signal that your hunger has been satisfied. Gratification is the signal that you have received nourishment.

Ironically, taking in nourishment is a learned skill. You need to learn to receive the food you eat, assimilate the love and attention you are given, experience and feel the exchanges and events you participate in, or else they cannot fully nourish you.

We cannot emphasize enough how important this is. When someone asks us how to create a more meaningful life we suggest this as a starting point: concentrate on taking in the meaning that is already there. Let the grass and flowers penetrate your awareness and bring you pleasure. Let the performance of everyday tasks gratify you sensually. Suspend your focus on larger containers for a time so that you can practice receiving nourishment in small and direct ways.

The practice of opening to gratification allows you to set down your sandbags and rest, so that you can see more clearly how to proceed in your life. You will not try to climb a mountain if you are dragged down by cares, expectation, and anxiety. You will not be able to make healthy, satisfying change if you cannot find some breathing space in your mind and present circumstances.

You might say: "But how will appreciating flowers or enjoying my ironing help me out of my destructive marriage and dead-end life?" In order to have the energy to change that life, you will need some fuel. *Gratification fuels you to move, to act, to try new things*. When nourishment registers in the mind, it then signals readiness to act. It you are stuck in mental torment, then your energy will be blocked or released in destructive ways. The only way to turn that around is by allowing the universe to nourish you in small immediate ways.

Your mind is a wonderful instrument, but it easily becomes congested and clogged with beliefs, understandings and expectations that block you from nourishment. Consider for a moment the difference between sitting in your house at night enjoying the night sounds and feeling the pleasure of being able to relax, and sitting there craning to listen to each sound because you fear someone may be trying to break in.

To what extent do you enjoy your experience and receive its gifts, and to what extent do you spend your time and energy struggling to change, criticizing your experience, and feeling short-changed? Your gratification comes in part from your willingness to be gratified. The more conditions you put on yourself, the less likely you are to be nourished by your experience.

Gratification is the filling of your containers. When you are dissatisfied with your life, examine your containers, but look also at your ability to allow them to fill.

A middle-aged woman came to us once and said: "I have been in therapy for years. I have found work that I am proud of, am in a good healthy relationship, have cleaned up past garbage with my family, do not use addictive substances, and try to follow my spiritual path as faithfully as I can. But I am still not happy. What is wrong?"

What was wrong was simple and sad. She had never learned to take in sensations on a basic, visceral level. She had been unsafe and abused as a child, so her sensual self was switched off to experience—even the appropriate and healthy experience she had learned to create.

Some of you were never given the freedom or permission to be gratified on a physical, sensual level. There is a strong puritan ethic in your culture that says pleasure is selfish and that taking the time to feel and assimilate experience (which often looks like doing nothing) is self-indulgent. Thus some of you never developed the mental and emotional habits or pathways that allow gratification to sink in.

Our sad friend never learned to be present in her life. She would make a mental videotape of her encounters with people, and later in the safety of her own room she would replay it again and again, using her mind to figure out what to feel and how to respond.

Most of you do not suffer such an extreme problem with your sensual circuitry. But many of you do suffer some blockage on this level and depend on ideas or abstract achievements to provide your gratification. The habits of distraction are so strong in your culture, that it is rare for you to do one thing at a time and truly attend to what you are doing. It is rare that you are alone in quiet circumstances, with few expectations pressuring you, so you can truly assimilate your experience. Yet your instrument requires this on a regular basis.

Gratification on a visceral, emotional level does not require exotic sensual experiences. It is really quite simple. It requires the nourishment of food, water, rest, activity, giving and receiving, all in their time. Gratification on the mental and spiritual level is more challenging for some of you, but also fairly straightforward. It requires you to think, listen, perceive, feel, express, imagine, create and define the moments of your life in a self-affirming and flexible way. When you allow each of these mental aspects space and time, and allow yourself to take each of these dimensions in, your life will feel meaningful as a lived experience, no matter how mundane or exotic its details. Your life will feel gratifying to you on its own terms.

Grounding

Slow Time Island

Shut your eyes and imagine yourself on a desert island. You are lying on the beach. The sun is warm, comfortable. The water is lapping on the shore, light breezes play over you, keeping you at a steady temperature. It is a perfect day, with a sky of bright blue. You have the whole place to yourself, nowhere to be, nothing to accomplish. A cool drink waits on a tray beside you.

And imagine that this is not just any island. It is a place called "Slow Time Island." Here time moves much more slowly than in your everyday reality. As you spend a minute or two of your normal everyday time on this island, it as if a whole day is slowly unfolding. Time moves so slowly that in seven minutes of your normal time, you can feel yourself taking a week's vacation on Slow Time Island.

Let yourself feel the week passing. Let your mind and body relax deeply with this vacation. Let your mind slowly untangle and sort through its confusions, your heart open gradually to this protective and utterly safe haven you have found. Let your breathing be guided by the lapping of the waves. Let the sounds of the surf be your lullaby.

As you open your eyes and return your awareness to your "normal time" surroundings, remember how wonderful it felt to be on vacation. Remember you have the power to visit Slow Time Island whenever you wish.

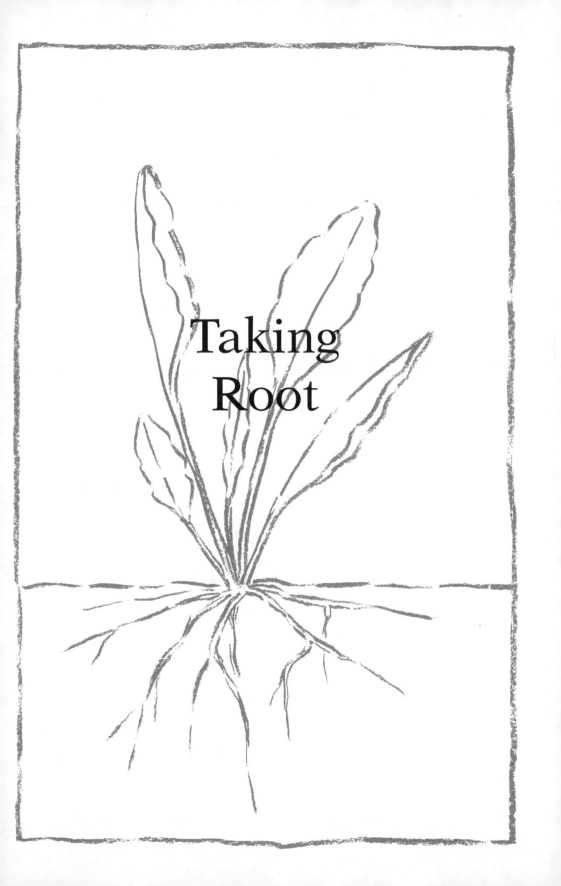

Taking
Root

Wiser Self Perspectives

Periodically, I go through what I dramatically label a *dark night of the soul*. It is an extremely uncomfortable time, when everything I say seems to dig me deeper into a hole, and every interaction seems doomed to failure. Machines break, plans fall through, my body sprouts unlovely symptoms. Despite my years of training and dialogue with the council, I start to wonder if my luck has deserted me, if my life is all wrong. I crave news that will make me feel better, I scramble to figure out what is wrong *out there* in my relationship, my job, my behavior.

Fortunately, these feelings pass and I see that what seemed all-encompassing and endless was actually temporary. My understanding was shifting, my hormones or physical being were out of balance, my mental pictures and ideas had pinned me to a course of action I couldn't accept or achieve, or I just plain ran out of steam for a while. The council advice I receive at such times is simple and thus hard to accept. They say "wait," "rest," "take time out to just inhabit your pain," "console yourself," "empty your mind."

When I follow their guidance, things invariably change. I stop struggling and something comes along to move me out of my dilemma. Usually I experience a mental shift, then willingness to accept the problem or loss, then some energy to act on my own behalf. Occasionally, I start struggling again, and it's like being in quicksand: I sink deeper into the muck.

For the longest time, I thought perhaps I was just a slow learner. Through discussion with my council, I could understand patterns in my feelings, motivations in my choices, karmic implications of events in my life, but I still found myself periodically depressed about my relationships, unsure about which choice was right for me, anxious over the outcome of some project, and wishing for the magical resolution, the right answer, the Great All-Knowing Voice which would assure me what was correct. I even found myself wishing I could go to someone like me for guidance.

Then finally, one day, I realized that I was never going to stop experiencing my dark nights and moments of insecurity. I was going to cycle into pain, dissolution, and muck on a regular basis, just as the moon cycles through dark as well as light. And I realized that it might be useful for me to change my attitude toward dark nights of the soul. I could see them as a temporary time of discomfort and blindness. I could see them as an obligatory time out. I could see them as fallout, like ash settling over my life after the eruption of a volcano. The weather patterns might change for a while and the landscape of my life would most probably change, but if I wished to benefit from my dark nights, I needed to stop seeing them as failure.

Over the past eight years, I've channelled psychic readings for over two thousand people, listening in as the council helped individuals to see their situations more clearly, in terms of their larger spiritual values. Some people were living dramatic lives: running from mafia figures, struggling with life-threatening illness, piecing together details of abuse that no one should ever experience. Others had more run-of-the-mill concerns: a boyfriend who wasn't very reliable, a decision to make about a promotion, uncertainty about how to deal with parents.

I listened as the councils (mine and theirs) helped each person to see where she was in her own cycle of light and dark. They shed light on the beliefs and ideas which were blocking movement or satisfaction. They showed how her particular character and energy engaged with the drama at hand. They suggested resources, productive mental stances, overviews, and reminded her of her deeper values or goals. They often took the questions someone asked, and re-framed them, showing which questions were more apropos:

"Will I get this promotion?"

"Do you understand where this promotion is leading you? If you take it, you are committing yourself to a certain course of action, toward which we sense you have great ambivalence. Try to clarify what "promotion" you would most truly wish to be awarded, apart from the job options at hand. It will guide you in your negotiations with your employer."

"Am I on the right track in my relationship?"

"Do you see the track you expect your relationship to follow? Do you see what goes into your definition of relationship? Let's explore those two things together. Each time you compare what you are doing with your friend to the monolith of RELATIONSHIP, you scare yourself with doubts. Stop for a moment and explore how "right" or "not right" your last interaction felt. Then we can look at what you can do to increase your comfort level within yourself, as well as in exchanges with your partner."

"Should I do x, y or z? I have to make a decision by next

week."

"We suggest you renegotiate your deadlines. You are not yet at a choice point, thus none of these can feel right, except in abstract terms. You are needing to clean out your mental baggage and integrate some of the lessons you learned over the last two years. You are too tired to start something new. When you are energetically ready for a new project, then you will be able to feel more clearly which of these you are drawn to."

"Should I go to Europe this summer?"

"Do you wish to go to Europe? A trip this summer represents new adventures and a certain amount of nostalgia for a time in your life when you were less attuned to dangers around you. Some part of you is craving the anonymity of travel in a foreign setting. Another part of you craves security. You see the option of staying home as one of work and drudgery. There is a certain sense of obligation attached: you should earn money rather than spend it, you should be practical rather than adventurous. Can you re-think the option of staying home, so it too addresses some of your present needs: security, time spent in nature, meeting new people. Then you will be able to weigh your two good choices and select one of them. There is no right answer here. Only a choice between two paths, each of which has valuable features."

Although I have heard the council continuously repeat the phrase: "there is no right answer here," I still find myself craving correct perspective, yes-no certainties and fool-proof choices. I guess that is something built into our cultural expectations of ourselves. But several years ago I finally understood how irrelevant the "right answer" search can be.

At that time, life offered me a challenge in which the council could bring me to a clearer understanding of both the advantages and limits of a wiser self perspective.

My friend who invited me to join her in Switzerland is someone I have known for many lifetimes; her fate is bound intimately with mine. The offer of time to write in Switzerland, coming as it did on the heels of a miserable breakup in my relationship, felt like one of those charmed synchronistic events that you read about in New Age books. I sat and meditated about the offer for an entire week, seeing all the powerful potential of the choice, and got a clear sense of direction: go to Switzerland.

I packed up all my worldly possessions and treasures, entrusted them to a small moving company with a good reputation and set off on my adventure with high hopes and magical expectations. At first, the experience unfolded beautifully. In Geneva, I gave lectures to a few local groups and began to receive requests for readings. I set wheels in motion to meet like-minded people, hoping to make friends. I began to take notes for this book and settle in to my new home.

Then, on the date my boxes were due to arrive but didn't, I discovered the mover had cashed my check, stashed my belongings in a warehouse in L.A. and promptly declared bankruptcy. The ex-mover assured me, when I called him, that he had been working a second job to earn the money to transport my load, so I could expect it in six more weeks.

Winter was approaching and all my winter clothes were in the boxes, along with my computer, on which I was supposed to be writing this book, my manuscripts, journals, and personal mementos.

I tuned into the council to ask: What does this mean? Did I do something wrong? Do I have some weird karmic connection with this man? Will my belongings ever get here?

It would have been nice to get a clear answer, preferably good news. What good are all-knowing guides if they can't save you grief? My council said, **"We cannot say at this time whether your goods will arrive. But we would suggest this to you. You have a choice about how you participate in this drama. You can suffer great anxiety from not knowing, or you can do what you can, and make do with what you have."**

I could see they were right, I could make do with what I had and avoid suffering. My friend loaned me a computer, pretty basic but serviceable, and a winter coat. I decided that either my belongings would arrive or they wouldn't and there was no point mourning them until I knew what would happen. It was an exercise for me in mental discipline, to resist imagining the impact of a potential loss, and to stay with the actual, temporary loss on its own terms. The fact was, I had no need at that moment to re-read the lost manuscripts or possess the lost belongings.

A couple of months passed and I heard no news. I was doing my best to concentrate on other things, but the charm of being in a new environment had dimmed. Geneva had turned grey and cold, and people were polite but distant. I had come down with a persistent flu that wouldn't seem to budge. I experienced writer's block. Then I called the ex-mover and discovered there had been an error—my crate had been confused with another woman's crate and was on its way to New Zealand. The authorities, I was told, had been informed and were instructed to forward my goods when they arrived.

Again I asked my council whether I had done something wrong. Was this error a punishment for something? They said, mildly, **"The man is bankrupt in more ways than one. He is going through a difficult period right now. You are a victim of that. You have a choice in how fully you will take on that role."**

I decided to focus on other things and let time push this particular drama forward. After waiting another six weeks, I called Los Angeles again, only to discover that the ex-mover had disappeared, eluding police and creditors alike. The receiving agent in New Zealand, a nice fellow, broke the news to me: my crate was lost in a warehouse in Auckland. He was doing his best to find it.

I can't say there weren't difficult moments. I experienced some grief at the loss of all my writings and family pictures. But the council said: **"Your belongings are lost, but not destroyed. Stop asking yourself *why* this happened and concentrate on understanding precisely *what* has happened. You acted in good faith. Another person's failure has inconvenienced you. You do not yet know the outcome. This is not a moral failing on your part, it is just a twist of plot. Keep on reading."**

I was angry that I couldn't magically control this event, but I could see the council's point. I would be much happier if I could live with not knowing. For once I could see that I had a choice between faith and panic. Acquaintances asked me why I hadn't predicted this loss, or why my council couldn't locate the boxes for me. Good question. The council said, **"It would not serve you."** But at the same time that they were reticent on the question of missing goods, they quietly guided me out of my writer's block and into accepting a speaking engagement which opened the floodgates to the teachings in this book.

It took nineteen months for the Auckland immigration service to find my crate and the other woman's lost boxes, to ascertain which belonged to whom, to wait out the strike on the docks of Auckland, to pass the goods through customs and ship them on to me in Switzerland. By the time they reached me, I had replaced my computer and the clothes, had forgotten most of what else I had lost and had learned to make do without all of it. But the most extraordinary part of the whole debacle was how little I had suffered.

I had to pay nearly three times the original fee to get my

belongings back. A good portion of this was a charge for "storage" for the time the crate was lost in the warehouse at Auckland. In addition, several items had been stolen from the boxes, and the insurance policy was never bought, though I had paid for it. I asked the council whether I should pursue a lawsuit. They said, "You have been wronged by other people's errors and incompetence. They did not wish you ill and did not ultimately harm you. You had the choice to harm yourself in this matter, and chose not to. The money you have lost has been more than replenished by the work you were able to do during this period. Enjoy the amusing anecdote. Mourn the actual losses—which you will see are few. What would be the point of a lawsuit? There is no one involved unaware of his errors."

It would have done me no good to know ahead of time whether my goods would arrive or not. For one thing, the truth was more complex than that. And for another, the mitigating gift of the experience was to walk through it without knowing, to practice making choices in ignorance of the outcome, and to know I could choose my level of misery, no matter how much loss and cost I might suffer.

The experience brought me to a new understanding of myself. I learned that actual disasters involve steps and decisions and a certain practical focus. Much of the suffering I'd done in my life had been in response to my fears, imagined disasters, and my own dissatisfaction at the ways events were unfolding. I could look back at earlier difficult times and see how I had assumed pain and suffering were my only choices.

My council and my wiser self are available at all times to guide me. But it has taken me several years to learn that wise guidance is not directive. When I am suffering, I still want my choice to be taken over. I want to be told what to do, what will happen, what is right. I secretly want the council to fix things so that they will come out right. Instead, what I am given in those moments is a *perspective* which is most likely to help or heal me. When I am willing to take that guidance for what it is, a focus in the moment rather than a pronouncement about the whole situation, then it is useful.

A woman came for a psychic reading the other day and said: "I have questions about my relationships, about my work and what direction I should be going, about my family and how they are doing, and about my spiritual path." She paused, smiled, and said, "I suppose that's what everyone asks."

It is. And the way to get information on these important

dimensions of your life is to listen in to your wiser self. When you return again and again to this listening, over time a certain understanding and perspective builds up in you and informs your choices.

In the following two sections, the council discusses the issues clients ask about most frequently: love and change. I have found that clients, like me, are most interested in understanding their connections with other people, and their struggles to express their life force, which is an aspect of love. And they, like me, have wanted insights into the shifts and turns of plot in their life.

Thus the following two chapters compile much of the information the council has offered individuals and classes on these topics. As you listen to the council's observations, remember they are not pronouncements of The Truth. They are wiser self perspectives. You may find some of the insights and ideas taking root in your mind, giving you new perspectives on your own situations, helping you to see them in a more grounded, accepting way.

Love

Grounding

Grounding In Love

Close your eyes and do some breathing. Take a comfortable breath in, and out. As you exhale, you release tensions and let go of tightness you might be feeling. As you breathe in, take in some fresh air, some new energy, as best you can. And feel the circulation that happens with each breath, of bringing in the new and letting go of the old, over and over.

You may notice that at the end of each breath there is a pause. As you inhale, you hesitate while you assimilate what you've taken in. As you exhale, there is a lull as you rest empty. Those pauses are important. If you don't have spaces in your breathing, you will hyperventilate. If you don't make spaces in your life, between the taking in and the letting go, you "hyperventilate" in your life as well.

We ask you to take a moment to think about the people, the places, the objects, the animals you have loved in this life. Call up images of the various recipients of your affection. Then take a moment to focus on and feel the love for one of those particular people, objects, beings or places.

Explore that feeling for a time. What is it? Where is it located in your body, or is it in your body? What are the sensations associated with it? We are not asking you to find out what Love is, with a capital L, for all time. Just this particular emotional state you have focussed on. As you feel this love, what are your reactions, what thoughts creep in? Where is your attention? Sit with the feelings for a time, watching them move and shift.

Give that person, object, being, or place a gentle blessing, and farewell, and bring your awareness back to your room again.

Notice your breathing without trying to interfere with it or change it. Are you open in this moment, connected? What is the sensation in the area of your heart and lungs?

Love

Nearly all people we meet in body want insight into their love life. They want to know if they will find a partner, or if the partner they have found is right for them. They want to know if "this is all there is," or whether they can expect great passion and soul bonding. They want to understand the perplexing and complicated relationships they have formed with others.

While this preoccupation is natural, we want to enlarge the concept of love to encompass much more than what you do with partners or in relationships. Love is the activation of your spirit, reaching out to make connections. Love is the life force knowing itself. And in this broader view, love is your life work.

Whenever you take the moment to taste a tangerine and really know it, that is a moment of love. Whenever you are doing activities that strike the gong of your nature, that resonate with your spirit, you are experiencing love. You are each enmeshed in a web of connection, in a web of loving. Whenever you recognize the life force flowing—between you and another human being, between you and something you are doing—you are experiencing love. Your days arc full of opportunities for love: tiny filaments of connection, recognition, attention, the life force knowing itself. And so our goal in discussing love is to focus your attention on all the myriad filaments of loving that connect you in this life. Those of you who have pinned your hopes or aspirations on a single person, a single idea, a single form, a single role, a single job, a single definition, are ignoring your multiple connections and are moving toward malnourishment. What fully nourishes you is a multiple exchange: allowing your life force to flow in many directions, and to receive from many sources as well.

It is fantastic and special when you meet someone who awakens your whole being. That love is a gift, because it can remind you of how rewarding it is to feel your life force taken up and shared, or activated and intensified. But can you recognize that what that special person activates is there within you? It is your awareness of being awake and alive.

The passion, the high energy, the exuberance of falling in love is there for you throughout your life, if you can realize that it is not dependent on another person, a true love, a soul mate. Your soul has many mates, and other soul-stirring connections as well. Your job is to stay open, to allow yourself to be awakened and stirred to passion regularly: by activities you love to do, by foods you enjoy eating, by sights, sounds and sensations that activate your life force, by ideas, by music and poetry. By the unfolding of the miracle of life all around you.

Your love songs and popular literature brainwash you to look for a certain kind of love, certain promises and commitments, certain symbols of loving. But you can decide to grow beyond those limits, to allow in all your potentials of loving, and recognize that you can never run out of love. You can either open to it in all its forms, or else shut your awareness down as you wait for Mr. or Ms. Right.

We differentiate between Love, with a capital L, and love with a small l. Love, capital L, is the note of awareness sung by your heart. It is your life force, as it speaks within you, it is your soul energy. You do not have to work at getting Love; you are here as an expression of it. It is the feeling of profound magnificence when you see a sunset or stand atop a mountain or recognize the miracles of your everyday existence. Love, with a small l, is what you work at. It is all the activity you engage in to express your spirit, or to receive the expressions of other spirits.

It is love, small l, that tangles many people up, as their egos struggle to define their membership, belonging, security, right to be recognized, their assurance that they have a place in the web. It is love with a small l which people are engaged in as they try to shape and define their relationships, as they partner up for marriage, as they fall into a swoon over someone.

Although it is popular in your culture to dream and focus on having one special person to love, the reality is that you have many love partners. Can you validate all of them, on their own terms? Some of them you may live with, some you will work with, some you will have sex with, some you will help to die, some you will parent, some will parent you, some touch you briefly and then move on, others will teach you, mentor you, incite you to passions of the mind and feelings.

You may find someone who brings you home to your Love, whose Love you feel so strongly, that it seems that being together sets your souls resonating. You may find a person who brings you home again and again to inspiration and joy. You may choose to build a partnership or life with that person, if conditions are right. But the Great Love you are experiencing through that one person is possible with each person you allow into your heart and mind. It is the Love of awareness of the spirit. It is a reminder of your own being, and of your ability to receive the spirit of another. Your beloved does not set your soul resonating; she or he awakens you to the fact that your soul resonates of its own accord.

We spoke recently to a friend of ours who was deeply sad over the lack of love in her life. She said, "I understand what you are saying about loving my friends, family and activities, and having love in that way. But I still feel dissatisfied. I want a lover. I want a life partner. The other things just don't do it."

We do not mean to gloss over the yearning for intimacy that many of you feel in your life. It is ironic though, that we hear the same longing in our friends who do have lovers, who do have life partners they live with. Another person can bring you that sense of intimacy and completion for a time. And you are surrounded by media which insist that love is the answer, that one special someone will fulfill all your needs. But in actuality there is only one special someone on the planet who can bring you to a true and ongoing sense of intimacy. That is you.

As you practice loving yourself, with regular acts of kindness and self-nurturing, as you allow yourself to enter into Love with yourself, when you are able to come home to yourself authentically within individual moments, you create an anchored ego which is capable of receiving experiences of intimacy with others. Then the longing for that "significant other" decreases, because you open moment by moment to take in the significance of others.

Our sad friend was hooked on a picture of what she needed. She craved sex, but would not allow herself to have it without the prospects of life partnership. She craved life partnership, but barely had room in her life for friendship with herself. She felt inadequate in this coupled society, and craved a partner who could make her feel more adequate. She was tired of being single in a society that seemed geared toward couples, and wanted to stop feeling like an outsider. She couldn't seem to meet someone who was both available and decent.

There is no doubt that her grief and longing were real. But our experience is that grief and longing are conditions of your mind and understanding. They can arise as easily when you are coupled as not, whenever you get disconnected from your root system and start looking outside yourself for that primary nourishment.

What our friend needed most was to enter deeply into the sadness and cross it to the place where she is connected to all-that-is. *When you can't work outward, work inward.* She needed to meet and comfort the panicked and abandoned self inside, who keeps whispering "I want love, where is it? It will never come." In that state, she had no room for exchange with others. That yawning hole can never be filled by another person, no matter how committed or affectionate they are.

This is the good news and the bad news. The good news is that love is all around you. You can't fall out of the web of loving and connection. You can only forget or block your access to it. And the bad news is that love doesn't come in one large, neatly wrapped package. It comes in millions of small packages. Even your life partner, should you choose to have one, will only be able to promise and deliver loving one moment at a time, one transaction at a time, one awakened feeling at a time. And ultimately, it is the entire universe of connections which is your truest life partner.

Self-Love

A cliché of the self-help movement is the injunction to *love yourself*. At the risk of being in vogue, we join our voices to that particular chorus. Practice loving yourself, yes, and what we mean by that is to engage in regular acts of kindness and attention to yourself. What we mean is to take regular trips inward, sitting quietly with yourself, feeling what it feels like to inhabit your body, your mind, your sensibilities. What we mean is to learn to fully use yourself, pursuing all your talents and interests. When you love yourself, you try, thousands of times a day, to receive your being as it unfolds and expresses itself through your two earthbound selves.

We hear two common objections when we suggest that at the center of a spiritual practice is the ability to love yourself: 1) "That is selfish. A real *me generation* attitude"; and 2) "I've tried to love myself better, but I just can't—I don't know how." We would like to address both of these.

"That is Selfish."

We are not suggesting, when we say self-love is crucial, that you become selfish. Selfishness is the behavior of a Self which is in pain, which has unfulfilled needs and can't see beyond them to a fuller participation with others.

We are suggesting that you work to become centered and grounded in yourself: aware of your needs and desires, attuned to your feelings and physical energy, responsive to your emotional, physical and mental requirements in any given moment. There is no other way to be if you wish to be healthy and alive. For if you are not centered in the Self, you are nowhere. You cannot be centered in the Self next to you or in an idea. You must be centered in yourself or you have no instrument.

But the irony is that the more centered in the Self you are, the more translucent you become; your Self comes to resemble more and more the Buddhist concept of "no-self." The more centered you are, the less attached you become to the particulars of your personality or lifestyle. You feel your nourishment rising from your spirit, you see the details of your life as notes in a song, not as the song itself. You are more able to know yourself as energy in motion, rather than as an object which must be maintained.

A musician can't play beautiful music without much practice and attention to the instrument. And you can't work effectively in your world without practice and attention to your three selves. You are taught not to be self-centered as a way to remind you of your obligations and interdependence with others. But you must take active responsibility for your Self if you wish to make some creative contributions to the larger endeavors. If you do not focus on the Self and keep that Self functioning, balanced, contributing in a centered way, and receiving energies with pleasure, then you block your own human exchange.

There are people who are altruistic, of whom you would say, "They are not self-centered at all. They are very much aware of and focussed on others." There are two ways to do that. One is to be such a bright shining star, so full of your own spiritual abundance, that you just feed the system because you resonate splendidly. That is healthy altruism, but is not, when you examine it closely, selflessness. It is an advanced form of self-fullness.

There is another way to be altruistic, by getting so involved in the needs, concerns and energies of others that you don't have time or energy to focus on yourself. It's a bit parasitic. The mind that is unattended develops a warped sense of what is right or wrong, good or bad. Often people who are overly-focussed on the needs of others will do wonderful acts, but those acts set up great obligation in the people who receive them. Ultimately this kind of altruism interferes with the free will and free expression of others, and becomes selfish in other, more hidden ways.

Anyone who dislikes herself, who has low self-esteem in this life will automatically skew and misinterpret all of her experience to a certain extent. The same is true of people who are overly focussed on themselves, without practicing self-love. If you are not at peace and at home with yourself, then everyone else's energy will knock you off balance. You will either have too great a need for the input of others, or be unable to take in the gifts of attention they give you (or both). The practice of self-love frees you to have a larger participation with others.

You can only be aware of the cosmic level of life through your instrument of awareness, which is the Self. This is why we insist that a spiritual practice, a humanitarian practice, begins with a practice of self-esteem. It begins with acts of deep courtesy and compassion for yourself.

"I don't know how."

Self-love is a practice that goes far beyond gazing at yourself in a mirror, treating yourself as a lover, or whispering affirmations. We remind you of our definition of love: making connection with the life force. The life force knowing itself. You practice self-love by regularly bringing your attention and awareness to each of your three selves. You practice self-love each time you allow your committee of three to work together. You practice self-love each time you authentically connect with your body, your awareness, your essence.

Think about how self-esteem, self-love, develops in a young child. She needs to receive attention in order to feel she has value. She needs approval of her actions, her ideas, her presence, in order to feel she has membership in the family, school, neighborhood. She needs security, a sense that she is going to be taken care of, get her needs met, and won't be capriciously hurt. She is more likely to learn to respect herself if she has good role models around, adults and other children who like themselves and are able to be generous and receive her presence with pleasure.

In order to learn to like herself, a child also needs to feel engaged with her environment. When she is bored, she feels dull and lifeless, not a state which generates much connection with her life force. So she needs many moments of stimulation and challenge that call forth her talent, allow her to experience success, offer her an expressive outlet for her particular energetic note.

You also need all these things (both from yourself and from others) to practice self-love and maintain self-esteem. You internalized the habits of attention you received as a child, and tend to treat yourself in similar ways now that you are an adult. And if you didn't grow up loving yourself as a child, for whatever reasons, circumstances and experiences, then you are working from a shaky base now, and need to be particularly compassionate and kind to your ego and gatekeeper who are doing their best to serve you, but may never have learned how.

In order to love yourself, you need to be using yourself.

You need to learn to read the gauges of your imagination, emotions, thoughts, actions, intuitions, desires and sensations and respond to them. You need to recognize in all these messages the many aspects of your nature craving to be heard, honored and expressed. If you feel artistic urges, it is an act of self-love to allow yourself time and energy to play with artistic forms, even when you have no training or technical skill.

If you are talented in something, for example the use of language, then you will feel loved only if you are using this talent, to talk, write, interpret, read, play in the realm of verbal expression.

Listening to the energies of your earth elemental self, truly inhabiting your body, increases your self-esteem. A body which doesn't receive direct attention and the chance to be in *body time*, feels distinctly unloved, and produces all kinds of unlovely symptoms to express this fact.

Your talking self, too, needs to find herself in situations which excite her imagination, allow her to express the different characters or aspects of self she is developing. She needs a stage to act upon, occasions to be her various selves, and she needs to be protected from situations which do not allow her to be herself. These latter also erode self-confidence and self-esteem.

Imagine for a moment, that you could set aside all your financial requirements and present commitments. Imagine you could design your ideal setting and schedule. What would your day look like? Who would you choose to have around you? What balance of interactions and solitude might you choose? What would you seek to learn, explore, experience? How would you like to be seen and acknowledged by others? While you may feel frustrated with the distance between your ideal and your reality, as you identify what your three selves are craving, you can begin to see both smaller and larger ways to engage and fulfill your inner imperatives.

Self-love is fostered by good placement.

You need to feel your own powers taken up and shared. First you need to recognize your own powers: we have referred to that again and again in this book. But you don't live in a vacuum, and you also need to feel that you have an effect on others. You need to feel them receiving you, accepting you, approving of your nature, thoughts, and actions. You need to feel that others want you around, and have some need for you. Therefore it is a deep act of self-love to pay attention to where you place yourself, both the physical settings and the social ones.

*You have a **habitat** that best suits you, not only a particular kind of geography and climate, but also a*

social, emotional, and energetic habitat in which you
will feel most alive and most supported.

You may feel truest to your nature in the midst of a bustling city, or you may feel yourself more alive in a rural, bucolic setting. You might feel awakened and enlivened in certain groups of people, or recognize that in fact you begin to shut your heart down whenever you are with more than one other person.

There will be a pace of life at which you feel loved and supported, and paces which are slower or quicker may make you feel invalidated or unappreciated.

You may be deeply aware of your physical surroundings, and have great need for aesthetic sights. You may, on the other hand, be comfortable in a cinderblock building with no windows, as long as you are in a certain intellectual or emotional atmosphere.

Do you see the connection between your habitat and self-love? When you are comfortable, at home, being yourself, then your heart opens to yourself and others. And when you are a fish out of water, struggling to feel at home in a setting which doesn't particularly support you, it is hard to feel your life force taken up and shared. And it is all too easy to feel there is something wrong with you, and embark upon mental monologues of self-criticism.

We are not suggesting you must rigidly control your surroundings. We are suggesting that it is an act of self-love to recognize, seek and affirm surroundings which appeal to you. It is an act of self-love to like where you find yourself, and the self can feel negated when you place yourself repeatedly in settings where you feel unwell, unwanted, or invisible.*

Self-love is an attitude and mental habit.

How much do you trust yourself? Do you make regular resolutions about how you will change, or are you able to accept and enjoy how you are? If we were to wave our magic wand, freezing you as you are this minute, how much of that self could you accept and embrace? Would your body be fine the way it is, would your daily habits, your mental image of

---

* While we are addressing this issue on a personal level, it must also be addressed on a social level as well. We acknowledge the particular tragedy of those individuals who are trapped by their history, skin color, or special needs in situations where they cannot thrive. Internalized racism, homophobia, class values, and expectation create a two-sided coin of rage and self-hatred that affects all of you. The plight of individuals interweaves with the social values and choices of the collective. It is valuable to recognize how you contribute or detract from the creation of healthy habitats for all.

yourself, your achievements, your faults and strengths all be acceptable and enough for you?

As we have said, the self responds to approval, and shuts down in the face of criticism or disapproval. Some of you have mental habits which are not, when you look at them closely, very self-affirming. Each time you look at your body in the mirror and notice its flaws, each time you treat yourself like a wayward, unruly, out-of-control person by making new rules for how you should behave; each time you take yourself to task for making a mistake, you are eroding your self-esteem.

You live in a culture which is addicted to self-improvement, and so it may feel natural to constantly look for ways to improve yourself. You are encouraged to think in terms of making something of yourself, becoming a somebody, getting somewhere; and the implication behind these expectations is that you are not enough, nobody significant, and nowhere adequate at the moment.

It seems perhaps outrageous to suggest that striving to be better is an insult to the Self. But in fact, your pleasure and power rest in the present moment, with your Self exactly as you are. So if you are able to celebrate yourself today, while also setting some long-term goals, this attitude is not a problem. But many of you who feel unloved and unappreciated by others do not recognize that you are under-appreciating *yourself*.

There are two aspects to this notion of self-love: what idea do you carry about yourself; and how do you treat yourself on a moment-to-moment basis? As you work on your mental self-love, you are working both to improve your picture of yourself (your self image) and also to move toward greater acts of courtesy, compassion and respect in your moment-to-moment transactions with yourself.

Self-hatred, an extreme failure of self-love, often arises when you disinherit parts of yourself. Whenever you say, "I should be more...," "I hate it when I...," "If only I were...," you are letting one or all of your three selves know they are inadequate, insufficient, not enough. And they will hate that judging mind, which seeks to annihilate them. So you have the self hating the self. The criticized self hates the critical judging mind and vice versa.

Self-love, on the other hand, is a policy of mutual appreciation. As you validate your three selves and their behaviors, with either acceptance or compassionate recognition, those selves love each other and open in the warmth of the exchange.

A Self who doesn't like herself has somehow set or accepted conditions that she can't live up to. So you have a choice. You can either get rid of the conditions or get rid of the self. Some of you are so hooked on the conditions—"I won't be good unless I have my PhD." "I'm not really living if I don't have a partner."—that it feels easier to get rid of the self. You slowly annihilate yourself with self-hatred, misery, and a contracted heart rather than give up your ideas of what *ought* to be.

You may be thinking this is easier said than done. Those mental conditions relate to the values you learned in your family and in response to your experiences and observations in life. They are tenacious. We suggest you try an exercise to break yourself free of your social values. Imagine yourself as different animals in the zoo. What are the habits and conditions which make you a *good* bear, a *good* walrus, a *good* ibex? Then as you find yourself making a judgment about yourself or another person, ask yourself which creature might appropriately possess that quality. Picture that creature's place in the whole ecology of life forms. Since your mind is probably freer to embrace the diversity among animals, it can help you begin to appreciate the diversity among people as well. Let there be room in your understanding for all qualities, and let there be compassionate understanding in your heart for all types of behaviors.

What role does change play, in trying to love yourself? Change rarely happens when you beat, bribe and cajole yourself into it. Change arises when you are able to embrace yourself exactly as you are. The three selves who feel received and supported just naturally grow and expand and feel open to trying new things in an atmosphere of approval and love.

Safety is a vital ingredient of self-love.

What do you need in order to feel safe? Your body needs nourishment, rest, activity, protection or support in the face of extreme sensations. Your mind needs to set conditions for the life you wish to live and then work to fulfill them. Your spirit needs to feel that it can flow and be expressed.

You need to experience connection, receive nourishment from your open heart and the hearts of others. You need to have boundaries, and know you can maintain them. You need to know that you belong somewhere, and that that somewhere is a place where you can get your needs met. You need to have faith in something deep within yourself, and faith in something larger than yourself.

A sense of safety arises when each of your three selves can trust the others. Your earth elemental self feels safe when she knows that talking self will not put her in danger, push her past her limits of strength or energy, commit her to projects which erode her health.

Talking self feels safe when she can feel anchored in the body, when she has a way to understand and interpret the messages she is getting and sensations that arise. She feels safe when she has learned to protect the body from dangerous others, when she believes she has a home in her own body, in a physical space, in the hearts of others, in the shared dramas, in the cosmic scheme of things. Talking self feels safe if she knows how to set appropriate boundaries and limits, and how to create appropriate challenges and risks for herself.

Wiser self is safety, since on the level she resonates, there is no illness, death or pain (as you know it). Instead there is blockage or flow, all held within the larger awareness of their place in the scheme of things. The safety of wiser self can be felt whenever the other two selves listen inward for it, or honor their own safety needs.

What does safety have to do with self-love? It is an act of deepest self-affirmation each time you allow your earth elemental self and talking self to work within their safe parameters. Each time you act to preserve the sanctity of your three selves, you are permitting connection, and love.

Security is a matter of balance, and being anchored within your own source. It is a matter of access to those things which nourish you, the inner sources as well as the outer ones. It is the ability to set limits which keep you safe.

Setting limits will keep you safe if they are limits which fit you. If they are too narrow, the life force can't resonate very well, and so you block off love and fulfillment. And if they are too wide, you will feel dwarfed and threatened. For example, if you say, "I can only like people who have gone to college," your spirit will rebel, and you will feel parts of yourself disinherited. If you say, "I must try to love everyone," it is a limit which will not keep you safe. You will rebel and shut down whenever you meet someone whose energy is invasive and is more than you can handle at the moment.

Setting limits is something you do to protect yourself rather than to critique or rebuke others. When you say, "You are overwhelming me," you are criticizing the other person and it can cause even more energetic struggle with them. But if you say, "Excuse me, I'm getting tired and need a break," you are setting a limit.

Loving yourself with safety means unlearning the habit of invoking danger fantasies, in which you imagine, "What if I get fired from my job and...." When this type of fantasy arises unbidden in the mind, it is a signal that one of your selves feels unsafe and needs attention. She is trying to practice her responses so she can trust herself better.

Developing a sense of inner security means consulting your own perceptions and inclinations, listening to your heart when your mind starts reeling with fear and prophecies of disaster. If you can interrupt your disaster scenarios with the recognition that a gatekeeper alarm has just gone off, it will rob them of their power. If you focus on your panic feelings, and turn off the sound track provided by your fearful mind, you can address your insecurity directly and viscerally. If you can recognize when your mind is starting to use scare tactics, you can return your attention to the present moment: what is physically threatening or protecting you now, in this precise minute? Each time you listen to your gatekeeper without reacting blindly to the various alarms and messages, you strengthen your sense of security.

Self-love deepens when you learn to acknowledge and work with your present experience, even when it is not what you would wish.

You affirm yourself more deeply when you stop trying to change your reality by wishing things otherwise in your life. If you are sick, you are sick. There is no point in engaging in self-recrimination. If you are lonely, you are lonely. When you can address that sensation and experience it, rather than scrambling blindly to remedy it, you will find a way to authentically move beyond it. If you are depressed for the fifth time this year, there is no need to tell yourself it is disgusting, or that your life is a failure. Instead, recognize that the depression is there for a reason and serves a purpose. It is not a punitive "lesson." It is evidence of either lowered or logjammed energy in your physiological or emotional habits. When you stop wasting your energy fighting what is, then your self feels affirmed and can move through to a new state.

Your selves do not like to feel abandoned by others or by your conscious awareness. Your body does not like to be ignored or tuned out when it is speaking to you with sensations, your mind does not like to be trivialized or laughed at when it is expressing feelings or concerns, your wiser self does not like to be muffled by mental or physical garbage.

The practices you use for avoiding pain or joy or self-awareness—the distractions, drugs, and mental blocks you put up—do not help you to trust or love yourself. In fact they generally erode your self-esteem. Just recall for a moment the self-disgust you felt last time you went on a spending spree.

But when we say that self-love is supported by the ability to work with and inhabit your present experience, we are not suggesting a fatalistic, punishing attitude that this is your lot and you must accept it. Rather, we are suggesting that you cultivate a gracious acceptance of your human nature and reactions. When you accept and investigate your pain rather than fighting it, you will be able to release it sooner. When you recognize how the present conditions have served you and abandon perfectionist notions of how your life ought to unfold, your Self will actually be freer to fulfill your dreams and desires. Acceptance and compassion are necessary qualities in learning to love yourself.

You stay healthy in love if you can love others without getting lost.

It is delightful when you can feel your connection with others and open to their perceptions, ideas, invitations and love. It is sad when you open to another and in the process lose track of your own perceptions, ideas, feelings. When you feel drowned-out by another person, no matter how much you admire them, it erodes your ability to love yourself.

Loving yourself is a prerequisite to loving another person, because if you don't love yourself, the other person's energy and mind will overpower you. This causes your gatekeeper to shut the gates.*

---

* If you have grown up in the shadow of others and never learned to listen to your own truths, then your gatekeeper is more likely to respond to powerful others by opening the gates too far. Your heart will shut down, and you will operate in panic mode, without knowing why.

So the romantic notion of getting lost in another person is an extremely unhealthy fantasy. Instead we encourage you to fantasize about getting *found* in love, both in your relationship with yourself and in your healthy connections with others.

It is within balance—of giving and receiving, of hearing the self and hearing others, of taking in and putting out, of loving and feeling yourself loved—that the connections of spirit can be maintained.

When you are balanced in yourself, as honestly as you know how, you attract others to love who respond to that balance. If you try to attract someone when you are in an unbalanced state, the connections you make will reflect that imbalance. For example, if you react to your anxiety about being single by dating everyone you can find, you generally end up with a partner who is attracted to your anxiety and need rather than to your healthy fullness. Or your partner may be so insensitive that he or she is oblivious to your anxiety.

If you make an effort to spend some time with yourself, loving and consoling that anxious mind, then you are more likely to meet your dates with a clear, loving and balanced judgment. You will make choices that reinforce your strongest truth.

In general, your relationships reflect your state of emotional and spiritual health. So if you want intimacy, you must work with your ability to allow intimacy in.

A Small Exercise in Self-Love

You may feel, after reading all of this, that self-love is a lot of work. But we do not wish to leave you with that notion. There is a lot you can do to radically improve the amount and quality of love in your life. And there is also something very simple you can do in any moment to come home to love, when you can't handle any of these thoughts and mind forms. Simply open your heart. Because in the opening of the heart, the energy flows and the life force automatically starts reaching out and making other connections.

How do you open your heart, especially if you do not feel safe? We suggest you take one hand and cover your heart with it. Then you take your other hand and cover your belly, or your solar plexus region. There is an energy center right there where your ribs meet. In covering the heart and solar plexus you create a completed circuit within yourself.

When you cover your heart, you are bringing your attention in to your heart. When you cover your solar plexus you are cutting out some of the world's influences. You hold yourself in and cover your heart, so that the warmth and energy that are coming out of you are being fed back in, through your hands, to your body again. It's like creating a little pressure cooker there where you can build up feelings of openness. You can relax, come home to yourself.

It is a very physical, basic way to pay attention to yourself in a moment. It is the same attention as the attention of the mother's womb to the fetus. It is that very physical love that many of you forget in your everyday lives, which you can come home to. You can love yourself with your hands, you can love yourself by putting a blanket around you or by embracing a pillow or stuffed animal. Because in that moment the energy that is coming out gets sent back in to feed the whole.

Let the love build up, helping your heart to open. Helping you to relax. Know you're a little protected. Your hands act as a temporary gatekeeper, deflecting incoming energy. It can calm you and bring you home.

This exercise is an extremely simple daily practice. You draw back from the dramas out there, and you come home to yourself, which will teach you everything you need to know. The information you need for making choices is all right there, expressing itself minute by minute if you can just pull your focus back to the minute, close enough to hear it.

Bonds and Relationships

&

When you look at a blade of grass you see a single stalk. But in your mind's eye you can see its roots intertangled with the other roots under the surface of the lawn. You would laugh at the notion of a blade of grass picking up and walking away, because it is so thoroughly interwoven with its fellows.

You look very much like a blade of grass to us, apparently free to wave in the wind, but in fact greatly bound up with your fellow creatures in a massive energetic root system. These roots are your bonds with others.

A bond is an energetic connection. When you come into body and into your identity for this life, you already carry thousands of bonds: you have the soul bond connections of your fellow council members, you have the spiritual bonds formed through many lifetimes of activity, and you also have bonds of resonance with others who vibrate at a similar pitch.

You continue to form bonds with others throughout your life. A bond is created by affinity. Whenever you feel an affinity with someone, you are creating a potential bond. Whether it be an affinity of interest, outlook, life circumstances, personal style, affection, or even suffering, the bond comes into being in a moment of recognition of another.

Not all bonds are operative at every moment. They are activated through your *attention*. You pay attention to somebody and your energy goes out and touches them. Have you ever looked up in the midst of laughing to yourself over something, to notice another person also laughing? In that moment, a charge runs through the bond of shared amusement. You feel a slight warmth and connection with that person.

You activate a bond, a linkage, with your attention. You then further energize that bond with your *intention*. So when you are looking at someone you create a temporary connection to them. When you consciously direct your laughter and warmth toward that other person, in a spirit of affinity, then you are energizing that bond. You are sending them a message along the connection that has been forged between you.

If you are sending your warmth and shared laughter along an affinity bond, the person you are sending it to often feels your intention to connect, and looks up to meet your eye. This can further strengthen a bond, if the person chooses to acknowledge it and send a responsive signal back. They can also choose to disengage from the bond by sending you negative signals: breaking eye contact and looking displeased; shutting down their heart to you in that moment.

Not all bonds are comfortable for you. When, riding a bus, you notice an unwashed, unkempt stranger, you may feel a connection and even empathy. But if that person directs her attention toward you, tries to activate that bond by entering into more purposeful eye contact with you, you have a choice about whether you allow that bond to become a vehicle for more direct communication.

Denial or refusal of a bond is not always comfortable. You may feel shame, or anger at the person for wanting something from you. This is natural. You are sustained by your bonds with others, and the breaking of even a subtle affinity bond is uncomfortable. Your three selves seek, feel and wish for connection, even when your mind refuses it.

When you connect with a lover, a partner, a friend, an acquaintance, a pet, you strengthen your bonds by paying attention to them over and over again. You vitalize the bonds with your approval, recognition, warmth, joy, celebration, sharing, and also with your fear, anxiety, and negative judgments. With each strengthening of a bond, it will feel more solid and permanent in your mind.

Once a bond is established (or if it already exists), you can send energetic messages along it, even if the person is not present in the room with you. You can send loving concern to your friends and relatives. You can send warmth and approval to your role models and colleagues. You can also send anger, disgust, and other negative or non-affirming messages.

We do not recommend that you make a practice of sending out your negative intentions (which are somewhat stronger than your negative thoughts and feelings), but as we mentioned earlier in this book, you can't really harm another person with your thoughts. For one thing, the person receiving your thoughts has a screening mechanism to determine whether you truly mean harm. And your bond is like a telephone wire connecting the two of you; that person has some choice in whether or not she picks up the receiver. So although a sensitive person is not comfortable receiving another's ill will and pain (and needing to block that bond for a time), it won't actively harm her.

What makes a bond strong? Two things: a history of connections, or a strong potential to connect. And because your potential to connect varies from person to person, you will feel stronger bonds with some people than with others.

You may meet a perfect stranger and feel an instant bond with her. You may, on the other hand, have a friend or family member whom you have known for years and still feel very little bonding; the energetic link is just not that strong.

The bond you share with someone is not necessarily reflected in your relationship with them.

Relationships are not the same things as bonds. You may feel a strong bonded connection to someone with whom you can't actually get along that well. Why is that? Because when you relate to someone, you are building a shared form — a ship—that will carry the cargo of that bond. Sometimes you are just unable to find a form, a pattern of relating, a personality mesh, that allows you to adequately express the bond between you. Sometimes you can only build a little canoe to carry this bond, and the canoe tends to tip and sink.

This example will explain our metaphor. Imagine you meet someone at work with whom you interact once a week, and that's how you know her. But say that every time you see her, you feel a strong connection: you love her. You don't know why, you just feel warmth and love, and would like to know her better. That is a pretty strong energy for that tiny frail work relationship to hold. That relationship of talking-once-a-week-in-a-work-context can't hold the intensity of what you're feeling. So what do you strive to do? You strive to build a different *ship*, a form big enough to express and carry that energy, to do justice or honor to what you are feeling.

Perhaps you ask that person out for coffee and get to be friends, because a friendship is a slightly larger ship than a workship. And at some point you may begin to feel the friendship is too small to carry the whole cargo of feelings. You're feeling sexual, you're feeling love, and you're wanting larger time chunks and larger commitments with that person. You try to build a love relationship to carry and do honor to that bond, to give you a form through which you can express the energy and connection you are feeling.

Some of you have had the frustrating experience of meeting someone with whom you felt a strong bond, and discovering there was just no way for you to get to know her. She was busy, committed elsewhere, infirm, or you met her in a context where it just wasn't appropriate to build a friendship. In those moments it becomes clear that sharing a bond does not necessarily mean that you will share a relationship of some sort.

Sharing a relationship does not necessarily mean you will feel a bond either. Have you ever experienced the frustration of building a relationship that was a very large ship, but somehow had a very small cargo of connecting, of bonding going on? Here you had this large commitment of time, energy and expectation, but not much true exchange was happening. The love was not passing between you, the bond was not alive enough to fuel the relationship, and so you felt empty, despite the commitments that had been made on both sides.

The ideal situation is to learn to build relationships that can carry your bonds. The more flexible you are in relating, the more creative you are in finding forums for interaction and exchange with people, the more likely you are to do justice to the bonds you feel, and have relationships that reflect true intimacy and connection.

If you are aware of bonding and relationship-building as two separate but interrelated activities, you have a better chance of true connection with other people.

Relationship building is a skill that you develop with practice. There are so many variables to healthy relating. You need to know yourself and your own limits, so that you can allow a smooth give and take, without abruptly shutting the other person out (or letting her too far in, before you are sure you wish for the connection). You need to be aware of your feelings and fantasies, and communicate them (when appropriate) to the other person. You need to be able to manage your time, your activities, your energy in such a way that there is room in your life for that other person.

You need to be conscious of the parameters of the roles you play, both the formal roles such as mother, sister, lover, colleague, and the informal roles such as caretaker, confidant, and scapegoat. When these roles don't allow you a full enough expression of your feelings and bondedness, then you need the flexibility and creativity to change them.

Expectation and your mental picture of a connection have

a lot of impact on how you relate to another person. Have you ever met someone you found attractive, and after only one or two encounters mentally married her, bore four children, and walked hand in hand into old age together? Much of the disappointment of love and the pain of relationships arise when your expectations and mental pictures don't match the actual experiences you have shared with another. Or else the pain arises when you each interpret experiences differently.

The fine art of relationships is created as you communicate: affection, feelings, expectations, perceptions, desires, hopes. It is the stuff of which your loving exchange is made.

But we would suggest to you that, in learning to recognize bonds, you are learning to start at the center and work outward. The more you can start at the bond level and slowly build a slightly larger and larger *ship* to hold that bond, the healthier your relationships will be. If you give yourself the time to discover and assimilate some truths about others—their ability to be there for you, your ability to be there for them, your mutual ability to take each other in, your respective ability to take responsibility for yourself—then you are less likely to suffer the shocks of disappointment or betrayal.

It is possible as you build a relationship with someone, that the bond will strengthen. It is also possible that in the course of building a friendship, the bond will dissipate. You can only know the outcome by exploring the potential for expressing that bond. That is why it is important, as you build a relationship, and feel connection to another, that you not make promises you can't keep. Sometimes love does die, feelings that were intense fade, your desires shift, and you need to move on.

Not all bonds yield ships. Not all ships are long-lasting. But all bonds and all relationships, no matter what their length or intensity, are valid. They are all expressions of the human exchange you are here to engage in. When you are aware that some bonds are there just to awaken you for a short time, some relationships will only allow you to make a limited but instructive exchange with someone, then you have the basis for learning to benefit from all your roots and all your connections in this life. You have a basis for taking in love on all levels and in many forms.

Ways of Loving

🌿

Love is something you do with your whole being—- it is mental, emotional, physical, energetic, and spiritual—because it is the activation of your life force. So when we refer to ways of loving, we are talking about all the ways you can work with love, to deepen and enrich the experience of making connections in your life.

Think for a moment about your heart area, that region of the body most often associated with love. This center contains two of your most vital organs, your heart and your lungs. Both of these organs are constantly pumping, in and out. The lungs pump air (spirit) into the body and out again, the heart pumps blood (life force) in a constant circulation.

Neither organ is just pumping in or just pumping out. No wonder you associate love with your heart. Love too has an in-out rhythm to it. You cannot always just put love out. You cannot always just take love in. It flows in and out of you, and circulates through your awareness.

That means, in terms of a relationship, that there will be seasons to the relationship. There will be rhythms that you can recognize and identify—of giving and receiving—with each of the beings, places, objects and activities with which you are seeking to connect.

No one will be perfectly open to you, nor will you remain steady and constant in how you feel toward another. There will be fluctuations in your feeling that reflect the opening and closing of your heart, the taking in (and assimilating) of influence, the closing down (and resting empty) as your heart follows its natural patterns.

We have noticed that some of you struggle against natural love rhythms, striving to give love at a time when you have none to give, trying to demand love at a time when you really need to be resting empty. You feel rejected when your friends or partners lose interest in you temporarily, which is natural in any healthy relationship. You may find yourself panicking and turning to new people during those times when your own affection and interest flag.

Who can you open to? How, when and under what circumstances are you comfortable being open? Pay

attention to these rhythms in yourself, to the opening
and closing rhythm of your heart and of your being. And
as you open, you take someone in and feel the
connection. As you close, you gently make a separation
and know yourself to be at home alone. You can develop
a sense of groundedness in yourself, a sense of being
centered enough to ride with your rhythms and those of
other people as well. As you do, you strengthen your
ability to take love in and learn to more fully trust the
ways another person is loving you.

One aspect of the love force that is not very well understood by some of you is that when you love someone you are taking them in, you are opening to them. You are *recognizing* them, *receiving* them, *acknowledging* them. How many of you think of love as an energy that you *put out* toward someone, like a golden ray of caring streaming out of your heart? It's a cultural image of love to "shower" someone with love, to put out energy. And in fact the image has some truth: when you open to someone, what comes out is warmth.

But the goal is not to generate the warmth and put it out there. The goal is to open and take connection *in*. And that is the gift you give when you love someone. You *receive* them. When you love someone you are seeing them, you are hearing them, you are celebrating and cherishing them. And that is a tremendous gift.

The two most challenging parts of love, for most people, are learning to take things in and learning to allow yourself to be received by another. How often during your day do you receive a kind word, a smile, a moment of affection, a sign of appreciation, the attention of another, the approval of another, and just brush it off? It is easier to complain that that special someone isn't giving enough, isn't behaving properly. But when you feel a deficit, it is rarely because one person is failing to love you properly; it most often stems from your own inability to assimilate love and connection from many sources.

How often do you gloss over those moments of being listened to, being told you are important, being received by the many people around you, and end up feeling "nobody truly loves me," because that one special person isn't available, or isn't receiving you in the precise way you would like them to.

Most of your successes in love come from those

connections and exchanges you are not trying to control
or change. And most of your love woes stem from trying
to manipulate love to fit your mental ideas of it, and in
the process missing the rich and varied forms of loving
that are available to you throughout your day.

You have been pushed in this culture to think of love as
something you do with one other person. Yet if we gave you a
garden and said, you may plant only one seed, you would be
pretty disappointed. It would be a waste of the land. When you
plant a garden, you plant many seeds, and all of those grow and
nourish you in combination. By the same token, in your life,
you will have many loves. To say that one love is more important than the others, or should be, is to deny the multiplicity
of yourself.

We aren't trying to say that you can't make commitments
with people. But you each are linked in the web of connection,
so your love work is to find those connections. Start watching
people loving things. Watch the ways people have of expressing their affection, of receiving other people, of receiving themselves. Watch people walking through the woods drinking in the
green beauty. Watch people playing with their dogs.

In the following pages we offer you a brief observation
guide, to help you gain insight into the ways of loving that are
available to you, to help fertilize the soil of love. When you can
diversify your focus on love, then you are less likely to feel you
are suffering its lack.

Awakening

Awakening is the aspect of loving that is most closely
aligned with what you know as "falling in love." This is when
someone or something wakes you up. You fall in love with
someone, and all of a sudden the world comes alive. Life feels
glorious, colors are more vibrant, other people take on a warm
glow, you become either intensely dreamy or intensely aware.
It feels so good it hurts.

The illusion is that that particular person is incredibly
special, unique and suited to you. In fact it is the feelings you
are having which are special. Your heart has opened to allow
someone or something in, and the connection you feel can be
more intense, more mystical, more charged than anything you
feel in your normal state.

It will happen repeatedly in your life. Most people are awakened at regular intervals, by another person, by an idea or project, by a beautiful sunset, in a moment of epiphany. Your heart opens and you find yourself flooded in love. The gift and the purpose of this state is to show you your own heart. To show you your potential for awakening, and also to show you the potential of strongly valuing people or experiences "out there."

It is part of being alive to find yourself jolted awake, jolted into a heightened awareness of another being or of your own passion. It is lovely when this heightened state is shared, when you can use it to start a relationship with someone, or to deepen your intimacy and clarify your goals. But it is not necessary for the awakening to be mutual. You can still benefit from it greatly, if you do not get trapped in your expectations of what your awakening will bring you.

Awakening serves the purpose of bringing you home to your own heart, your own capacity for caring, for feeling connected, for feeling intensely about something. It is like a bright spotlight which illuminates your vision for a time. It is your heart, celebrating its ability to open.

But it is easy to get addicted to these feelings and try to hold on to them at all cost. It is easy to get fixated on the object of your affections, on the person you have fallen in love with, on the place or idea you have opened to. And if the other person does not reciprocate your feelings, you can experience strong grief and sorrow. When your heart, following its natural rhythms, gently closes again, you may suffer deep disappointment as the glamour fades and you are faced with ordinary, everyday feelings about your beloved.

When you awaken to another person, it does not mean that you must run off with her, and form a life together. It does not mean you must hop into bed with her to consummate the connection. It does not mean that you have received a sign that a match with this person would be a match made in heaven. It is not a message from your wiser self that this person is a soul mate. But it can certainly feel this way.

Awakening is merely (and splendidly) an opening to your own potential. It shows you something of what you want, often mirrored in your beloved. It shows you your own readiness to open sexually, or seek partnership, or have an adventure. And when the conditions are right, when the other person is trustworthy, free to make a commitment to you, or free to honor that bond without harming others, then it is perfectly appropriate to use your awakened energy to forge a new relationship or fuel an adventure.

If the person is not truly available, however, or not really capable of sustaining the type of relationship you are seeking, it is important to recognize that while *awakening* energy is a blessing, it can also be a curse. It can motivate you to suspend your judgment, take risks you aren't really prepared to take, behave in ways that are humiliating, push for something you don't necessarily want in the long run.

As a high energy state it is useful in forging new bonds, or motivating you to crack old forms in your life and try new things. It is not useful if you allow yourself to go crashing into walls, if you don't recognize and honor that it is a special and volatile state. When you are in love, you may want to throw cares to the winds and follow your impulses. It is easy to overextend your physical limits and lose track of your mundane concerns and commitments.

The energy of awakening, of falling in love is glorious and limited. You will do it again and again; it is like the springtime, and comes up seasonally in your garden. When the flowers come up you can't hold onto them. You can celebrate them, you can take pictures of them, you can remember them. Then the petals fall, the leaves wither and the plants are plowed under in preparation for next year's planting.

Nurturing

When you are yearning for love, what is it you want? Is it sex you are craving? Good conversation or attention? Companionship? Is it a sense of identity, conferred when someone recognizes you and acknowledges you as special? Often, what you are craving in your yearning for love is **nurturing**.

Nurturing is a form of love that you learn when you are just a fetus, being held and cared for in your mother's womb. You have warmth, you have nourishment, you are safe. You are enclosed within the in-out pulse of another's being. This is nurturing: being held, having your needs met, being cared for; it is the physical basis for love.*

* This does not have implications for the political question of the morality of abortion. Although a fetus is an earth elemental spirit, like the insects, plants and other earth elementals it has a much more fluid and flexible conception of life and death than your talking selves comprehend. Some wiser selves choose to form an earth elemental fetus, then terminate it in order to re-experience just that portion of your reality, without

You each have this physical basis for love (though sur-
vivors of fetal drug or alcohol poisoning may have some special
challenges), no matter what further love experiences you have
had in your life, no matter how warped your experience with
love may have been. And because you have a physical basis for
love, you are capable of learning a healthy give and take, a
healthy style of loving as an adult.

*The desire for nurturing and nurture stays alive in
you throughout your life. It remains as a yearning to be
held (and hold), to be deeply and entirely received, to be
mothered, to be encompassed in the life rhythms of
another. Nurturing is an affirmation of the living
creature that you are.*

Nurturing is the form of love which intersects most clearly with need. You each need to be touched. You each need to
know that you are safe and protected. You each need to be
affirmed emotionally and physically, and held within the
awareness of others. When your needs are getting met, you feel
loved. Many of you carry the expectation that you will get most
of your nurturing from your lover. We would suggest that you
expand this view: that you receive nurturing from friends, from
relatives, from colleagues, from the environment you live in,
from nature, from yourself. Once you are an adult, the entire
world is your womb and is capable of nourishing you.

You provide nurturing for another person by embracing
them for a moment. You give it to your lover, not just in the
heat of passion, but in a quiet moment of intimate connection.
You nurture a friend each time you reassure her and let her
know she is valuable. You can give it to a stranger in a moment
of empathy or recognition.

Within nurturing is a key to a very physical kind of love
which each of you can practice every day. If love is opening and
receiving, then what allows you to open and receive? What
opens you is connecting to the in-out pulse of anything that has
an in-out pulse. So any time you attune to a living energy, you
are practicing a form of very physical love that will nourish
you. If you are feeling unloved, lie on the grass and feel the

intending to create a full-fledged committee of three. Sometimes the formation of an
earth elemental fetus is accidental and not appropriate for the earth elemental or talking
self of the mother. Sometimes the pregnancy is a talking self drama engaged in by the
mother for purposes of her own growth and evolution and was not intended as a choice
to mother a new human Self into the world. Each of these cases is individual and must
be evaluated in the context of the mother's life and understanding.

earth. Or sit next to a tree and feel the pulse of that life form. Or sit with a pet, sit on a bus and feel the life around you. And feel that you have life within you. Allow yourself to be held and taken in by your surroundings.

Allow yourself to notice that you are breathing, and the person next to you is breathing, and the person next to them is breathing too. And you are all breathing the same air. The commonality of that can trigger your very basic, physical sense of nurture that got coded into you as a fetus. It was developed in any physically healthy womb, no matter what your mother's attitude toward you, personally.

When you are feeling a lack of love in your life, nine times out of ten you are experiencing a craving for nurturing. And although you may be anxious to find a partner, or angry at the partner you have for not meeting your needs, there is a good chance that the lack of nurturing is coming primarily from you.

We have addressed this at length in the section on self-love. When you forget to nurture yourself, in minute and specific ways throughout the day, when you are at war between your body and your mind, then it will feel like what you are missing is love from others. In those moments it is helpful to remember your power to nurture yourself. The more willing you are to engage in small acts of nurturing yourself, the more available you will be to participate in a true give and take with others.

Discovery

Because your need for affection and nurturing is so strong, it often overshadows another important aspect of loving, that of **discovery**. Curiosity is built into your system. You have a deep need to understand what makes people tick: how do they see things? What are they really like? How do they organize their lives? This curiosity is one of the reasons you form friendships, affiliations and groups with people. Your need to discover how people work leads you repeatedly into new exchanges with others.

In your family, you learned certain patterns of interacting with people. You learned what is acceptable or not, what is "normal" (in that setting), what is "weird," what to expect from an exchange. If your family was healthy, then you probably got a chance to discover that there were many acceptable ways of connecting and exchanging with people.

If your family was dysfunctional or alienated, then you didn't get much opportunity to discover what kinds of exchanges could bring you pleasure, warmth, support, affection, stimulation, calm, security. You may have learned to wall yourself in behind a whole slew of attitudes and behaviors which originally kept you protected, but now just keep you isolated from others.

Whatever kind of family you grew up in, you are carrying a set of mental criteria for who can love you, and how, and when, and these conditions often serve to limit the amount and quality of intimacy you are able to have in your life. You have your ideas about your kind of people, drawn in part from your experiences, but also from the prejudices you learned at home and in school, and the images which have bombarded you in the media.

Discovery is the name we give to the work you do to break out of your mental limitations and conditions for love. Each time you invite someone to lunch just to get to know them, each time you date someone and keep an open mind about where things will lead, each time you are willing to explore your assumptions about people, you are giving yourself a new opening for love in your life.

Discovery is also the work you do to open up your self-image. Each time you choose to try a new activity, take a new direction in a conversation, explore your feelings about something, you are fertilizing the soil. In such a mind, love can truly take root and grow.

We have met several people who have said to us, "I don't understand. I am reasonably attractive, fairly friendly, and very successful professionally. But I can't seem to find the right person, can't seem to attract a partner." In each of these cases, the person was not lacking an ability to be affectionate. They were blocking love with their own perfectionism, their own mental conditions. Not only were they tremendously hard on themselves, but also tended to be too judgmental in meeting others. They had a list of criteria for acceptance, and each time they met someone new, they would mentally tick items off a checklist.

This habit, while being a form of self-protection, creates a barrier to establishing a loving exchange. If you can develop the spirit of discovery, you can learn to live with the unformed aspects of a relationship long enough to let something new emerge: new patterns, new bonds, new ways of relating. So if

your old ways of relating do not yield you the kinds of relationships you would like, or the amount of love you feel you
need, then it is perhaps your sense of discovery which needs
some attention.

Companionship: Shared Experience

Why do people who own pets have fewer heart attacks
than those who don't own pets? Because the companionship
they get from their dog or cat meets an emotional need. **Companionship** is a love need you can easily fill from moment to
moment, day to day. Each time you sit in a restaurant with others and feel the exchange of forces all around you, each time
you invite someone to go for a walk, each time you sit in a
meeting at work, a need is being met in you. The need for
shared experience.

Every time you walk out of your apartment, and there is
someone in the elevator with you, you are sharing an experience and you are creating a bond. That bond is something
energetic, perhaps temporary, but it is a moment of connection. That bond nourishes you in subtle ways. And over time,
the impact of all these momentary bonds accrues and you
begin to feel yourself *companioned* in this world.

It is true that when you are craving companionship, you
are generally craving something that runs deeper: good conversation, a committed friend, someone who shares your interests and is interested in you personally. But this type of companionship builds on the base of shared experience. It is useful
to stay in practice, interacting, allowing the little exchanges in
life to mean something to you.

Love often grows unexpectedly out of shared experience.
Why do people in movies who are trapped on a desert island
together tend to fall in love? Because the shared experience
allows them to forge a strong bond. So when you want more
love in your life, let yourself have more experiences with people. Ask yourself what types of things you'd like to be doing
with that mythical companion you are craving, and do as many
of those activities as you can with other companions.

If you picture yourself with your true love preparing dinner together, then invite an acquaintance over to make dinner
together. We do not wish to sound like an advice columnist
here; our point is not to send you actively shopping for a partner in all the right places. Our point is to encourage you to stop

shopping for a specific partner, and let yourself have the companionship and shared experience you are craving with multiple others. When you do, unique bonds will form that carry their own satisfactions.

When you break your craving for love into its component parts, you can address it. Instead of focusing on the love you are not finding, shift to the experience you are having with love, with connection, with recognizing your life force taken up and shared. As you do this, you open a doorway to deeper love, and further connection.

You will feel more love in your life if you have ways to share experiences with people and allow yourself to value those experiences you are having. Your work setting may provide some good opportunities. Have you ever had the experience of making a friend through work whom you realize you would never really choose to know otherwise? Each time you allow your experience to instruct you in love, you grow richer and more capable of love in your life.

Internalizing and Anchoring

Love doesn't do you much good if you can't take it in. It may not feel like a love activity, but stopping to feel is a crucial part of evolving as a loving and beloved person. How often do you brush off a compliment, saying "it was nothing"? How often do you miss a kind and loving exchange with a friend because you are anxious about what your partner said yesterday? How many times, after you have had a nice interaction with someone you like, do you turn around, get on the phone, and dissipate the energy before you have fully felt it?

We are suggesting that you consciously take the time to stop, to grow moony, to realize something feels good and to float with that feeling. Take the time to **internalize**, to let it become part of you, that love, those feelings, that connection.

Taking time to internalize is a far more important part of love than most of you realize. You are doing it for yourself and for the other person. For yourself, you are giving your mind and emotions time to realize that a connection, a love transaction has occurred. You are allowing the feeling of connection to work its way kinesthetically through your system. You need to digest love just as you need to digest food; otherwise it can't really nourish you.

For the other person in the interaction, the sense that you are taking in their compliment, gesture, sign of affection, and truly feeling it, is a great gift. As we have said, one of the best ways to love someone is to receive them. As they feel their compliment received and savored, they too feel loved. It strengthens both of you, and encourages further connection and exchange.

Stopping to feel your transactions throughout the day, even the difficult ones, allows you to keep your gates open to connection with others. It keeps your focus balanced, between your feeling self and your thinking self. Many of you work in places that expect you to remain in thinking mode full time. Some of you have adopted a persona or personal style that is head-directed. Over time if you stay in your head too much, you can fall greatly out of balance. Not only does the cerebral focus make it difficult for you to assimilate emotional exchanges, but it begins to skew your perceptions of what you need.

Many of you have much more love in your life than you are capable of taking in. You feel frustrated because your partner or family or friends aren't loving you the way you wish to be loved. They feel frustrated because when they do show their love, it's never enough. You still want more. Practice taking in what you have. Even if it is flawed love, even if it is clumsy and seems like selfish love. Take it in and let it nourish you. Over time, you reduce that sense of deficit in you, and grow clearer on what is truly missing. Most often, the missing link is your own ability to assimilate your connections with others.

Anchoring is the security that comes within yourself when you are loved. Why do you want someone to love you? Because it makes you feel secure in a certain way and because you need love. Why do you want to love someone else? Because it makes you feel connected, anchored in this life.

If you had a parent who loved you very much and was a pretty decent parent, then you probably internalized their love as an anchor within you that makes you feel secure. So when you find yourself in a scary situation, the love and support you received from that parent anchors you. You can allow any love experience that is working for you at the moment to become an anchor within you.

If you have someone who loves you and believes in you, it is easier to go out and take risks in the world. Knowing someone loves you is a reminder that you are part of the web, that you are held and protected. Why is it you feel so betrayed when someone stops loving you or turns their attention to someone else? Because you feel excluded from the web. You feel dependent on that bond to support you emotionally, socially, even financially. And if it fails you, you feel the pain of separation and isolation.

But if you can internalize the love that has been given, then the security is within you. Each time someone loves you or acknowledges you in a moment, that is a gift. They can't take it back. In the next moment they can change their mind, but you have still received the feeling, the connection and the affirmation. You can still let it nourish you.

Every moment of love that you take in, receive, internalize and work with, helps to build that anchoring and security within you. It helps you to consolidate a clear sense that you are lovable. That you are human, and part of the human exchange. That you are grounded in a loving universe.

Those of you who have had serial relationships rather than one long sustained one, we say to you, "Don't see that as failure." See that as a chain of beautiful pearls that adds up to being beloved, being lovable. That is what anchoring is about. You internalize each of those connections as it happens, and then you anchor that connection in your sense of self, so that you feel secure and can take risks. So that you carry inside yourself the knowledge that you are lovable.

Structuring and Commitment

Whenever you meet someone you like, you need to create a **structure**, a context for getting to know them. Some of these contexts are ready-made: you are on the same sports team, you work in the same corridor, you live on the same block. Some contexts naturally support the exchange of affection and the growth of love, others make it nearly taboo. Often a good deal of your thought and creativity is called for to build the right kind of *ships* to carry your relating.

Love can be supported or choked out by the forms you create for knowing and interacting with someone. If you are an overworker and spend long hours at your job, you aren't leaving much time or energy available for a real give and take with friends or family. If you spend too much time with another person, and the bond is not strong enough to fill the space you have created for it, then the satisfaction of that love can easily dissipate and get lost.

There is a myth in your culture that if love is true, it can surmount all obstacles and triumph over adversity. In fact, love is a lot like a plant—it needs a nourishing soil in which to grow. It can sometimes crack the cement of your blockages and rigidity, but it can also wither and die when over-exposed to the elements or under-watered. Love is not a feeling that exists separate from the reality of your time, space, resources, commitments, or mind set. It is often the connection that you are able to establish because of your use of time, space, resources, commitments and mental expectations.

Imagine you have just met someone new who you would like to get to know better. How are you going to go about it? Where will they fit into your life? What other commitments have you made, that must be honored or changed as you shift your time, energy and thinking to let this new person into your life?

Most of you have furnished your life with plenty of commitments. You have a partner, you have children, you have work colleagues, friends, associates, family. And sometimes all these commitments and structures hem you in. You don't have time to get to know someone new. You don't have emotional space for yourself. You don't have energy to be open to others. In such a circumstance love can become diminished. The resentment and obligations you feel make it hard to take in and celebrate the connections you have made.

Connecting is not a permanent state. It is something that happens in a rhythm, alternating with disconnection. So you connect to your partner, and then disengage for a short time, and later re-connect. The forms that you make, the official relationships such as marriage, live-in partnership, friendship, family relationships (any links which are not secret ones) are meant to provide security. They offer a forum where you can connect and disconnect repeatedly.

But often what happens is that you get lazy. You let the formal commitment serve as the connection. So instead of truly engaging with your marriage partner on a regular basis, you spend most of your efforts on mutually maintaining the box: the married behaviors, your couple identity. In such an atmosphere, some love deepens but most drains away. That person no longer feels exciting to you or dynamic or special. She starts to feel like furniture in your life, rather than the precious, ever-changing person she most truly is.

Love is more than a matter of gazing soulfully into another person's eyes and feeling the life force ebb and flow between you. It gets expressed through a myriad of exchanges: whenever you share a task with another person, whenever you engage in conversation, whenever you attend events together you are fertilizing the soil for deeper and more engaged love. Structuring your life so that these events take place, working with your energy so you can be truly present with another person, managing your time and money so that you can afford to participate fully, all become crucial support tasks in love. Even making sure you get enough sleep, that you moderate your intake of stimulants, and keep up with the details of your life have a great impact on how available you can be for love in your life.

And when you have made room in your life for friends and significant others, the type of commitments you make with them is also important. There is a trend in your culture to ask commitments of people, to promise to stay forever, to create a hierarchy of love, so that others know where they stand with you. The fact is, your sense of need, interest, and connection will shift and fluctuate over time with each person you know. Like a boat that can bob and float on the tides, your relationships and commitments need to be flexible enough to float with these shifts and changes of energy.

We encourage you to work on inner security, and try to be a bit more flexible about the commitments you make. Can you commit to being present with someone and honoring the gift of her love, without promising that you will always want what you want today? Can you be clear with yourself and others about what limits you need to set, so that you are not wasting energy on confused expectations and feelings of betrayal?

Years ago in your culture the expectation of roles was much more fixed than it is today. People were expected to marry, stay with their partner for life, and adjust themselves to fit the demands of the marriage. Children were expected to continue living with or near their parents, building a life which intertwined with their parents' lives. People were expected to stay put geographically, for the most part, and maintain friends and connections for life. There was not as much mobility in changing jobs, dwellings, or social setting either.

But all of those forms are breaking apart. You may view it as a sign of alienation, but we view it as a positive trend. There is a real move toward finding more genuine choices in your life. If a marriage is an empty form, you are more free to let go of it and seek your love and connection elsewhere. If you outgrow your job, it is becoming more acceptable to move on, try a new kind of work. You are encouraged to travel, to see many options, to form the life which expresses your nature.

Within this shift comes the responsibility to invent relationships and design commitments as you go along. Together you and your partners need to define what your friendships, loverships, marriages mean, and how you wish to behave toward each other. Together you must work on communicating clearly, solving problems that arise, and juggling the various obligations that tug at each of you. It is not an easy task. Many of you suffer great growing pains in trying to make contemporary relationships work.

One of the best tools you have for building relationships that mean something is your ability to communicate. In the shifting patterns of energy that you share with someone, only clear and ongoing communication can keep you each relatively secure. It is no longer realistic to see a relationship as an object to be maintained. Instead, what you have with someone is a commitment to engage with them as best you can, over time. Communication, skillful structuring, and love are the glue that hold these efforts together.

Collaboration

True joy comes from merging your spirit with another human being. A wonderful vitality is created when you put your energy together with others and feel your efforts feeding something that is greater than the sum of its parts. Have you ever sung in a choir, and felt the surge of power that comes when your single voice joins a swell of voices and produces a spectacular sound? Have you ever marched in a candlelight parade, carrying your one single flame, and turned to see all around you a river of light in the darkness?

Collaboration is a form of love where you feel your powers taken up and shared. Not all group efforts are collaboration. Some are competitions, or petty dictatorships. But a true collaboration can be immensely satisfying, and make you feel wonderful connection and love.

When you join forces with a partner—be it a friend, lover, relative, colleague, stranger—to accomplish a task or share your strengths, a special bond is developed that nourishes you deeply. This is very different from the energy created when two people are focussed exclusively on each other. Collaborative energy reaches out and nourishes others. Closed circuit energy will feed you at first, then quickly burn itself out. It is often annoying or repelling to others who witness it, for you are social creatures, connected in multiple ways, and are not really designed to exchange all your forces with one other person exclusively.

One of the advantages of a form like marriage is that you can merge your energies with your partner and find the strength to try things and take chances you wouldn't dare to take alone. Whenever a friendship, partnership, lovership is dynamic, it allows the participants to feel this increase of potential, this touchstone of strength and support.

But you needn't wait until you find a marriage partner or true love before you build collaborative relationships. You can practice collaborating in all your connections with people, sharing a focus on something outside your two selves, and feeling the deeper bonds that form through that shared experience.

Each time you collaborate to solve a problem at work, each time you cooperate with neighbors to make your living area better, each time you play sports on teams (or in loving competition), each time you share spiritual practice with others, each time you join in a political movement and collaborate on working toward shared goals, you will find you are forging bonds with your fellow participants. The act of collaborating gives you a sense of membership, which is an important key to feeling secure in this life.

Competition, on the other hand, when it pits one person against another, may motivate you and energize you, but it rarely leaves you feeling loved and connected. In any situation

which demands losers as well as winners, all people are ultimately losers.

*Examine when and how you join forces with others.
Are you able to merge your efforts with theirs? Are you
able to see the value of each person's contributions? Are
you able to feel the pleasure of participating, rather than
getting focussed on the ego fulfillment of being singled
out as the star?*

The more you allow yourself to truly collaborate with others, the more capable you become of letting love grow in your
life. Building relationships that endure and are consistent in
your life requires you to merge your identity (not permanently, but from time to time), into a focus on shared purpose or
greater good. When you are able to do this, then the relationship can last, and can nourish you.

Love regularly changes its face. If you see only the full
moon, then you don't appreciate the beauty of the new moon,
or the waxing and waning moons. If you see love only as the
rush of passion, then you miss seeing love in all her phases.
These activities we've talked about are all phases of love. Love
itself is permanent. Your job isn't so much to create it as to
enter it, open to it, recognize it, strum it like the strings of a
guitar.

Love is a shifting energetic dance, and if you are seeking
love as an object, a particular person, a fixed commitment in
your life, you are going to miss the other more subtle loves,
the moments of connection and recognition. If you are too
focussed on a single relationship, then it will betray you and let
you down, no matter how perfect the partner is. You are not
designed to hang from the web by only a single thread. You
are designed to be interconnected in a myriad of ways.

So if you want to know love, you need to move your focus.
If you want to know love, you have to open your heart and
close it and shift and work with love. If you want to know the
mysteries of love, then you need to learn that each relationship has its own significance. Each encounter with another
human being has it own value. When you celebrate love on its
own terms and celebrate life as you encounter it, then it will
yield more love than you can possibly imagine.

Conditions of Loving

❧

If you are interested in spiritual practice, you have probably been told that you should learn unconditional love. You should somehow be able to love all people and all creatures, without judgment. An enlightened being, you have been told, loves unconditionally.

But if you have ever tried it, you know this is not easy. For one thing, the heart seems to behave like a sea anemone, closing when approached by anything intent upon touching it. And besides, the universe seems to delight in sending especially tough cases to test you: the co-worker who has few boundaries or limits, the emotionally disturbed friend whose life is so tangled that any help you try to give just pulls the knots tighter, the crazy person making a beeline for you every time you are in a hurry trying to get somewhere.

We would like to suggest that an enlightened being does not really love unconditionally at all. The enlightened being is skilled in loving *conditionally*. She or he is able to recognize with love and compassion all the conditions of this world of yours, conditions created by these minds of yours, and is able at the same time to hear the divine heartbeat within it.

So-called unconditional loving is actually a combination of two things: being able to recognize the humanity and life force within all creatures, and being able to recognize and stay present for the conditions people create. So if you wish to learn unconditional love (or merely feel more open to love), you have two tasks: come home to your heart frequently so that you can better feel your connection with the divine, and work with the conditions of your mind that obscure your sense of connection to others. Until you are able to love the conditions, by which and through which you connect with people, it is very hard to love beyond the conditions.

Conditions are the criteria your mind—your gatekeeper—uses for accepting or rejecting connections with others. They are the containers your mind creates, the shape it gives to reality. So as you work with your gatekeeper, and your mental constructs about the world, you are actually learning to love more fully. It is your mind which obscures or opens your access to your heart.

Take a look first at your expectations of yourself in the realm of love. Who do you think you ought to love? When and under what circumstances do you feel you should love them? What does it mean to love someone; what are the behaviors, the attitudes, the commitments you expect of yourself when you love someone? Look also at your expectations of others. What do you expect of and from someone who claims to love you? Do you have the same standards for how someone should love you, and how you ought to love them?

Many of you see love as something which should just open up the floodgates of your being. If you love someone, you feel you should share your energies, your time, your belongings unstintingly. Some of you see love as a prize, to be bestowed upon certain special people when they have proved their trust-worthiness. Others of you see love as an emotional stance in life, a certain warmth and openness you feel toward people, a certain acceptance.

Love can be all these things, but doesn't need to be all these things all of the time. As we have said, to love someone is to feel your connection, to allow exchange, to receive some-one's being. Your gatekeeper, in protecting you, will work out the limits of that connection, exchange, and receptiveness, to sustain the sanctity of yourself.

So the first place to work with love is in the conditions you are willing to accept in yourself. It is pretty common folk wisdom that you tend to dislike those aspects of others that you dislike in yourself. If you reject another person for being too aggressive, you are probably having trouble accepting your own aggressiveness.

Beyond that though, you will also reject any energy, qual-ity, or trait that you don't know how to receive. The greater your repertoire of what you can receive, the greater your abili-ty will be to love.

We have already asked this of you: how much of yourself are you willing to receive? How much of yourself do you accept? The conditions you put on yourself, for love, for approval, for success and failure, for safety, for "enoughness" are the conditions you put on loving. Each aspect of yourself you learn to accept increases the ease with which you will open to that aspect in others.

Consider for a moment the aspects of yourself—and others—you love or reject. Start with your **body** and **physicality**. Your earth is peopled with all kinds of bodies in all kinds of conditions. It seems so basic to appreciate the creature elements of yourself, but are you truly open to all the ways you are? Most of our friends in body look in the mirror and tear themselves apart with criticisms: they are too big or small, those wrinkles seem ugly, the signs of usage and weariness seem unattractive or unwelcome.

The scars, scabs, wrinkles and sags are part of your living creature, as are the illnesses, deformities, and individual differences. We were working with Ellen on this concept recently when she had a headache. She was angry at herself and the universe for her pain, and did not feel particularly charitable toward her body or toward others. In that state of mind, very little opening of the heart can be felt, very little exchange can happen with others.

We said to her: "You have a headache, why not love it?" She said to us: "Forget it. I don't love this headache, I don't want a headache." We came back to her with a different message, because for her the idea of loving is attached to liking, and approval.

We said, "Can you take in that you have a headache, that that is your reality, that your head has its limits, and it has reached its limit? Can you take in and honor the self that needs to rest, because it has a headache? Can you lovingly open to the need which is there? In recognizing that need, you open to the self that has a headache. You open to the headache."

You would rather not have a headache, but when you accept fully that that is the condition there in the moment, when you accept it on its own energetic terms—you can explore its energy. You can see that it moves and changes, and the headache is not exactly a headache at all. It is a series of messages from the body to itself, and from the body to the talking self, and the headache can become as interesting a situation to explore as other things you would rather be doing. When you open to the situation which is there, while not exactly liking it, you open to acceptance and a particular form of love called compassion.

When you learn to accept all the aspects of your physical condition—including and especially your discomforts—then you have a way to open to others in

*their physical conditions and discomforts. You can see
with loving compassion (not pity) those who are
differently-abled, who are hurting, or twisted in their
own knots. You can recognize the difficulty many
individuals have inhabiting this physical reality, and you
can open your heart to that recognition, and learn to
reach out, rather than draw back from such people.*

It is a natural tendency to avoid discomfort or pain. The more able you are to stand steady with your discomfort, to accept your pain as part of the ebb and flow of life force, the more likely you are to open to and stay present with uncomfortable situations. The less energy you spend avoiding your pain—and that of others—the more you will find your way through to greater ease and comfort. And loving.

Your gatekeeper will tend to reject and repel the unfamiliar, so the more willing you are to investigate what is unfamiliar (rather than avoiding it or blindly rejecting it), the more likely your gatekeeper is to accept it, and find ways to stay open.

This is especially true in the realm of **ideas, thought forms** and **mental habits**. How many people do you reject because they are stupid or fascist in their beliefs, or have different religious or political persuasions? It is ironic, but the more you fight against certain ideas, the more your own mental patterns come to resemble them. For example, if you find yourself rabidly angry about neo-nazis, you may find your heart just as constricted, and your mind engulfed in very similar energy.

We are not suggesting that you must embrace all ideas and ideologies within your own belief system. We are suggesting that you learn to investigate the mental conditions people put on their lives, and explore how those conditions might serve them. When you can remember someone's humanity, while understanding your objections to their mind frames, then you become more capable of dialogue and opening. You are less likely to be engulfed or hurt when you come in contact with thought forms you dislike.

*One of the most dangerous aspects of an idea is
that it can shut down your access to your heart and
wisdom. It can cause you and others to react, rather
than choosing your actions. So if you refuse to react
when confronted by another person's ideas or prejudices,*

and if you refuse to react to your own ideas and
prejudices, then you can grow larger in mind and spirit.

Your judgments harm you even more than they harm the people you are judging. They close you down. They limit your ability to love and explore. They clog your energy in physical tensions which can impair your physical health. But it is not likely that you will be able, merely upon our recommendation, to drop the habit of judging yourself and others. It is a habit which gives you the illusion of being safe, special, powerful, connected. It is a habit which gets deeply ingrained in your mind.

We recommend instead that you gently and lovingly invite yourself to substitute observations for judgments. To say to yourself "That person is intensely focussed in his mind," instead of "What a fanatic." Begin a process of noticing when you make a judgment, and tagging it. We suggested to Ellen that each time she caught herself judging someone and measuring their worth, that she just mentally send them a flower. She would think, "What a phony." And then, noticing what she had done, she would apologize to the person in her mind, and offer that person a lovely lily. This helped her to open her heart again. Then she would investigate her own reaction.

What does it mean when someone is a phony? It means someone is uncomfortable, doesn't know how to act. When you remember, with loving recognition, the times you have not known how to act, then you don't need to reject or shut down to the other person's humanity or your own. You can recognize and acknowledge their behavior or attitude for what it is, a sign of discomfort (or greed, or anxiety, or manipulation), and remember all humans practice such behaviors from time to time.

There are times when you will have so many judgments that you will find yourself sending whole bouquets and florist shops in your mind. Those are the times when you have a message that your ego and gatekeeper are needing some attention. For some reason you do not feel safe, secure, or grounded. And your judgments serve to signal that fact.

A mental stance which helps to break down the
need to judge and criticize is that of "bearing witness."
You are a visitor to this strange planet with an amazing
variety of life forms and expressions. Can you bear

witness to what is, without needing to judge its value?
Can you stand and watch someone else's pain, in
recognition that all people have pain, in recognition that
it is not necessarily your task to change them or fix them
or cure them? When you learn you can just bear witness,
as a compassionate observer, when you let yourself off
the hook of obligation and responsibility, you free
yourself to find true responses.

Perhaps the most difficult conditions to meet with equanimity are the **emotional** and **energetic** ones. Have you ever had the experience of interacting with someone, and finding yourself getting more and more tense, without realizing why? Often you are responding to emotional or energetic signals from the other person which are extremely subtle. She is broadcasting her pain, discomfort, need, and restlessness, and it is difficult to stay open, without soaking in her energy like a sponge.

Once again, we remind you that it is not necessary to abandon your limits or boundaries in order to love, accept, and exchange with another person. In fact, it is one of the arts of loving to learn to maintain your own sense of self, your own perceptions, your own energetic truth, in the face of the blasts you sometimes receive from others.

Awareness helps to protect you. When you see that someone is troubled and is putting out difficult energy, you can just gently remember your own truth, and let their energy pass through you. You can remember to bear witness to what is true for them, without needing to take on that energy as your own. You can remember the times you have felt those things for yourself, and how blocked the heart was in those moments. And you can stand safely shielded in your own heart, without needing to close it down.

It is a wonderful challenge to you to learn to hold your own in the face of shifting emotions and energies. The more you work with your own shifts, of course, the more skill you will have in recognizing others. It is a bit like surfboarding, learning how to move your feet, working with the winds, and maintaining a balance, so that you don't get dunked and drowned in the waters of someone else's emotional state.

Do you understand that the chemical or mental conditions that have triggered their emotions do not have to prevail over your system? In the face of someone else's difficult emotions or invasive energy, return your attention to your breathing. Listen to your heart until it finds its calm and steady rhythm. Use your ability to communicate: "I need a moment to think." "Slow down, I'm not taking this in." "What is it you are asking of me?" And through these efforts you allow yourself to stand steady in the face of uncomfortable energies.

The worship of **personality** and **social roles** is strong in your culture. How often do you find yourself dismissing someone by saying, "She's obnoxious," or "He's just a drop-out." You did not invent the conditions which constrict your heart and make it difficult to love. They are rife in your culture, in the hierarchies and systems and competitions which set people up against each other.

Unfortunately, each role or personality trait you reject (for yourself or others) acts to obscure your heart. Each time you pass a drunk on the street, and shut your mind and heart to him, you are also shutting your mind and heart to everything else too. It makes you less tolerant of your own vulnerabilities, your own needy, out-of-control moments.

Can you learn to explore personalities and roles as costumes people put on to express aspects of the human spirit? Can you see them as tools that people use, either skillfully or not so skillfully, to meet the basic needs that all human beings share: the need for love and exchange; the need for comfort and security; the need for self-protection; the need for stimulation and calming; the need for nourishment and nurturing?

When you find yourself behaving in a way you hate—flirting perhaps, acting clingy, bragging, being selfish—can you ask yourself what need that might be addressing, what purpose that might serve (or be trying to serve)? What old habit are you repeating? When you see another person accepting or playing a certain role or position in society, can you see them as holding up that piece of sky on behalf of the whole planet? That role exists because the talking selves of your planet have created it. Can you listen to the messages and reminders within each role, without detesting the being who inhabits it?

The question is frequently asked of spiritual teachers: "But what of the rapist? What of the murderer? Isn't it all right to hate them?" Hatred is the force *they* are expressing; they are enacting their own sense of violation and indignity. It is fine to decide that rape, murder and violation should not be part of human exchanges. And there is no reason why you should stand unprotected in their presence. But the energy you put into hating, dehumanizing, and refusing to recognize the hurt and wounded people who perpetrate the crimes, is the same energy that feeds the crime.

We do not ask you to automatically accept and embrace difficult energy. Recognize it. Listen to it. Observe the angers, hatred, desire to harm others, feelings of violation, disrespect you carry within yourself. As you work to heal them in yourself, to embrace them as human feelings and transform them, you will learn to see these individuals more clearly as human beings inhabiting a very painful and closed reality. You will begin to see ways to work in your culture to open that reality up.

As you open up your ideas about the various roles people play, as you get to know people more fully, you are studying human nature. You are learning the reasons why people do what they do, and choose what they choose. And you learn to accept that the different choices people make will not annihilate you. You will learn to see—and open to—the essence behind the forms.

This business of loving conditionally to grow beyond the conditions is a lot of work. It is the work of deepening your understanding and awareness of the human valences, and of growing more precise in your recognition of who people are and how they are constructed. What allows you to open to love is a detailed and intimate knowledge of how to keep yourself safe, how to protect your limits, how to say no when something is unsafe. What allows you to love is to develop a detailed knowledge of your heart, and how your mind affects it.

Listen in to the conditions your mind and your culture establish for accepting or rejecting connection. As you work to embrace physicality, diverse ideas, your need to make judgments, your emotional and energetic exchanges, the personalities and social roles you encounter, you can lovingly, gradually, open up some of those tight places in you which reject connection and exchange. You can open to greater compassion and wiser love.

Grounding

Touch Bath

Take a moment to get comfortable, wherever you are sitting or lying. If you would like to shut your eyes, do so. Take a few breaths, feeling the breath come in and go out, remembering that with the out-breath you can let go of tensions and random thoughts.

Then gently begin to touch one hand with the other. Bring your hands together, exploring, caressing. If you want, rub them together and generate a little heat in your fingertips. What does the hand feel like to touch, and also what does it feel like to be touched? Use a little movement and pressure to feel the energy, the flesh and the bones of your hand.

Wiggle your fingers around, to feel the sensations created as they move. Then start touching the rest of your body. Touch your arms and your face. Your neck and head. Feel yourself as a being of flesh and bone and blood. Feel this concrete self. Let yourself have the sensations of touch: of touching and of being touched, as if you were giving yourself a touch bath. Feel yourself awakening and activating the cells of your flesh, the sensors that are located all over your body.

In this society you are taught to be very timid about touching yourself. About feeling your own corporeal being. We invite you to take some time with yourself as a physical being. You can use your hand to actually wipe away tension, as if your hand were a towel, and your tension were perspiration.

Use your hands to do a little massage around your face, around your ears...then sit and feel yourself, feel the sensations in your body. All over, your skin takes in sensory information. Every part of you is one big receptive, sensitive being.

Sometimes it is so pleasing to come back to the physical home you created on this planet. Let your attention dwell in this physical body, with love.

The Turning
Wheel of Change

Grounding

Color Grounding

Shut your eyes a moment and feel your energy, whatever that means to you. You are looking for your energy of the moment, not your energy forever, to feel what it is doing now. See if you can imagine what color your energy evokes in your mind. There are no correct answers about what colors match which moods. What color do you feel at the moment?

You might see it quite vividly, within and around you, in your mind's eye, or you might see nothing but the darkness of your closed eyelids. But in your mind, the name of the color might come up. It could be a couple of colors.

How do you feel about this color and how does it feel to you? Is this the color you want your energy to be right now? If not, is there some color you are drawn to in this moment that you would enjoy feeling instead?

We're going to ask you to work with your breath to transform your energetic color. Start with the color you have now, and each time you inhale, imagine that color growing lighter in tone. Take another breath in, and feel that color become even lighter, as if it's moving toward the color white. As you breathe out, feel it settle in to that new hue or new tone you have seen.

It might take you a couple of breaths to hold a hue steady in your mind, then let another lightness in with the next in-breath. Feel the energetic color shifting. Move as quickly or slowly as is comfortable for you. Gently allow every couple of breaths to bring that color into a lighter and lighter hue, moving it toward the color white.

You may even take a moment with each hue, or tone, to see how it feels in your body. And when you have reached the color white in your mind's eye, rest there for a moment and explore it. Use your in-breaths and your out-breaths to somehow adjust the color, the brightness of it, the tone of it, until it is most comfortable.

Those of you who would like to be a different color, who have imagined what would feel good at this moment, use the same process. As you breathe in, gradually add a little of that pigment to the white that is in you and surrounds you, so that with each breath, you move yourself toward the color you thought might be preferable.

When you have reached the color you were craving, take a moment to feel it. What do your energy and body feel now that you have changed the color?

Then open your eyes, move around a little if you need to.

For some people, the shift from hue to hue is gradual, for others it happens right away. It is useful to pay attention to how it works for you, because it gives you some clues as to what most easily or best moves your energy.

Movement and Change

There is no such thing as standing still. Change and movement happen all around you. Your earth rotates every twenty-four hours, changing the amount of light and warmth available. It cycles around the sun, shifting through seasons of growth and fallow. And it cycles through the solar system, changing the subtle energetic influences upon it.

Within you too there is constant movement and change. The bodily fluids are circulating, carrying nutrients to where they are needed, and removing wastes that will not serve. Your cells cycle through formation, function, and disintegration to such an extent that you have a completely new set of cells forming your body every seven years. And your consciousness, attention, needs, desires and perceptions are also in constant movement and flux.

Life is movement. Life is change. So any change you wish to make takes place in the context of all the natural movements in and around you. If you wish to change some aspect of your personality or circumstances, it is crucial to understand this ever-moving context in which the changes you seek are happening.

Your mind has a tendency to get stuck on *always*, on a static picture of yourself and your conditions. But things are never static for you. Your comfort level shifts and fluctuates, your tolerance for certain tasks changes, your goals, ideas and expectations alter with time and experience. Even your deepest friendships vary with time, feeling more important at some stages and less important at others.

This means that time itself will bring about much of the change you wish, and you can listen to your natural shifts of energy to tell you which changes you are actually ready to make. Many of our friends in body suffer deeply from trying to control or change circumstances in their lives which they are not in fact ready to change. They try to push themselves to advance professionally, when in fact they are not really interested in greater challenge and stress. They try to lose weight and conform to some social ideal of beauty, when in fact they are still very dependent on food as a source of comfort.

Change is an addiction in your culture, and it is tempting to set goals to better yourself without stopping to appreciate the self that you are in this moment. Often, when you push yourself to grow or change you encounter deeply-held blockages and resistance. Your selves do not like to be pushed. And they do not respond well to rejection, criticism, and dissatisfaction. What they do respond to is support, affirmation, and change which is in tune with all of their needs and interests.

We have spoken of this before in other contexts. A self which is denied rest is going to crave rest. A self which needs the nourishment of creative expression will crave that. So when you wish to change, you can only change fruitfully, and with ease, in the direction your selves are needing and wanting to go.

Do you want to change a bad habit? If so, then you need to recognize the purpose that habit serves for you, and lovingly replace or supplement the behavior with others which will serve the same purpose. If you drink in order to feel more secure in a social gathering, then it is not merely a question of depriving yourself of your drink. It is a question of lovingly building up your self-esteem and social skills, so that you can learn to feel comfortable without drinking. If you drink to blank out or avoid the pain of everyday encounters, then you need to work on your self-protection, and give yourself permission to blank out (and rest), whether or not you take a drink.

Change is not a question of discipline, and does not come about in response to rigid rules or resolutions. Change happens organically, in the natural unfolding of events, behaviors, and desires. It happens when each small moment is lived differently, and these small moments accumulate. Change comes about when you are able to shift your balance of needs, desires, and mental understanding of what you need. When you do this you find yourself making very different moment-by-moment choices and decisions. If you wish to do things differently in your life, then you must treat yourself differently—with greater support, tolerance, and empathy. As you do this, you will notice the forms which no longer serve you dropping away. You will notice that little by little your uncomfortable circumstances can change.

Seasons of Change

There is a time to make an effort, and a time to be easy on yourself. There are times when you are open to changing, and other times when you are lucky if your resistance takes a nondestructive form. There are moments when you are ready to do things differently, and many others when you must instead be patient with old ways of being. Timing is perhaps the most crucial aspect of change.

Consider the plant processes of growth. They offer you wonderful insights into the nature of change. Early in spring, the sun's force begins to return, warming the earth and preparing it to receive the seeds. The earthworms get busy, aerating and mixing the soil. You too get busy, planning your garden, turning the soil, spreading compost.

At the right time, you plant your seeds, cover them, water them, protect them from birds perhaps. Then you wait. You do other things—repair your tools, work on your compost, water the ground, remove weeds. You don't really grow the seeds. They grow themselves when conditions are right for them. And at a certain point, tender green shoots emerge, reaching for the sunshine.

At first these shoots are tentative and delicate, but very soon they grow thicker, taller, and stronger, sending out leaves to catch the light of the sun. If there are too many shoots too close together, you must thin them, or move them, so that they don't crowd each other out and die.

Beneath the surface, the growing plants send down roots, ever more extensive to counterbalance and anchor the weight and size of the plant. The roots seek out nutrients in the soil, pull in moisture to feed the growing plant. The spring rains water the soil, replenishing it.

The season continues, unfolding according to the plan coded into the seed and the environmental conditions. There is a point when the plant sends out buds, flowers and fruits. There's a point when the fruits must be harvested or they will rot. And there's a time when the plant begins to die to the visible eye and go underground, finishing its particular life cycle. In its death it breaks down to fertilize the earth, which appears to lie fallow in the cold, darker months of winter. But this time, too, supports the future growth of the plants and health of the soil.

Your energy works much the same way as that of the plants, but many of you carry strange expectations of yourself which do not fit the nature of change. You decide to make a change in your relationship, and after two or three attempts at new behavior, you are angry because things still haven't changed. Yet you wouldn't go out to your garden and yell at the plants three days after the planting. You don't scream, "Where's the fruit?" and decide the garden is no good. That's because you have faith in the plant processes of growth. You know that a seed planted in decently fertile soil will grow. You know that there is much to do to support, nourish and care for the soil, but that the actual growing is up to the plant.

All change is a seed within you. It is a desire of your three selves working together to choose their reality. It is an idea, planted in the soil of your mind, watered and supported by your behaviors, and growing gradually to blossom and bear fruit in your everyday life.

All change goes through seasons like the plant. There is a time when you must prepare the soil, so that the change can be received in your life. There is a time to send out feelers to test for possibilities, just as you might test the soil. There is a time to upset the status quo, as you might turn and aerate the soil. There is a time to try new strategies, behaviors, attitudes, like the planting of the seeds.

And when those new behaviors take root, they will grow into new forms which split the surface of your life as you were living it (and frequently produce discomfort or anxiety in the process). You become the cultivator of the new forms, placing them, shaping them, training them to grow in new directions as best you can. As you do so, the anxiety abates, you become more comfortable. Your change becomes a solid reality in your life (or dies from unskilled attention and failure to thrive). It can even, like a weed, take over your whole life.

We do not wish to belabor our metaphor; our purpose is to heighten your awareness of the many phases you go through in making a change. The more conscious you are of the nature of the phase you are in, the more accurately you can adjust your expectations and actions to suit the season. Many of our friends in body suffer terribly through their barren seasons, or feel crowded and overwhelmed in the height of their flowering. They bemoan the times when nothing appears to be happening as empty or wasted, or fear it is a permanent condition. They expect themselves to change radically, without understanding that they must grow their changes, like a patient gardener, often through many seasons of effort.

Small Deaths

All change emerges from small deaths. The death of your interest, the death of your willingness to tolerate the situation you have been tolerating until now, the death of delight, engagement, fulfillment. Death, endings, completion of a cycle all require change, even when you do not wish it. And if you do not recognize that all things shift, alter and come to an end, you can feel quite resentful to find yourself in a barren place, craving or requiring change.

Do you understand what has died in your life, and the purpose it served, both literally and symbolically? Often you must go through a period of mourning, of letting go, of resting barren, just as some trees release their leaves and rest barren through the cold winter. Often you must take time to release your emotional and energetic attachment to the way you are doing things now, to make room in the soil of your heart for a new planting. And it is not very comfortable to feel disconnected or disaffected this way.

Just as some plants thrive in a cold climate with long barren winters and other plants can only survive in tropical settings where the barren season is not so apparent, your three selves will choose the kind of seasons they need. Thus you may know someone who has been out of work for over a year, and can't seem to attract the right sort of job, while someone else you know was able to send out a résumé and gain an acceptance while barely seeming to think about the change. You may know someone who got a new job while she was still busy and engaged with the old job, and someone else who couldn't find new work until he took the plunge and quit the old one, leaving himself unencumbered and free to change, prepare for different tasks, take on new risks.

You will each have your own relationship with change that is like the climactic differences. You may be the kind of person with distinct and harsh seasons, or you may have learned to work with change so smoothly (or naturally) that you barely feel your shifts. And yet most of you will choose, at some time in your life, to experience the shock of a sudden change, and to experience the smooth transition of an easy change. Can you look back at your life, and see which experiences fit which pattern?

Inner Change and Outer Change

There is a dynamic relationship between the work you do within your mind and imagination to prepare for a change, and the work you do *out there* in the world to make that change happen. It is like the interplay between the seed and its environment. One cannot really happen without the other.

Let us give you a specific example. Imagine you want to change jobs. The work you have been doing no longer satisfies you. It is natural, in the face of dissatisfaction, to begin dreaming of changes. You picture yourself doing something more stimulating. You imagine having a larger paycheck and more flexibility because of it. You see yourself surrounded by more interesting people or having more freedom, or clarity, or support.

Change almost always grows out of discomfort or desire. The discomfort is your emotional or mental recognition that you are outgrowing the forms that used to serve you. It is the restlessness of a talking self who requires regular change in order to feel alive and interested. It is the mental recognition of the limitations that keep you from growing or the physical protest of an earth elemental self who is not getting her needs met adequately.

The desire is the voice of your wiser self wanting to blossom more fully. It is the yearning of your talking self for greater security, greater participation, or greater fulfillment. It is the pull of your earth elemental self to find greater creature comfort.

It is often at the point where you recognize your discomfort or desire that you decide to actively make a change. You think, "I must look for a new job." You pick up the newspaper or scour the professional magazines for openings, and there is an illusion that you are at the mercy of the forces out there in the world, that you must search for a job slot and gain admittance. If you don't find something interesting, it is easy to get depressed or quickly discouraged.

This is the stage of change that many of our friends in body have the most difficulty with. They compress several steps into a single focus: finding the new job. Imagine re-framing this change into a series of steps: exploring your discomfort and desire for change so that you understand them more clearly; testing the soil for diverse possibilities; planting seeds and doing the physical footwork; occupying yourself while waiting for the seeds to grow.

Exploring your discomfort and desire for change.

As we said earlier, change is the context you live in. As you work at your job, even if the actual tasks and title don't change, the circumstances in which you are working do. Your boss has troubles at home and becomes critical and tense. A co-worker has an attack of insecurity and stops cooperating with you. There is a shift in the weather patterns, or availability of goods, or market for your particular service, and this shifting affects your ability to do your job well and your satisfaction with the tasks or environment.

If you leap in your mind to the thought "I must find a new job," you are presenting yourself with a premature "yes-no" solution ("Yes I can find a new job, no I can't") to what is generally a multidimensional problem. This kind of thinking can actually block your ability to work with change. The change you need is both more specific and more general.

Consider for a moment all the dimensions of your discomfort you might address and change.

You could ask to be moved physically, or to report to a different supervisor for a time, making a *placement* change. You might strive to *re-structure* your work, so that it has a different flow of activities, a different schedule or rhythm to it. You might work on your *attitude* to and *expectations* of the job (or yourself), so that for a time you see it as a place to practice your compassion, or an opportunity to work on your inter-personal skills.

You can change some of your *behaviors* or *habits*, and see how those affect the interplay of personalities and actions around you. You can change the *relationships* you have with the people at work, addressing the difficulties directly or building new alliances that can support you. You can shift your *focus*, using the slower times to develop new skills, and the more crowded times to relinquish some of your self-imposed pressures. You can work on your *self-esteem,* so that you are less affected by the difficulties or obstructions of others.

We are not suggesting that you do almost anything

*to avoid changing your job. A job change is often what is
called for. Rather we wish to point out to you all the
dimensions of change you might actually be craving. And
it is useful to explore which dimensions of your present
situation don't work and need to be shifted, so that the
new job or pattern is truly a fruitful change. Sometimes
it is not just the job which needs to be changed. Other
parts of your life may also need some reorganizing or
reframing.*

It is useful to identify the interplay of forces that make
you uncomfortable. It is rarely a matter of one person being
wrong and ruining things for you. There is your own physical
state to examine. Do you get enough sleep, nourishment, and
stimulation from both the job and other sources? How are your
friendships and relationships (at work and elsewhere) working for you? Do you understand what emotional and interactional patterns are being played out, and whether they are
echoes of other difficulties you have had (and thus an opportunity to learn some new responses)?

There is also the organization of the work to examine. If
you could rewrite your job description and reorganize your
work situation, what would they look like? What elements are
most important to you?

Testing the soil for diverse possibilities.

There is an ironic conflict at this stage of change. Once
you are in touch with your own discomfort and fantasies, it is
tempting to grouse and complain and to begin the process, in
your mind at least, of leaving your job. This type of venting
can help to relieve the tensions of the discomfort and help you
to let go of your attachment to the job. And yet your talking self
hates criticism and rarely tolerates a vacuum. She changes
most gracefully and comfortably when she feels secure and
supported, and when she can see something to change to. That
is why many people get fixated on a single solution (the new
job) without truly addressing the full scope of their needs and
desires. It is too uncomfortable to live with the uncertainty and
displeasure you have identified.

It is rare that you can make a fruitful change without
exploration and more information about what is available. The
exploration takes place in your imagination as well as out there
in the world. What would it look like to respond to your need
for lower stress by working three-quarters time? What would

you need to change in your habits in order to do that? Where else might the skills you have be useful, or what other skills might you like to have?

The work you do in your mind to recognize your abilities, skills, interests, needs, and desires, helps to prepare you for a change. The work you do to separate mentally from your past positions and job titles, and to recognize in a deeper way the qualities you are seeking, the type of setting you would like, the new areas you would like to learn about and explore, helps your intuitive self to guide you to fertile soil. The work you do to dismantle any rigid expectations you might carry, allows your telepathic self to send out messages that bring in interesting challenges.

Then when you go out to talk to people, put out feelers about changing within the same organization, or send out letters of inquiry or application (also useful tasks), the message you are putting out will conform to your energetic truth and will ring clearly for others.

Do you see that you are not entirely at the mercy of what is available? The fact is that your job search (or any change) is a combination of things: your own readiness for planting (or transplanting), the nature of the soil into which you propose to plant your change, the readiness of the soil to nurture the change, and the timing.

When you are planting your change in the correct soil at the correct season, it tends to take root and grow. The work you do to look inward, in your heart, mind, and imagination, helps you to recognize the seed of change your three selves are initiating. The work you do to look outward: to send out résumés, initiate a job search, and test for possibilities, allows you to discover if you have the training, experience, and energetic readiness to plant that seed where you think it needs to be planted.

When you allow yourself a period of exploration, of trial and error, attempt and failure, you are refertilizing the soil of your mind, turning it, waiting for it to become rich enough to accommodate your change. If you see your job search, your dating periods, your new friendships, your application procedures as a time of testing the soil, you are less likely to feel yourself unwelcomed or unsupported, less likely to judge your efforts as inadequate and undesirable if they founder or fail to yield permanent results.

Planting the seeds and doing physical footwork.

Our friends often ask us: Is this the right job for me? Do I have the correct partner in life? They are expecting a yes or no answer, but we cannot give that. Instead we re-frame their question as a discussion: in what ways will this job serve you? What are the dynamics of this partnership, and in which ways is it blocked?

There is a point when any change requires action. You can't experience how sweet the harvest will be if you haven't planted the seeds. You can't know for sure if a job is right for you (assuming it sounds like what you want) without trying it. The seeds must be planted and cultivated over time.

The crucial thing is to confront your fear of making mistakes, your belief that a seed which doesn't yield is a failure. When you are making changes you can expect that only some of the seeds will turn out right. A certain number of the seeds you plant will not amount to anything; they are part of the learning process.

If you are an active type of person, you may need to slow yourself down to take time with the earlier stages of change, but if you tend to live more in your head, you may need to push yourself into the actions of change. Be honest with yourself in this. When you wish to behave differently, are you willing to try the new behaviors repeatedly, allowing yourself the time to truly gain comfort and skill with them?

We often have students who have mentally rejected many fine changes and possibilities. They say, "I tried that, and it didn't work." But they forget that early tries may bear as much resemblance to the mature action as a seedling bears to a mature tree. They get stuck in an absolutist, all-or-nothing mindset that often leaves them choosing the old out-grown patterns of behavior over the new ones they so fervently desire. They forget that what they tried last year happened in a different context and with different timing than the same action taken this year.

If you stay flexible and open to learning as you try to make a change, you are more likely to get what you want. First of all, you can suit your actions and effort to the actual situation as it presents itself. And second, you can integrate what you learn, and shift what you want in response to your growth. You may say, "How obvious," or "Too simplistic." But we assure you, many growing pains and disappointments arise from trying to manifest what you want, and feeling punished or ineffectual when the harvest doesn't match what you thought you were planting.

The physical foot-work required in making a change is often like the weeding you must do to keep your garden growing. It is not glamorous, it can be physically tiring, and it often requires repetition, perseverance, and patience. You pull the weeds out one at a time. Similarly, you cultivate your changes one step and action at a time.

Occupying yourself while waiting for the seeds to grow.

This shouldn't be difficult, right? You have so many things in the back of your mind you would like to do someday. Yet how often have you had the experience of sending in an application, or going on a diet, or initiating a new practice in your relationship, and found yourself unable to think about anything else?

When you focus your energy too much on something you are trying to change, it often exhausts you, and sometimes actually acts to block the change. When you focus full-time on finding a new job, then all your eggs are in that one basket, and each disappointment or delay looms large and painful. When you initiate a series of activities to look for your new job, but also put time and energy into things and people that are more secure in your life, you have a better balance of joys and sorrows, and maintain a better equilibrium.

You do not go out to your garden every day to dig up the plants and see how big they are growing, because this kind of attention would kill them. Similarly, there is a certain faith you must practice, once a change is underway, that each little action, each moment of choice, will help to carry you in the direction you wish to be going. And when you are not actively working on your changes, then it is important to occupy yourself elsewhere in a healthy and wholesome way: exercise to let off steam, keep up with everyday tasks and obligations, support the body, mind, and spirit which are learning to express themselves differently.

Failure to Thrive

In our work we have met many frustrated people who

have repeatedly planted their seeds with few results. After sending out hundreds of job applications, or trying a dozen unsuccessful relationships, going on their fiftieth unsuccessful diet, or moving out of their sixth apartment in six months, they feel defeated, sad, and angry at the universe.

There are two reasons why people tend to get into this type of trouble. Either they are planting the wrong seeds, or their habits of caretaking are killing the baby seedlings as they grow.

What do we mean by wrong seeds? Your life purpose rises from deep within you. It speaks to you in terms of needs, inclinations, and desires. But your talking self develops ideas about what you need, want, or are inclined to do that often don't match this inner truth.

Everyone needs, for example, to be accepted by others. This is a need deep within you. But your talking self might have decided that certain professional roles will allow you to feel acceptable, and others will not. In your ambition to get to where you think you need to be, other values can easily get glossed over: the need to accept yourself as a human being, irrespective of your accomplishments; the need to make friends rather than compete; the need to focus on other areas of your life and use your time for other activities besides getting ahead; the need to slow down and work less.

Your gatekeeper hears these other needs within you, and filters the energetic messages you are sending out, so that you experience blockage, strange delays, setbacks, rejections, and disconnection. Your gatekeeper does not do this maliciously. It is charged with the task of representing all three of your selves and maintaining the sanctity of your whole Self. So when your personality self decides she wants something that will contradict some of her greater needs, the greater needs get broadcast around her, altering the message she is communicating to others.

When you have applied for hundreds of jobs and have not been hired, then you are getting the message that you are looking in the wrong places, or not clear enough on who you are and what you want, or too upset to be attracting others right now, or needing to focus on a different area of your life: your self-esteem, your spiritual life, your love life, your ability to take in the experience you already have, your fears of success and failure, and so on. If you feel unclear as to what needs are unaddressed inside you (and thus creating blockage), then it is a useful time to find a "coach": a responsible psychotherapist, minister, astrologer, psychic, or healer, who can help you to clarify which of your attitudes, needs, and beliefs are helping to cause blockage.

It is also useful to consider that you may just be in a barren season. You may be recovering from a loss, integrating some new learning, getting ready to make a quantum leap forward, trying to re-locate yourself emotionally, without recognizing yet where you need to be or what you truly want.

Some of you have no trouble planting the seeds, but they do not seem to yield a harvest. You find the job, but it turns out to be wrong for you, or untenable. You get into the apartment, and only then discover it is unlivable. You lose the weight, only to regain it with a vengeance. You find a lover, only to have the relationship go stale after a few weeks. If this is the case, then your failure to thrive is due to a mismatch: wrong seed, wrong soil, or wrong caretaking techniques.

Perhaps you are trying for jobs you don't really want to do, even though you are skilled at talking your way into them. Or perhaps you are not yet aware of what you need in terms of environment: it's the right kind of work for you, but office morale is low or the boss has an impossibly rigid ego, and you didn't know how to recognize that when you were interviewing. Or it is the right kind of work for you, and the environment is o.k., but you have developed a style of interacting and behaving which creates conflict and rejection around you.

These problems stem from insufficient training: your talking self never learned how to get her needs met and protect herself. Your self-esteem is too low to sustain you, so you drain the resources around you, then feel you are in a barren and unsupportive soil. You are cut off from your faith and internal sustenance, so you feel a need to control or manipulate your surroundings. You are caught in an addictive or compulsive pattern (of behavior or of abusing a substance) which keeps you from engaging in an authentic exchange with your co-workers.

When you do not know how to take care of the seeds you have planted, when you over- or under-water them, over- or under-feed them, dig them up to see if they are growing, neglect them, block them from sunshine, then they will eventually wither and die. Again, this is a juncture at which it is useful to take some lessons from a

*skilled gardener: a communication or group dynamics
course, a psychotherapist, a spiritual teacher, a support
group, a healing practitioner.*

When the process of trying to change leads to resistance,
further obstructions, and dead ends, you must confront your
illusions about yourself and how others perceive you. You must
confront your fears and how they hamper you. You must confront your communication skills or lack thereof. You must look
more deeply inside, to see if there isn't a voice there telling you
to turn in another direction. If you listen inward (on a regular
basis), being honest with yourself, you can determine which is
which.

The Magic in a Seed
The seasons turn and evolve automatically, without
human control. Your life phases too, will shift and evolve. The
barren season will give way to fertility if you do not actively
poison the soil. The seed unfolds magically once it has been
well-planted.
But it may be that what grows in your garden is not what
you expected. You may set out to change jobs, and end up with
a new friendship or a new relationship with yourself. You may
be striving to shift your career, and find instead that your self-
image has cracked and needs reformulating. If you can recognize what is emerging in your life with the turning of seasons,
you can more accurately cultivate it.

*The wiser self receives all the seeds and desires you
plant. All three of your selves set about to grow the seeds
of your needs and desires on the mental, physical and
spiritual levels. But just as a raspberry bush takes many
seasons to grow and produce fruit, your desires too may
take some time and evolution to come to fruition. Before
you enjoy that job or relationship or new way of being in
the world, you may have to encounter thorns, brambles,
and creeping vines.*

So if you have planted the desire for a new job, you must
trust that that seed is planted somewhere. Then you will need
to attend to what comes up in the garden on its own terms. If
you get the weeds of despair, resentment and victimization,
you must work to clear them. If you get other plants, such as

new relationships at the old job, or a change in health, or a change of heart, you must work to cultivate, tend and train them in their growth.

Each of these manifestations provides you with information: about your truer and truest needs, about the fertility of your mind and environment, about your caretaking abilities. And with that information you can grow, adjust, and lovingly cultivate your creation-of-self.

You will be given what you need in this life, both in terms of resources and opportunities to express yourself. This is the gift of your divine being to your human self. But you are not handed a neatly-wrapped package of fulfillment. Instead you are given the soil, handed the seeds, and taught by the community of beings how to use the tools which will enable you to grow to fruition.

Ecology

The reason we have been harping on plants is because we want you to be aware of the immense teaching they hold for you. As you watch the plants around you (and within you) in their multitude of expressions, as you watch the seasons turn, as you watch the entire ecology of plants and animals interacting, you have profound teachers and teaching about the nature of being alive, the nature of energy, and the nature of change.

One of the reasons human beings suffer so much is that you have separated yourselves—in your thinking and value system—from that ecology, from that dance. You are a little like dinosaurs in that way, you are bigger than some of the other creatures, so you have tended to ignore the fact that there may also be advantages to being small. You are smart, but there are also advantages to being dumb. You may be able to verbalize, but there are also advantages to being other than verbal.

Each creature in the ecology of the planet has a place that is valuable and that contributes, and you have in your minds been lifted out of that. You have, through your culture's religion and philosophical beliefs, been placed as *caretakers of* (rather than participants in) the ecology of the world webwork of beings and creatures and substances. That is an incorrect placement. The more you think of yourselves as caretakers, the more you will miss the fact that you are being taken care of by those very plants and animals and substances you are trying so hard to control. You are within them, you are not around them or above them.

When you are felled by disease, struck by natural disasters, visited by loss, there is a genuine astonishment in many of you: how could this have happened? Why are you being punished? But there is no punishment in loss, decay, destruction, failure, breakdown, pain. It is a natural part of the ebb and flow of the life-force. A plant builds up its physical essence, it flowers, bears fruit, then decays and dies. That is natural. It provides food for the insects, animals and humans, even as they eliminate their wastes and fertilize the soil that nourishes the plants.

You might argue: "Yes, but human beings are different. We are more powerful. We can think and manage the other creatures and substances. We are superior." That reflects a certain value system which sets human traits up as evolutionally superior. Imagine for a moment a conference of germs, viruses and bacteria. There is a speaker saying, "Those humans are getting out of line. Ignorant creatures. They overrun their own food sources and destroy the earth which supports them. They are too blind to manage their own life force. We must be their caretakers, and help them to limit their actions."

It is very important as a spiritual practice, as a meditation practice, to focus regularly on the ecology of life forms, to undo the teaching of your culture that places you in the wrong relation to other life forms. When you are able to see your life in terms of a larger ebb and flow of energies, you have a basis for making wiser choices, and for recognizing the reasons for much of your misfortune.

We are not suggesting that you shouldn't care about your losses or decay, just because they are a natural part of the life cycle. You, like all creatures, are designed to protect and conserve your life form. There is a certain healthy narcissism that leads you to believe you are the most important beings in the universe. The weeds, too, behave as if weeds are the center of the universe and most important. That's why they crowd out the flowers. They don't know that to someone else those flowers are important. They are just trying to express their life force. But there are limiting factors within nature that come to cut the weeds down. You are one of the limiting factors to those weeds.

By the same token, there are also limiting factors that cut you down, as in your narcissism you grow and overrun other dimensions of the life-force. As your populations explode, there are viruses, there is conflict, there are the cultural breakdowns that come when systems get overloaded and collapse from their own weight. There is the limiting factor of destruction, (of health, environment, good relations with others) which results from the imbalances of some of your creations, technology, and chemical usage. You experience much stress from your cultural tendency to ignore the balance of life forms.

So as you deal with stress, with illness, with breakdown in communications, it is good to remember that these all take place in a larger context, and are due to imbalance of the larger movements of energy and expression around you. When someone attacks you, it is not a random, unmotivated act. Nor does it necessarily have much to do with you personally. Someone who gets pushed will eventually push back. Someone who loses will seek to gain, and someone who gains will tend to hang on to what he has. Sometimes to the detriment of others or the greater good.

When you see crime, illness, and failures of relationships in this larger context, it can help you to develop compassion. After all, you are each part of a larger context. That sufferer could be you, and on some level, that sufferer *is* you. His creative efforts to heal or alleviate his suffering can help to heal that imbalance for many. Your efforts to help him heal, to bring him into greater harmony, teach you and others more about harmony.

You are not a caretaker, you are being taken care of, and you must take care in your turn. Only in understanding that exchange, the doer and the done to, the perpetrator and the victim, the lover and the beloved, the giver and the receiver, the teacher and the student, the leader and the follower, do you learn more deeply how to work with your true nature, and how to recognize the effects of the changes you wish to initiate.

Larger Mind, Smaller Mind

When Ellen was a little girl, her mother made a dessert which she called "floating island." This was not the floating island you may be familiar with: little meringues on a lovely crème anglaise. This was vanilla pudding with fruit cocktail stirred into it.

While it is not entirely appealing as a dessert, we find this floating island useful to illustrate the concept of larger mind and smaller mind. Imagine you have been picked up by a friendly divine hand and have been dropped into a gigantic bowl of floating island. How disorienting!

There you are, treading pudding, and trying to get your bearings. Where are you? What is that smell? Isn't it familiar? If you are a brave soul, you might even take a small taste and realize that pudding seems to be a major component of this strange element you find yourself in.

As you look around you, you get the impression of large shapes, cubes and half circles, dotting the landscape. They don't seem to be moving, so you make your way, half swimming, half walking (there seems to be a strange hard curved surface at the bottom of this pond) over to the nearest cube. You poke it. It is soft and moist, and once again you daringly take a small taste and discover that you have just encountered a gigantic cube of pear.

How strange, you might think. Is that cube over there also a pear? You make your way over to it, and discover that no, this one is a peach, or a cubed semblance of a peach.

In these first moments, you are in *smaller mind*. You are smaller than the situation you find yourself in; you know very little about it. You have only the evidence of your senses to tell you what you are experiencing. Your mind has only bits and pieces of information that make no coherent sense yet, even though elements of the experience might be very familiar.

Your task when you are in smaller mind is to explore, to gather information. To find out where you can go and how you can get there. You don't know if the entire world is like this, or in fact just the portion of it you can perceive at the moment.

You don't understand where you are yet, so you swim a little further, and you discover some grapes, and three halves of maraschino cherries. Your mind is starting to map the environment: "pear cube here, peach there, cherry at forty-five degrees, another peach cube behind it...." As the map comes together for you, you switch into *larger mind*.

Larger mind comes into play when you have a mental image of the whole, when your mind has become larger than the situation. You know you are in pudding. You know where to find most of the different pieces of fruit. You know that if you want to get from grape number one to maraschino cherry number three, you have to pass by pear chunk number two and peach number six. You know how to locate the edges of the bowl. You may even have some idea about how you can climb out of this mess.

That's larger mind. And that's how you learn and grow. You move repeatedly from smaller mind to larger mind, and then back again. As you climb out of the bowl of floating island, you will find yourself in a new environment, requiring you to use your smaller mind to orient yourself again.

Your life is a series of movements from smaller mind to larger mind to smaller mind to larger mind. We hope our playful example is useful to you in recognizing this, because this movement between the two types of focus is important to understand if you wish to work well with the changes in your life.

Both kinds of focus are extremely valuable to you, and deserve your time and participation. Smaller mind is valuable because it is where you get the specific information to build your map. The more time you spend gathering sensual information and exploring without trying to interpret and place each detail into a framework, the more complete and accurate your eventual overall understanding will be. When you are in smaller mind, feeling, seeing, tasting, hearing, smelling and knowing in very direct terms, you are able to experience all the subtleties and impact of a moment. Smaller mind is a very direct experience. The Zen people call this *beginner's mind*. It is a highly awake mind.

When you are in smaller mind, you have to be awake to what is because otherwise you could drown in the pudding. You have to be alert, you have to interact and be right there.

When you go into larger mind, on the other hand, you can relax and make decisions more efficiently. You have a map of the whole and generally know what to expect. So your little computer mind says, "No need to be constantly on guard here, there are no pieces of fruit for another three strokes. If I keep lazily swimming in place I will be fine." In larger mind you can use your understanding to respond to your experience, rather than just reacting. You can set some goals, and see how to achieve them. You can see how to get out of the bowl, if you wish, which gives you a sense of security and mastery.

However, in larger mind you tend to be less alert and less awake, for the most part. You tend to ignore new evidence of the senses which doesn't fit your mental map, and tend to get more of your satisfaction from the mental calculations you are doing, rather than from the experience at hand.

We are not saying the smaller mind is better than larger mind. Each focus eventually leads you to the other. When you have too much time in larger mind, you eventually grow bored with your mental understandings, and a craving rises up in you for sensual experience, for new stimulation, for an encounter with something you don't quite understand. And by the same token, when you are mired in the senses for too long, stuck in smaller mind, you grow uncomfortable, craving clarity and understanding. Craving mastery.

In your culture, there is a great preference for larger mind. Those of you who have the big picture, who can make connections and show how things work, who are masters of something and who can produce are considered valuable. Your time in smaller mind is less valued, the fool, the beginner, the child, the person who is directly awake to the experience-of-the-moment, is considered "less than" in your culture.

You are more often paid to produce than to explore. You are more often paid to analyze and summarize than to experience and broaden your scope. This is an ignorance on the part of your culture.

If you leave a job or relationship, it is natural to thrash around for a while, not knowing where you are, or what you want your life to look like. When you have finished a time in larger mind, it is natural to be in smaller mind for a time. But smaller mind is uncomfortable for many people. They do not enjoy confusion, feeling lost, feeling like the new kid on the block. They do not feel they have the right to be a beginner and to explore and investigate. They do not allow themselves to *not know* who they are or what they want. Instead, they cling to old larger-mind maps that will no longer serve them. They jump into new relationships with people who are very similar to their ex-partners. They jump into new jobs that use their already-developed expertise, rather than taking on whole new realms or challenges.

From the time you are young you are taught to fear smaller mind, and to push toward larger mind. Remember the ridicule or stigma of not knowing the right answers in school, of not understanding things the right way socially? Your culture prides itself on its larger mind structures, on its world view and the body of knowledge it maintains. It makes fun of cultures whose way of life is more oriented toward moment-by-moment experience and the smaller-mind focus.

But we assure you, smaller mind is not less than larger mind. It is equally important.

In your culture, there is a movement to push children into larger mind quickly, to get them to talk earlier, teach them what you understand to be facts about the world sooner, get them reading as quickly as possible. And this pressure short-circuits their smaller mind, which is one of their most valuable resources. When children are allowed to explore and interpret for themselves, to tolerate not knowing, and to go through the process of constructing provisional understandings over and over again, then they are more creative and flexible people as adults. Their ability to stay with direct experience and to be within it allows them to develop a broader base for understanding, a more personally meaningful map of experience.

This concept of smaller mind and larger mind is useful in helping you understand your changes. If you know which mind focus you are in, in relation to a particular aspect of your life, you can make clearer choices about how to act, and what you are trying to accomplish. For example, if you have just met a new person and realize you are still in smaller mind as you relate to her, then you can see that your task is to spend time exploring and experiencing things with her. You can put aside the desire to know exactly how she will fit into your life; you don't have enough data and are not ready to make larger-mind decisions about her.

If you find yourself bored at work, you can look at how

many of your responsibilities you have already mastered. Are you in larger mind, ready to break through to a new smaller-mind challenge? Are you holding on to your areas of expertise to such an extent that nothing new is penetrating your awareness?

If you find that you and your partner have been spinning your wheels, going over and over the same old details of an argument, then it is useful to recognize you are still in smaller mind about the issue, and have not yet broken through to a larger-mind clarity. You can recognize that you are not yet at a point to make decisions about the situation. You may need to wait until you are more able to re-work and clarify your mental maps.

What do you need right now in your life: additional smaller-mind explorations, or more larger-mind synthesis? You will probably have a mix of both kinds of focus. You might be in larger mind with your job, feeling competent and together, but in smaller mind in your new relationship, still at the stage of getting to know the other person. It is good to have a balance in your life between feeling competent and having a sense of the scheme of things (larger mind traits), and feeling challenged by new unknowns (smaller mind).

You don't really control your shifts from smaller mind to larger mind and back again. The wheel of consciousness turns and you weave naturally between the two. If you find yourself unable to comprehend what is going on in your life, then relax, realize you are still in smaller mind, and shift your focus to what is in front of you. Let your wiser self guide you one step at a time. ("Turn right." "Try this." "Let go and sleep.") If you find yourself attaining a clarity and perspective on your life, then you are in larger mind. There is no need to try to hang on to it as a fixed map of reality. Just enjoy it, and play with the ideas and insights that come to you. Give yourself daydreaming time to shift your larger understanding in response to your insights. Soon enough you will step out into the unknown again.

Motivation

We mentioned earlier that you are usually motivated to change by desire or discomfort. Perhaps that seems too simplistic to you. Lots of things can influence your choices: pleasure, anxiety, intellectual goals, greed, shame, generosity, friendship, avoidance. The list of such influences is long, and at its core are two seemingly contradictory pulls: a desire for security and rootedness, and a craving for expansion, growth and stimulation.

Your nature embraces and requires these two apparent opposites. They serve to keep you in a moving balance. You will try something new, then feel a need to stop and assimilate that experience or else to return to some old familiar ground. You will find yourself wanting to reach outward, while at the same time resisting and pulling back too.

This isn't because you are a wayward or fearful person, unclear about what you want. You have this set of oppositional pulls built into you and if you learn to work with them, they can serve you, helping you to maintain balance. When you can't embrace and work with the opposites and contradictions in your nature, they can just as easily work against you and thwart you.

What are all the opposites that affect you and are true for you? A need for activity and for rest. A craving to take in and release. A desire to follow rules and to break rules. A pull to reach out and to reject. A yen to speed up and slow down. You naturally enact all of these pulls in your shifting motivations.

If you see yourself as only needing to express yourself, or only wishing to follow rules, or only able to resist and reject, then you aren't allowing your self-image its full scope. If you were to create scales, where one member of the pair is at one end, and the other member at the other, you could begin to identify where your needle of self-understanding chronically points. And you can begin to see where your expectations of yourself are getting stuck.

If you pressure yourself to be always good, then the part of your nature which craves the *bad* (that is, the iconoclastic or lazy or inconsiderate qualities you have assigned to this word) will clamor to be heard and honored. If you push yourself to be productive and expressive, then the part of your nature which you might term *lazy* will assert itself and demand some time.

Thus you don't fight laziness (or any resistance) by being more determined and disciplined. You fight, or in our view honor, laziness by indulging it for a time, giving it a place in your mind and behaviors. Once it has asserted itself, it recedes as a motivation, and the natural desire to produce emerges again, refreshed.

When you find yourself doing self-destructive acts, it is because there is a pull in you to de-struct, even as there is a pull to construct. So your task is not to fight self-destruction, but rather to give it a healthy outlet. Allow yourself to vent bitter and angry feelings in your journal, then imagine them being dipped in a "well of resolution" where everything melts down to neutral and becomes plain energy. Take a break from all the constructive plans you have, and allow yourself to rest empty, in nothingness for a time, with no thought, no activity or decision required, no expectation. This too is a form of de-(con)struction. Give yourself time to finish and close up old business, throwing away old papers, saying goodbye (at least within yourself) to relationships which no longer serve you.

When you think of many of the so-called bad habits you have, you might notice that they serve one of two purposes: to turn you on, increasing the heat, or to turn you off, decreasing the heat. It is like that flame which inflates and deflates the hot air balloon. Your nature waxes hotter and colder as you steer your way through life. But somehow, you get hooked into patterns of turning on or turning off that don't always steer you where you want to go.

If you drink, smoke, overeat, or take a drug to calm yourself, then you often impair your ability to handle both excitement and calm. Your whole relationship to stimulation and calm becomes skewed, because these substances tend to cause your flame to stick at inappropriate levels of calm or excitement. If you spend too much money, hop into bed with strangers, or talk compulsively as a way to express your excitement, you often find yourself out of balance between giving and receiving, knowing and being known, putting out and taking in.

Thus a key to healing your bad habits lies in learning to address your needs in other ways. If you eat compulsively, for example, it is often a sign that you need to calm yourself and don't know how to do it except with food. It is sometimes a sign that you crave input, you want to let the world in, but are only able to take food in. It is sometimes a compensation or shield; you are bombarding yourself with food, (a source of nourishment) to counteract the sense of bombardment you feel from energies which seem to take something away: criticism, internalized parental messages, too much work, other people's needs.

All bad habits and negative tendencies are an attempt, sometimes misguided, to find balance between your need for security and your need for stimulation. What makes them bad habits is that they don't rebalance you correctly. They make you feel better in the moment, and then worse in the long term. They knock you off balance more than they help you to get grounded and grow.

How do you sort out your motivations? In general, you are motivated by your needs. These express themselves through cravings, which draw you toward energies or substances you need. When the system is in balance, or well-tuned, you can trust your cravings to tell you what you need.

But once the system goes out of balance, or if you are not very clearly attuned, then your internal communications appear to go haywire. You will crave both what you need and its opposite, and many things in between. You will crave substitutes and symbols, rather than the true, balancing substances. You will crave destruction and failure as much as fulfillment and success.

For example, if your system is overstimulated but basically attuned, you will crave rest, quiet, emptiness. However, if you are not basically balanced or attuned, and feel overstimulated, you may just as easily crave further (or different) stimulation.

Your cravings are reliable messengers that something is out of balance and that something is needed, but they are not always reliable as to what you truly need, or what you should do about it. When you feel cravings for sweets, it may be a physical hunger, but is more often a symbolic message that you want something "sweet": love, rest, water, release. When you crave a life partner, you may in fact be ready and willing to build such a partnership; on the other hand, you may be craving a sense of security, or membership, or social sanction. You may be craving an antidote to some inner voice accusing you that being alone is not valid. You might even be needing more alone time, and craving partnership as a skewed, guilty expression of that.

But we do not wish to imply that there is something wrong or immoral about you if your cravings are skewed and you are not in balance or attunement. You live in a culture which bombards you with stimulation, which teaches you to want and consume but rarely to truly assimilate and take in, and which demands that you put out or produce prolifically as a sign of your worth. In this atmosphere, it is no wonder that many of you find yourself craving things your intellect tells you are not really right. It is no wonder that many of you get hooked on ideas and self-images that you think will meet your needs, when in fact they are constantly letting you down. It is no wonder that so many of you are caught in compulsive and addictive vicious cycles.

We feel that one of your greatest spiritual tasks is to learn to work with motivations more clearly. To learn to attune your mind to your creature self and work out clearer communications. To learn to accept the conflicts and opposites within you and begin to work with them differently, lovingly, with acceptance and honor, rather than self-criticism and blame.

Needs and Symbolic Needs

Your needs are really fairly simple and straightforward. Your earth elemental self needs food and drink, rest and activity, a balance between what it takes in and puts out. It is designed to let you know these needs clearly, through sensations and cravings.

Your talking self needs stimulation and self-expression. She needs to be able to plan, take part in, and later evaluate or reflect on experiences. She needs to spend part of her time attending to the earth elemental self, and part of her time traveling in the symbolic, imaginative realms.

Your wiser self needs to have a clear exchange and working relationship with the other two selves. It pulls you toward certain energies which are an expression of your nature, and nudges you toward experiences that can help you to grow in awareness.

When you are attuned to these three selves, and have learned how to meet these needs in healthy ways, then you will find you have a natural rhythm to your life. There will be cycles of challenge and relaxation, of build-up and release, of striving and attainment. You will hear clear messages in your mind about what to do, or not do, in any given moment. If you are in a state of balance, then you can trust these messages to guide you clearly.

When there is blockage to this flow, then alarms will probably go off in your gatekeeper mechanism, flooding you with bad feelings, fear, shutdown, unrealistic bravado, or any number of reactions you learned to feel in response to imbalance as a child. It can feel as if your whole world is wrong or bad, even when the problem is something as simple as not having enough sleep, or not spending enough time in healthy exchange with others. It can be difficult to trust the voices in your head because their suggestions can often lead to further trouble and imbalance.

There are two things which generally block or unbalance you: *bad habits*, behaviors which address short term cravings at the expense of your longer term welfare; and *bad symbols*, goals, thoughts and expectations which you set up as conditions in your life and which frustrate or block you rather than enabling you to grow.

We have referred to bad habits already, citing the chronic use of stimulants and practices which leave you muddled and over-excited or overly calm. We call these *distractions*, because they are not really bad in and of themselves; they are only a problem if they distract you from finding and maintaining balance in your life.

When we say *bad symbols*, we are talking about the thought and belief patterns which don't really help you to grow and circulate. For example, although you need exchange, there is no rule in the universe that says it must come from a marriage partner. This is only one symbolic expression of exchange. Someone else may feel this need fulfilled through money transactions (another symbol), or shopkeeping, or pleasant conversations with others.

It is absolutely natural for your mind, and especially your talking self, to assign meaning to symbols. You do it in learning language, in learning the shared values of your culture, in representing your experiences and the meaning of those experiences to yourself. The problem arises when these symbols block you from fulfillment, when you put yourself on automatic pilot while you strive toward things you think you need, rather than listening to and honoring your authentic need of the moment.

When you decide that you can't feel secure unless you are earning a certain amount of money, this is a symbolic motivation. When you decide that in order to stay fit you must run half an hour a day, this is a symbolic motivation. These symbolic motivations can serve you, if you hold them as loose goals and are still able to listen to your truth of the moment. But how many runners injure themselves because they push themselves to jog even when their body is clearly protesting? How many people find themselves financially solid but unhappy, because they got carried away with earning money and didn't attend enough to social or physical needs?

There is a tendency on the part of your mind to decide what you need in order to feel happy and fulfilled, and to get stuck in those symbols: I need love, I need respect, I need to live in this city, I need to hold that kind of job. There is a tendency on the part of the ego to try to stockpile the commodities it thinks it needs. To crave more and more symbols and expressions of love, money, respect, stimulation, much more than you can truly assimilate or use in a given moment.

The process of finding balance, and healing your woes, is a process of coming off automatic pilot. You need to work with your earth elemental self, no longer driving the body, but following its lead. And you need to examine and learn more flexibility with symbols, so that you are able to participate in a moment-by-moment exchange in your life. You need to let your efforts go toward meeting actual and immediate needs, rather than ignoring those needs to work toward symbolic goals.

It takes a leap of faith to believe us when we say you will accomplish much more if you are balanced. The student who says, "I can't sleep, I don't have time," deprives herself of the inner balance and resources to actually learn. The spiritual practitioner who says, "I must meditate two hours each day", is pressuring herself to fit some ideal of accomplishment. If it unbalances your life to regularly allot two hours to meditation, then the pressures of that imbalance will eat into your serenity and concentration and greatly diminish any meditation benefits.

If you wish to make change, or adjust to change in your life, then there are two questions to ask yourself: 1) Am I attending to my creature self, and listening to its messages accurately? 2) What symbols am I attached to at this moment, and are they increasing or skewing my grief and troubles?

Often you will find that the symbols you are attached to are not just grandiose goals for achievement. They are also small stubborn expectations or ideas. You find your serenity eaten away because you are worrying about what someone said to you yesterday, and what it really means. You feel anxious because you aren't accomplishing enough right now, and feel you ought to; you are stuck on a mental symbol for *enough*. You criticize yourself for how you look, unable to reconcile your actual appearance with the symbolic look you carry in your mind. You are eaten up with anger because a certain person isn't behaving the way you think he should.

Hanging on to these symbols does not effectively change your reality. It just causes you grief and discomfort.

We are giving you a profound key to change here. It is not a matter of forcing or controlling a change. It is not even a matter of having clear goals and knowing exactly what you need in order to fix your life problems. It is a matter of working your way back to your natural, balanced motivations, and letting them guide you. It is a matter of listening to the cravings and voices in your head, and *interpreting* them rather than reacting or following blindly. Are they pointing you in the direction of health and balance, or are they just signaling your imbalances to you?

As you learn to make this distinction, and work with balance, you come into clearer contact with your wiser self and your inner authority to guide your life. All healthy change flows naturally from this act of centering, of attending to the self in the moment, of balancing your powers and working with them.

Security

Traditionally when people think of security, they think of having enough money in the bank, owning a comfortable home, gaining assurances that they may continue in their job, knowing that someone will take care of them if they become ill or frail. Yet as we say this, you can probably think of someone who has all these things and yet does not feel particularly secure. You may also know someone who does not have all these things, but who appears nonetheless to be secure.

Security is a state of mind. It is a belief that you are safe, that you have what you need, that your abilities will serve you, that your environment will continue to yield nourishment and support. And for each person, security is a relationship you have to your own life force, and to the arrangements you make for expressing that life force.

It is important to explode some of the myths of security, if you want to find your way home to true security and to natural motivations. Let us look at the popular beliefs we have mentioned.

Money can be useful. It can buy you adventures, comforts, access to experiences. But each of you has a relationship with money and exchange that is a mix of what you bring in with you to this life, and what you learn in your family and class background. You may be able to recognize that there are many people with a golden touch, who seem to earn money without even thinking about it. There are others who have chosen on some deep level to explore deprivation, and no matter how much money they earn, it seems to slip through their fingers. You will know still others who suffer because they have self-defeating money habits and never learned how to make their peace with money and money concerns.

Some of you need more money than others, because the activities and objects which satisfy you cost more or less. But many of you get hooked into stockpiling money for your old age, or saving it so as to carry a certain status in other people's eyes, or striving to earn larger salaries so that you can occupy a certain social stratum. And these tendencies to stockpile rarely match your actual financial needs. Think about the person who worries regularly about saving enough money for retirement, only to die young. Think about the person who saves less than enough for retirement, and then finds herself creatively addressing the problem (or even inheriting money) when she is nearly ready to retire. Think about the parent anxiously saving in order to accumulate an inheritance for his children, while at the same time too occupied to attend to them emotionally.

Our point is not that saving money is bad. Our point is that it is an individual matter to determine what relationship to money will support your security and peace of mind, and which relationships to money become a form of bondage and constraint. How many people do you know who yearn to break out of their mold and try something new, but don't dare, for fear of money problems? Even when they look at their situation more carefully, and see they have family and friends who could come through in an emergency, they are not able to trust. Even when they see that they have always in the past managed to earn enough to meet their needs, they are hooked on a certain symbol of money and stuck in their mold.

The other symbols of security that we mentioned are similar. It is nice to have a comfortable home, but what is your real need for space, belongings, ownership? For one person a lovely home is an artistic expression, and for another the same home is a slavery, constraining her time and requiring more work hours or maintenance effort than it is worth. Some of you have deeply examined your relationship to your environment, and have found many ways to make any space you find yourself in a home. Others of you are stuck in expensive, tasteful, but emotionally barren environments which do not at all make you feel secure, except in a symbolic way. Some of you need a steady home base in order to feel secure. Others are more nomadic by nature, and would be happier with regular changes and moves.

It is nice to think that your work efforts are appreciated, and that your skills are embraced by others. But for many of you *job security* is the worst trap of all. Holding on to the same job for years and years, or even staying within the same company, is stultifying for many people. There are a few souls who flourish in uniformity and consistency, but many of you need far more change and more diverse change than your society encourages.

Some of you are most alive when doing precisely the work you do for your job. Still others of you have more diverse needs for stimulation and expression. We often meet friends in body who say "I wish someone would pay me for making friends, and dabbling at my various hobbies and interests. These are what I really value in this life." We wish someone would pay you for precisely what you value as well. And so for most of you, it is a creative challenge to find the mix and balance of work and leisure activities which give you true security in your sense of time well-spent.

How can we convince you that you will be taken care of in this life? That you have the power to form bonds, to make alliances, to help others, to be helped in your turn? When we mention this to someone who is insecure, despite a history of family and friends and social membership, we always hear the same response: "But think of those poor people who end up alone, lonely, eating cat food."

We think of them often, indeed. Suffering exists in many forms on your planet, and is often caused by the greed and imbalances in your cultures. It is caused by your collective ignorance of the ways of nature and disrespect for your planet. It is caused by groups that stockpile at the expense of other groups. It is caused by individual and mass cruelty and denial of social inequities. It is caused by fear, and noninvolvement, and insularity. It is contributed to—never cured—by your refusal to embrace or trust the portion of the web which secures and holds you.

While it is our job, and yours, to work to alleviate these sufferings and instances of individuals failing to thrive, it is also our job and yours to celebrate the human successes, the ways in which your individual being is thriving and able to help others to thrive. When you hear the phrase "There but for the grace of God go I," it does not mean that God has somehow singled you out, while ignoring others. It means that by participating in "the grace of God," you are able to avoid some of that suffering. It means that by allowing the divine force to guide you, by seeking authentic motivations and treating yourself with extreme compassion and courtesy, you are inviting that energy into your part of the web. You are strengthening your portion of the web, the web as a whole, and also your own true security.

Someone who is attuned to her spirit, body and mind, and spends her efforts integrating them, is led from one secure situation to the next. But the security is not a promise of wealth or status or shielding from pain. It is a promise of inner resources to deal with whatever you encounter or create in this life. It is a promise of a sense of inner rightness, and serenity, that goes deeper than any symbol of security such as money or status.

Do you recognize that when you see so many individuals who cannot be secure in your society, it is not a proof that you should not feel secure. It is a challenge to you to practice authentic security, emotional, spiritual and physical security of the moment, and then teach it to others. There are many wonderful programs which offer you examples of how security may be spread and extended: groups of individuals give their time and physical labor to help poor families build themselves a home; parents who have learned successful ways to support their children go out and visit other families who are struggling; wife abusers who have realized they are sick, have sought help and then in gratitude extended their learning to others; addicts of all kinds have found spiritual and practical techniques for breaking their addictions, and have gone on to reach out and help others.

Your security comes from your ability to participate in the web of connection. It comes from your mental serenity, when you are able to break through mental conditions which block you and come home to yourself, attending to yourself and others in a balanced way. It comes when you are freed from a slavery to symbols, or to past hurts, or to harmful practices and ideas, and are able, one moment at a time, to practice supportive thinking, self-respect, faith in the strength of your divinely-guided selves. Your security is strengthened when you find in yourself a willingness to learn, to be human and accept your flaws and strengths, to listen inward, to make mistakes and learn from them, and to embrace and honor your contradictions.

"But How?"

This is the question we are asked again and again, when we point out to someone the beliefs and behaviors that unbalance or thwart her, and suggest she work on changing them. We have tried to point out a myriad of techniques throughout this book, to answer the question "But how?" We do not offer our techniques as a slick package, or as a clearly laid-out program. The process of change is an individual, often messy and meandering process. But we would like to suggest here some thoughts and questions to keep in mind, as you strive to change:

• Can you first recognize and accept the qualities, characteristics, situations or behaviors that you wish to change? By accept, we do not mean embrace or find desirable, we mean recognize the purpose they serve, their origin, the gifts they have given you, despite whatever liabilities they contain.

• Can you release yourself from perfectionistic expectations? Are you willing to allow the change to grow and evolve, and seek its own forms in your life?

• Can you focus on the *essences* you desire, rather than the forms. If you want love, do not confuse it with wanting a specific love partner. If you want to feel good about your body, do not confuse that with losing a certain number of pounds. If you want to feel successful, do not bond it irrevocably to a specific job title or accomplishment. Leave an opening in your life to get your needs and desires met in diverse ways, and even to occasionally find that what has shifted is your attitude: you no longer find the old status quo problematic.

• Take stock of your mental habits and the running commentary in your head. What is it saying, to what extent is that causing or exacerbating your suffering?

• Learn to work with your gatekeeper. We cannot emphasize this enough. When an alarm goes off in your mind or emotions, learn to recognize it is an *alarm*, not the *truth*, and give yourself time and space to explore what that alarm might really be telling you. When you panic, thinking, "My partner no longer loves me," take time to identify the emotional basis for that thought: an announcement of insecurity, an indication of waning desire or hope on your part, a fear of disapproval. And then parent yourself in that moment with attention that reinforces security, affirms desire and hope, counteracts judgment with kindness and compassion.

• Remember that security is learned as an infant, when you can be fed, held, burped, cuddled, guided to rest, stimulated in response to your needs. When you hear a physical, mental or emotional alarm going off, check to see if you are taking good care of yourself in this moment, and if you are not, do your best to move toward a better balance of feeding, resting, reassuring, challenging, knowing and feeling.

• Allow yourself to feel pain and discomfort, and move through them. They are like quicksand, the greater you struggle against them the deeper you sink. So when the alarms go off in your mind, emotions, or body, remember that pain is not punishment, it is not evidence that you are bad or unworthy. It is just pain, one condition of this shifting, moving reality you are co-creating. Instead of struggling against it, investigate it, explore it, breathe into it, and watch it shift and change. In the investigation, you will see whether it is the kind of pain which must be attended to by others (such as appendicitis, or emotional alienation), or a messenger of a condition that will shift and change as you alter your thinking, efforts, breathing, attention.

• Realize that often the harder you try, the more success eludes you. The stress factor is important to consider in making a change. Women who are unable to have babies often get pregnant once they have given up and made the decision to adopt. Surrender and release of the stress of expectation is an important part of any change.

• Remember that all true change goes through cycles and seasons, and has its own rhythms. Cultivate the attitude that you are there to *chart* the cycles and rhythms, rather than control or produce them.

• Remember that each person's journey through this lifetime is unique. You are not here to replicate your parents' lives, nor to go where everyone else is going. You are not here to keep to some developmental timeline, or to chalk up certain milestones and accomplishments. You are not climbing a ladder, and your life does not need to evolve in complexity or sophistication or arrival. Each moment is an arrival on its own terms. The constellation of *arrivals* created by your various projects in this life may form a picture discernible to others, or may not. Your life here is just as valuable if it is a grab-bag of experiences, all speaking to you in some way, as if it adds up to a grand statement or achievement.

• Often what seems to be the problem is in fact just a piece of the problem, or even a distraction. As you reach out to solve your problems by seeking greater balance and recognition of your inner authority, stay flexible to how you define your problems and needs. Sometimes a troubling experience is problematic because you are not willing to feel troubled for a time and explore that feeling. There is nothing wrong with the experience itself.

• Often the best way to deal with blockage is to allow it to be there. If you are blocked in your creativity, don't force it. Focus elsewhere for a time. Go for a walk, pay your bills, find something you do feel willing to do, and do it. Sometimes activity in an alternate realm creates more flow and circulation in all parts of your life. And when you stop treating blockage as failure, you invite the scared, blocked self to feel safe enough to choose its own moment to move and change.

• Remind yourself regularly that you are a multidimensional being. When you find yourself putting too much weight on a particular symbol of success or safety, take the time to start collecting evidence of other things which can give you pleasure, satisfaction, or security. Get a glass jar and put in a bead for everything, from the Sunday *New York Times*, to caterpillars on the sidewalk, which is able to touch you and give your life meaning. In this way you will have a visible symbol of the richness you are capable of perceiving. If your problem is too much negative thinking, then toss in a bead for every positive thought you recognize wafting through your head. Let it be a task of collecting security, satisfactions, positive outlook, rather than striving to achieve them.

• Imagine you opened your door one day, and found an infant on the doorstep, with a note saying "I've been abandoned, please take care of me." How would you do this? What skills would you need to learn, how would you need to change your time and habits, what kind of help would you seek?

Sometimes your infant or child-self dumps herself on the doorstep of your consciousness and says, "Take care of me. I need a parent." In much of your work to solve problems and make changes in your life, you will find moments where what is needed is to stop, provide yourself with good parenting, and adopt some abandoned portion of your mind or psyche. It is not cheating to admit you need help, you never learned how to parent, or that you feel resentment at having been handed such a monumental task. On the other hand, it is not particularly helpful to open the door and toss that needy self back out into the cold. Do what you can, recognize it is sometimes an overwhelming job, and realize that all around you there are others in very similar predicaments. It is useful to share skills and resources.

One good thing is that the needy self within is often satisfied by far briefer attentions than an actual child. Five minutes of rest will often satisfy a screaming self who wants you to leave work and never come back. Ten minutes of calm breathing and loving holding in your imagination will often bring enough reassurance and strength to get you through what earlier felt like an impossible meeting or confrontation.

• Insecurity has many faces: fear, anxiety, bragging, over-attachment, over-distancing, bravado, wild high spirits, worry, depression, negativity, greed, jealousy, lust, aversion, clinging, anger, resentment, rock-solid assuredness, and so on. It multiplies in the face of judgments and perfectionism. It responds to loving, kind, compassionate recognition. It dissipates as you find ways to ground yourself in authentic moments, and to acknowledge the authentic and very human gifts and contributions of others.

• As you work to change, you repeatedly acknowledge the light within you and around you, and the ways that light gets distorted. You work with your light and your shadow as equal partners in the wholeness of being human.

Stress

✿

We invite you to join us in an experiment. Pretend you are reaching out to pick up a ball. Feel what happens to your muscles as you reach out and as you grasp it. Now, wind up to pitch, and throw the ball. Do you see what happens to your muscles as you let the ball fly?

Your body has several sets of oppositional muscles that work together. As you reach out toward the ball, you can feel the muscles on the outer part of your arm tighten, while the inner muscles release. And as you pull the ball into the wind-up for a pitch, the muscles on the inner portion of your arm tighten, while the outer muscles flex. As you throw you can feel yet different dynamics between the releasing muscles and those which are holding your arm in place.

Now try this: stand upright, relaxed, and notice which of your muscles are tensed and at attention, and which are loose. Lean slowly to one side, as if you are about to fall over. Can you feel the muscles tensing and straining to hold you?

Your body is the place where stress registers, and it offers you a good lesson in how stress works. In your body, each action requires some stress and some relaxation. Some tightening and some release. In your life too, you need to engage and disengage in a balanced way.

Stress is a signal of preparation. You are holding a ball and are ready to throw it. Can you picture how it would feel to get stuck in that position? Your muscles would begin to ache and shake. The tension would radiate down your arm and back and take over your whole body. Your mind might begin to fill with frantic and anxious thoughts pushing you to let go.

On a mental, physical, emotional, spiritual and creative level, some of you are chronically stuck holding the ball, ready to throw it, but lacking the time, the appropriate outlet, or the courage to release your energy. Your mind or personality is stultified by work or relationships where you are not allowed to express yourself fully or honestly. Your body is tense and sore from holding in thoughts, feelings, fears, unfulfilled expectations, and even from plain old-fashioned lack of exercise. And so you suffer the sensations of stress.

Stress is a signal of imbalance. As you lean to one side, it requires more and more energy to hold yourself up without falling. In all areas of your life, wherever you are out of balance, you use more and more of your physical and mental energy to keep yourself from crashing. Imbalance can be a question of too much or not enough. If you are over-working, it takes more energy to keep going in all areas of your life. But if you are under-employed, under-stimulated, that too creates stress. Stress, the messenger, tells you that you need some movement, activity, exchange.

Stress has many symptoms. You can feel tightness in your muscles, shortness of breath, aches, pains, fatigue and physical weakness. You might notice that your senses have dulled, your vision is slightly blurry, your ears are ringing or muffled, your sense of smell is off. You might on the other hand experience a heightening, becoming hyper-sensitive to light, easily bothered by sounds, smells or sensations.

Mentally, you might notice your thinking grow fuzzy or vague, your mind running in anxious circles or fixated on particular details. You may feel anger, resentment, boredom, fear, vindictiveness, self-righteousness, indignation, or heightened cravings. You may feel drawn to grand gestures, defiant symbolic actions, letting people *have it*, jerky headlong actions, escaping or hiding. You may find yourself mired in confusion or depression as well.

As stress increases, it manifests as symptoms of illness. Your body gives out, so you are forced to rest and create the conditions for rebalancing yourself. Your body ejects food and wastes in an effort to cleanse itself and purge the stresses. Your immune system goes on *red alert*, exhausting itself and reacting allergically to things in an erratic manner. You might injure yourself as stressed muscles have trouble keeping their balance. You might grow tumors or cancers as your body copes with over-drive — the continuous releases of stress-induced adrenaline. Or your body may succumb to a virus or infection, switching into low gear, and leaving you feeling as if someone pulled the plug.

As stress remains unresolved in your system, it skews your appetites, your judgment, and your ability to relate to others. It blocks your ability to meet needs, and to carry through on projects and plans.

With all these dire effects, you might be asking: how can I get rid of the stress in my life? The ironic thing is that it is not a question of getting rid of stress. Stress is a messenger, and stress is a healthy part of any action. The muscle that tightened to throw the ball is taking on necessary, useful stress. The problem lies with muscles that don't release again. Muscles that are under-used. Muscles that are used incorrectly.

In dealing with stress, the goal is to harness it and respond to it effectively. To use it as a motivator and messenger, and to find the balance of stress and calm, of build-up and release, which works best for you. It is a matter of responding to the stress with creative uses of your mind, body, resources and imagination.

It may come as no surprise when we tell you that each of you has your own tolerance level and comfort level with stress, based on your nature and experiences. Stress is partly physiological, partly energetic-temperamental, and partly a result of learned behaviors and expectations.

One infant tolerates lots of noise, momentary discomforts, or upsetting experiences with equilibrium and calm. Another may be set off by seemingly innocuous stressors, and take hours to regain her composure. Your nervous system was created to reflect some of your spiritual goals and your energetic nature. Then it was tempered and trained by the environment and nutrition you received while growing.

Do you have a sense of your natural temperamental stress level? Are you naturally calm or high-strung or somewhere in between?

Your blood sugar metabolism, hormonal system, and physical circulation of nutrients, oxygen, and energy also profoundly affect your stress level. Some of you can handle sugar, caffeine, chemicals in food or polluted air without over-stressing your system. Others of you cannot. These stressors knock you off balance to such an extent that you are chronically flailing physically or emotionally, trying to rebalance yourself.

There is an interaction between your mind and body that is profound. Too much (or not enough) emotional stimulation can unbalance your body's systems, and too much physical imbalance can trigger emotional storms. Which comes first? It doesn't really matter. Some of you learned emotional patterns in your family that have progressively knocked your body out of balance. Some of you were born with physical sensitivities that affected you to such an extent that you were never able to learn how to gain emotional equilibrium.

Your search to understand your stress is your
search to understand your physiological and emotional
nature: what you came in with, what your particular
balance points are, and what you do in response to stress
as an adult that may not be getting your needs met.

While stress is perhaps triggered by bad arrangements, difficult situations or specific troubles, ultimately it is caused and released by the stance you take in life, by your reactions to situations, by your own particular sense of need, balance, and imbalance.

For one person, to be caught in a traffic jam is a stressful nightmare. For another person, it is an opportunity to listen to the radio, muse about life, or just relax and wait. For one person a low bank balance will set off alarms of panic and physical tension, and for another, it can be merely a motivator to get on the phone and find some extra work.

In learning to manage stress, work with it, and use it productively, you need to first recognize what your stance is: whether you are chronically living at too high a stress level, a comfortable one, or one that is too low.

Since stress can block change, use up your energy, or skew your judgment, it is important to sort out which stresses are healthy for you, and which are not. No change *out there* is really going to solve your problems for long if your real problem is an unbalanced stress level inside you.

If you are generally a tense person, you will feel stress and doubt, even when fabulous changes come into your life. If you are regularly out of balance physically, you will feel the symptoms of this whether you take six months of vacation or only six minutes. If your chronic stress level is too low, you will respond limply no matter how many exciting projects you undertake.

Just as your body and mind interact and affect each other's expression of stress, your mental state and your life interact. If you have a chronic attitude of fear or doubt, your life will generally feel difficult, and you are more likely to find yourself encountering problems.

If your life feels unlivable, you can look for ways to change it: cut down on commitments, re-schedule your time, alter your pace, change your work, try to let go of bad habits.

You can also look for ways to change your attitude and your internal stress level: meditate, exercise, go for psychological counselling, use your imagination to release pent-up stresses and anxieties, breathe more fully, improve your nutrition and habits of sleep, and so on.

You will generally find that if you address the **inner** *stress you are feeling—physical, emotional, intellectual, creative—the problems you wish to solve in your life will shift and begin to resolve themselves. On the other hand, addressing your* **outer** *problems only sometimes heals and affects your stress level.*

How do you address your stress? Look for ways to release what is pent up inside you, and ways to stimulate what is under-used in you. That is the broad answer.

Take a minute and shut your eyes, and ask yourself what you want in this moment. Often an image will rise to mind. This image will embody some of what your system is craving, in terms of release or stimulation. Imagine what rises to mind is a picture of yourself skiing, in Switzerland perhaps. It is mid-summer and you are in downtown Manhattan. What can you do with this image?

Use it as information. You are craving isolation in a beautiful place, you are craving exercise. You are craving the challenge of a difficult slope, you are craving cool air. You are craving travel. You are wishing to recapture an emotional state you experienced last time you were in Switzerland. Perhaps you are merely craving escape.

Now, in your imagination, spend a few minutes giving yourself what you crave. Take yourself off to the slopes and feel yourself skiing to your heart's content. Sometimes the imaginative response to a craving will help you to move blocked energy and release stress. Sometimes it won't.

You may need to go find some air-conditioning for a time or splash cold water on your face. You may need to look at your calendar and plan a time to get away, as soon as possible. You may need to pick up the phone and make contact with someone who shared your Swiss idyll. You may need to go for a walk, and shake the sawdust out of your limbs. You may need to play a quick video game to get your blood pumping and your excitement level back up.

There is no clear formula we can give you for dealing with

stress. What we can suggest is to become aware of it in your body and mind, and begin a regular practice of responding to this messenger as creatively as you can. If you are tired and drink coffee, you may find yourself more perky, but nine times out of ten you will increase rather than decrease the stress in your body. A few minutes of calisthenics, a quick walk, some breathing exercises, a two-minute catnap will address your imbalance and re-vitalize you more effectively.

If your life is out of balance, and you have several people making demands you can't respond to, you may need to take some time re-balancing your mind before you are ready to take action. Write in your journal to explore the pros and cons of each request. Go out and gather several objects from nature and make yourself a mobile, noticing which elements you use to balance out which others. Go for a long swim, letting your problems and the demands trail away from you in the water.

Because all stress manifests in the body, it is almost always useful to respond to it physically in some way. Sleep, drink some water (for better circulation), breathe in more oxygen, stretch your limbs, walk, run or swim.

And because all stress affects your mind, it is useful to work with it mentally or emotionally. Center your mind on a single thought for a time, and just rest there, allowing the other swirling thoughts or images to eventually calm down. Reaffirm your faith, hope and positive feelings, and give yourself an opportunity to vent, in a way that isn't harmful, any negative thoughts and feelings. Re-frame the problem or situation, cutting it down into manageable parts. Rethink your goals and expectations. Forgive yourself. Forgive others. Let yourself off the hook, or re-frame your hooks.

Stress is a sign that your spirit is being blocked or thwarted in some way as well, so any spiritual or creative work you do will help you to release stress. Prayer and the practice of faith can help. Reading spiritual reminders (in small enough doses to really assimilate) can help. Doing most forms of art, in a spirit of play and release, can help.

When you are leaning too far to one side, and are about to fall over, you do not have to think about which muscles to move. Your body automatically knows what to do to re-balance and right itself. Sometimes your muscles are responsive and you are able to right yourself, sometimes you pull a muscle, sometimes you fall over.

Similarly, your system will often be able to guide you in the release of stress, in the actions which will re-balance you. But sometimes you will find that you need to question your attempts to release stress: do they give you the release (or stimulation) you need, or do they cause further trouble? Are your emotional, mental and spiritual muscles in good shape, or are they letting you down?

If you are not sure, then focus your efforts on keeping a good balance of release and stimulation in your life. Focus on *rotating the crops* of your activities, projects and endeavors. Let yourself go through seasons of activity and rest. Let yourself be helped and supported by others at times and stand on your own two feet at others.

Find activities which either symbolically or directly provide counter-balance in your life. If you spend all day putting out energy with people, take some time after work to take in the calming sounds of music, or the not-human energies of plants, animals, minerals. If your work keeps you focussed on numbers all day, take breaks to stimulate your creative self: read an occasional poem, make designs with colored pens, listen to the radio for a while.

If you have spent a few hours trying to untangle a difficult problem, pull out the iron and let yourself relax with the ease of ironing out wrinkles. If your relationship seems jumbled and confused, take some time to sort through your overloaded closet, bringing order to the chaos and giving your mind a rest. Or else go for a drive in the country, and enjoy the simple calm of an environment in equilibrium.

When your mind is in turmoil, spend some time with something that touches your heart, an activity or release which allows you to open your heart and dwell there. When your heart is in turmoil, find something that focuses and rests your mind: a crossword puzzle to solve, a book that offers some light reading, a household task which will make you feel efficient and productive for a while.

Any activity which counterbalances your excesses offers you the chance to move or calm energies in your body, mind, or spirit. Rest gives you an opportunity to listen in to the minute-by-minute conditions and just observe them. New mental understandings and imaginative play help you to unlock a stressful stance or attitude. Physical exercise can help you get energy circulating. Spiritual practice will help you to tune in to your own wisest guidance and to find your way home to calm.

Grounding

Stress Inventory

We would like to invite you to participate with us in a short exploration of your stress. We ask you to shut your eyes for a moment. Take a deep breath. And go inward, inside yourself. We are going to guide you on a little tour through your body and your energetic being, starting with your head.

What we would like you to do is just gently touch different parts of your head with your consciousness, with your attention, and see if you feel any stress or tension. What sensation is there? You may want to touch that part of the body physically, to help you guide your attention there. You may find that distracting. Play around with what works for you.

We wish to guide you in taking an inventory of the stress you might be expressing in your body at this time.

Take your attention to the top of your head. Feel your scalp. Sometimes, in order to feel what is happening there, you can move it a little. Get a sense of whether it is tight or loose, hot or cold, loose or tingly. What is happening there, in your scalp?

Remember to keep breathing. And if you have stress you do not want in your scalp, you can send it out with the out-breath. Take a deep breath and just release the stress. It is not necessary to release it, but that is an option.

Next we ask you to feel your brain. Are there places where it is tight, or loose? Hot or cold? Open or closed? It is a funny sensation perhaps to be feeling your brain, rather than thinking of or looking at it.

Remember to breathe.

Then explore around your head; perhaps you'd like to check out the mask of your face. Your cheeks. Your eyes. Your nose. Your jaw. What about your lips, is there tension in your lips? How does it feel under your chin? The top area of your throat?

How about your ears, what do they feel? If you wiggle them a bit, it might be easier to locate them.

Remember to breathe.

What is going on in your neck? The back of your neck? The sides of your neck? Your throat?

What we are doing with you here is just guiding you through an inventory of sensations, to locate stress or tension in your body, and to help you recognize what is happening in your body. If you wish, you can try to characterize the sensations, going beyond "stress" or "no stress." For some of you this will be an easy task, and for others it will be difficult to take your attention into a specific area and feel what is happening there. You can practice it over time.

What is happening in your shoulders? Are they in their most natural position, or are they out of place? How about your shoulder blades? Your spine? Is there tension somewhere in your spine? You can take a run with your attention from the very base of your spine, slowly but steadily moving upward, just to see what you feel. The muscles? The nerves?

How about your arms, your upper arms? Try tensing them on purpose, then releasing. What do you feel? Your lower arms?

Your wrists...turn them slowly. Your hands?

Your chest. How do the sensations change as you breathe in and out? Remember to breathe.

What is happening in your belly? Do you notice change or movement happen, as your attention sweeps through. Do you notice transformation?

Now your hips...what is tension like when it is in the hip?

Your pelvic region...your left leg, your left foot...your right leg...your right foot...?

Then bring your attention for a moment to your lungs, and the area where you breathe. And see if there's tension there where you breathe. In...out...a couple of times.

Then open your eyes. You may have grown sleepy with this exercise. Sometimes when you direct your attention inward, and you've been working a long hard day, it can make you go right to sleep. So you might need to shake a little, or move around a little bit to get the kinks out.

Distractions

There are certain mental habits that we find often signal an imbalance in your life or can actually cause imbalance. We call them distractions because they can draw your attention away from listening to your three selves and their communications. We also call them distractions because they are often a call for help or a gatekeeper alarm, yet the focus they suggest is probably not your real problem or concern.

What are some of the common mental habits that function as distractions?

Worry is usually a signal that you feel insecure, but most often what you are worried about has little to do with the actual source of insecurity. It is common to have pet worries. You feel tired so you worry about your children. You feel needy so you worry about your bank balance.

Comparison of yourself with other people, especially people you look up to or down upon is an easy way to lose track of your originality or to make you feel disconnected. "What do others think of me?" "I'm not as professional as Janet." When you find yourself invoking comparisons instead of appreciations, making judgments of yourself based on how others act or look rather than on how you feel and want to feel, then you have a lovely signal that you aren't paying enough attention to yourself.

When you fill your mind with **expectations**, about how things should be, or how events will turn out, or how you will perform, you are short-circuiting your ability to directly experience something, draw value from it on its own terms, and then evaluate it. Some of you are afraid to meet life directly, afraid you won't know how to take things, or won't get your needs met. Setting expectations that are too high or too low is a good distraction from this fear, but often makes it a self-fulfilling prophesy.

If you find yourself making **value judgments**, it is usually a signal that you are not assimilating pleasure very well. Somehow you are undernourished, and so the judging mind sets out to sort your experiences and evaluate them as a way to verify or refute this sense of deprivation. But putting other people down, criticizing and critiquing all that you encounter, can truly waste your time. It serves more to push the world away than to satisfy your cravings and need for connection, commonality.

Someone who feels good about herself on her own terms doesn't need to pass judgment on others. It is more productive to learn from others' foibles, or to practice compassion. Passing judgment is often a signal that you need to differentiate yourself from others. We suggest that when you find yourself doing it, stop to affirm your special qualities directly.

Telling, keeping, or **creating secrets** can use a lot of your energy, make you feel special or part of an in-group, and give you a false sense of power over others. But it, too, is a good distraction that over time undermines your sense of security, connection, and power-from-within. If you are telling this secret about Sally today, what is she likely to be saying about you? If you are getting a charge out of intrigues and bartering for information, then it skews your sense of satisfaction in everyday exchanges. It drives up your need for drama, makes you feel special for the wrong reasons. That makes it harder to enjoy open, more honest exchanges. When telling or keeping a secret is harmful or manipulative to someone else, it also harms you. With the exception of loving surprises such as secret birthday gifts, intrigue is evidence of insecurity and disrespect.

Future tripping shows you that your mind is uncentered, or that you are somehow uncomfortable in the present. "Next year I'm really going to have a great year because..." is a good hint that there is something you are not able to accept about this year. Focusing repeatedly on the future, or on the past, crowds out the present. It is a mental habit that distracts you from your present needs, interests and dissatisfactions. It is sometimes valid to look ahead, or to review past experiences. That has a very different tone from future tripping (or reminiscing) when used as distractions. Can you see the difference?

What if...is a mental habit which is productive, if you are trying to develop your imagination, brainstorm, expand your ability to visualize things. When it is used to invoke disaster scenarios, or grandiose hopes, it is more a sign from your gatekeeper that your boundaries feel threatened and your sense of self is not clear enough. Your mind tends to practice "what if" scenarios when it wishes to substitute specific fears for generalized discomfort or dread.

Sex becomes a distraction when it is used as a mental preoccupation. Your sexuality is a potent force in you, so when you are using it and enjoying it in ways that don't harm you or others, it is a wholesome activity. But when you find yourself making sexual innuendoes which are not really invitations, or cracking nervous jokes about sex, or focusing on the sexual dimension in moments when that is clearly inappropriate, then you have another signal of insecurity and power which is out of balance.

Do you ever find yourself exhausted, feeling hemmed in, and **compulsively running over schedules or budgets** in your head? Sometimes it is useful to re-schedule or re-budget your time and resources. But many people find themselves planning, arranging and re-ordering their existence over and over again. It is a signal that they feel out of control and fear their needs won't get met. When this is happening to you, finish your latest budget, if you must, then lie or sit down for a few moments, breathe deeply, and listen to the emotions that are churning in you. Move out of your head into your heart.

Money is a favorite distraction for couples to use when arguing. Yet the conflict is rarely about money alone. It is generally about power, security, love, communication, and other dynamics of the relationship. Just note when your mind takes off on schemes to make, spend, or invest your money. Is this a distraction from your feelings and your more immediate needs? In some families, money is used as a substitute for love, or as an excuse for lack of love. If you are unable to think about money, or find yourself thinking about it often, then you are probably getting signals that there is more to this symbol than meets the eye.

Many people's **preoccupation with love** has very little to do with a clear effort to improve the love and relationships in their life. It is a distraction, an anxiety alarm on the part of the gatekeeper, saying that person feels inadequately or incorrectly connected to herself (first of all), and to others (secondarily). So when you find yourself obsessing about another person, about what was or wasn't said, about when and how you might fall in love, realize that you aren't doing much to allow love in. You are actually distracting yourself from love, and from your power to connect to something in the present moment. Much of the mental obsession and preoccupation with love that people indulge in acts to reinforce the conditions and limitations they put on their heart and mind.

It is not surprising if love is a big issue for you and occupies much of your mental energy. It is through loving and being loved that you first developed, or failed to develop, a sense of security. It was a major arena for developing self-esteem, and learning to use your feelings. So when self-esteem is challenged, or feelings of inadequacy come up, many people find it most comfortable to worry about these in the form of love fantasies: she loves me, he loves me not.

Compulsions and **addictions** are a mental problem as well as a physical one. It is important to realize that any substance or behavior you turn to repeatedly to meet your needs can become unbalancing to both your body and mind. This is easier to recognize with alcohol or heroin than with golfing, complaining or excitement. Yet almost any mental or physical habit can be used compulsively.

When you feel compelled to run six miles a day in order to live up to some ideal shape you should be in, this is a compulsion, and a distraction. When you run six miles every day out of enjoyment, it is not problematic. When you find yourself needing to run six miles each day in order to fall asleep at night, or feel good about yourself, it is creeping toward addiction and is a distraction from your other needs.

Compulsion or addiction is not a sign of weakness or lack of will power. It is a signal of imbalance and insecurity. It is often an effective, but painful, distraction from thoughts and feelings you don't know how to face.

Other people's problems are often a lovely, tempting distraction. If you can fill your mind with worries about your neighbor's sick cat, or your friend's turbulent love life, then you can make your own problems feel small in comparison. You can feel helpful, and loving, while forgetting to notice that there is a self inside who wants your help, love and attention. There is a difference between compassionate concern for others, and getting distracted from your own life and center by back-seat driving in other people's lives.

We have already mentioned **perfectionism** as a mental attitude which can distance you from the moment and your direct experience. If everything is "not there yet," or "not good enough," that is a signal that you have some real imbalances in your sense of Self. You are probably carrying too many symbols of what is acceptable, and feeling chronically inadequate. Perfectionist messages are rarely about the person or situation you are judging. They are signals of discomfort, alienation, and fear.

If we tell you that **illness** can be a real distraction, you might feel we are being extreme. Of course you are distracted when you are ill. But how many people do you know who seem to start sprouting symptoms, and anxiously testing their body for signs of illness at what appear to be convenient moments? Illness is a message about stress. So when you get overly focussed on the diagnosis and treatment of specific symptoms, it is easy to overlook the ways in which your mind, body and behaviors were out of balance and contributed to the physical breakdown or release.

People who have been abused or molested as children often find themselves sprouting symptoms (somatizing) as a signal that old feelings or memories are trying to come up. There is nothing wrong with this at all; it is a self-protective alarm system. It is useful to listen to the physical symptoms not just as symbols of something, but as a direct request from your earth elemental self to slow down, rest, take greater care, and release unhealthy stress for a time.

Jealousy is a distraction which arises when someone else is getting attention you want or feel you need. It is not generally a warning that the other person is bad or harming you. It is a message about your own need, your own longings, your own lacks at the moment. So whatever you can do to reassure yourself and meet your needs of the moment will eventually release your mind from its preoccupation with someone else and his accomplishments and gains.

When you know your needs will be met and that your imbalances are only temporary, then jealousy tends to dissolve. You can feel blessed that the other person is also getting her needs met. It is only when you are insecure that the jealousy comes up and appears to be the problem. It is a very primordial kind of signal.

Fear, like jealousy, is a basic mental habit, and a favorite gatekeeper alarm. But the danger it signals is rarely as dire as it feels. Fear is expressed through bodily sensations which are fairly intense. In a natural context, when it was a signal for predators and life-threatening dangers, this was appropriate. As a signal for mind or ego-threatening dangers, it is less effective. You can learn to receive the message of fear, calm down the physical symptoms, then choose a response that is more appropriate than aversion, shutdown, fight, or flight. Fear is a direct request from the earth elemental or talking self to the wiser self for support and reassurance.

The ego doesn't like to be insecure, so your gatekeeper throws out these smoke screens of distractions. A distraction gives you the illusion that if you solve this particular problem, or resolve this particular need, you will be cured, healed, fixed. But worry, jealousy, fear, sexual obsession, and these other mental habits have not generally solved your problems in the past, and will probably not do much for you in the future. They are useful in that they are safe, old, familiar thought patterns which your gatekeeper can flash into your mind whenever there is something that seems unsafe or unfamiliar. They are habits you fall into that often tend to make you more unstable and more uncomfortable than before. They often have the effect of skewing your perceptions and spoiling your enjoyment.

What you can do to get out of these mental habits is to recognize them when they occur. Stop to see what purpose they are serving this time, what they are really signaling. Then address your needs with more appropriate responses.

> *When you think, "My neighbor is really messing up that big contract," take a deep breath and allow yourself to figure out what has threatened you or made you insecure, what you are needing right now. If you can't think of anything, you can still reinforce the* **gates of your being.** *Just acknowledge that you must be feeling insecure. Send a moment of blessing to your neighbor ("May she be guided to the choices that are best for her"). Then repeat the blessing for yourself. "May I be given what I need. May I be guided in the choices that are right for me." "May my wiser self take care of me, and my neighbor's wiser self take care of her, so it isn't my job right now."*

In the process of interrupting your distractions, and working with them as gatekeeper alarm signals, you rob them of their power to unbalance you. Instead, you use them as gifts, opportunities to bring your attention once more to each of your three selves, and their needs. The process of paying attention to your distractions, and responding in a loving way, becomes a curriculum of self-healing. It is a process of opening up dialogue with your gatekeeper, and re-working both the signals she feels a need to send, and your understanding of what it is you are actually receiving.

It is a process of re-working your sense of security from the inside out.

Activism and Global Change

❧

It is difficult to feel at peace and relaxed in a world that seems torn apart by turmoil, cruelties, and power struggles. Yet you may have noticed that throughout this book we have encouraged you to focus on your own personal moments and situations, to learn how you use each of them to increase or tarnish the quality of your experience.

We do not wish to imply that it is inappropriate to focus on the world concerns, or to have a global perspective on change. It is important that each of you who feels drawn to do something to better the world situation may find some way to make a contribution. It is our belief that your first and most essential contribution is through your very being. You are resonating your being forth, and you are creating part of the web of connection. The more effort you put into allowing your resonance to express itself through everything you do, think and say, the more likely you are to contribute in both concrete and abstract ways to the larger good.

Spiritual seekers who come to hear us speak are often deeply moved by a passionate sense of concern and curiosity about the planet. What is happening right now globally? Are there mystical themes unfolding that we should know about as we choose how to serve humankind? These are noble intentions and valuable questions.

The world is gradually waking up, and as it wakes up, you are more aware of the problems, the sense that the world is falling apart. It is like the uncomfortable sensations of pins and needles you experience when your leg has fallen asleep and then begins to awaken. It is painful, and it is a sign of life and circulation.

The conflicts you see are a result of the creative spirit accelerating its resonance. They are the careening of ideas, practices, and power dynamics that have been nudged into new relationships and are trying to find their balance. They are the destruction of old forms, cracking so they can reformulate. They are the shoots of seedlings that have been planted and may or may not thrive. They are the release of noxious fumes from stalemates that have been broken.

Let your imagination play with the events and activities on the global stage, and find ways to clothe and understand the dramas taking place. But realize, as well, that it is not your job to comprehend, in the sense of taking everything in and creating a cohesive pattern of it. Your world is in the process of moving from smaller mind in its understanding of individual needs and priorities, to building a larger mind map. This emergence into larger mind will happen of its own accord, and will reflect the quality of time you, and people like you, have spent honoring the smaller mind explorations upon which the new structures will be based.

There are times when the answers to problems lie in re-structuring situations and re-allotting powers. And there are times when resolution must be pursued by seeking greater wisdom, insight, information, awareness, experience. In your own life you are called upon to work on both these skills. The more you are able to address your own outer forms, and their relation to your inner life, the more you will be able to contribute wisely on a larger scale.

Imagine you are on a boat, cast adrift with all your fellow human beings. The boat is careening wildly and in your opinion, threatens to capsize. What can you do?

You can try to take over, shouting instructions to others and pushing people to obey your sense of what will save the ship.

You can run in a direction opposite to the one you feel is most unbalanced.

You can take yourself to the middle of the boat, on the assumption that one fewer person is causing the boat to sway.

You can panic and scare others around you, possibly awakening awareness to the dangers, but most likely causing greater confusion.

Do you see what a great number of choices you have, as you seek to help the world and make a good effort to keep the ship from sinking?

The world is tipping back and forth at the moment and threatening to capsize. Your task is to learn how to live in such a setting: how to maintain a moving balance, how to work with the volatility of this boat, how to do what you can, but also how to recognize your inter-dependence with each other inhabitant of the boat.

One of the big problems on the planet at this time is that there are many individuals who do not realize that they make a difference. They don't see that their choices and actions contribute to the tipping and destabilization of the boat. There are people and countries who will rape and pillage the earth, or rape and pillage others, because they do not see how those others help to keep them afloat.

So if you wish to save the world, you can work to realize your own interdependence with others. Not just in fear at the doom and destruction you perceive, but in celebration. Look for ways to strengthen and illuminate your connections with others. Look for ways to celebrate the web of connection and share that sense of celebration with others. Look for ways to spread awareness rather than fear or panic.

There are many teachers at this time, both in body and on the inner planes, who are whispering guidance to all who are willing to hear it. We are working with those of you who recognize that each individual pebble affects the mosaic, each strand can strengthen or weaken the web. There are other teachers working to help organize movements of intention, like those individuals at a demonstration wearing the orange arm-bands, trying to move the crowd in directions that have been planned ahead of time to facilitate a peaceful march. There are still other teachers whose job it is to resonate certain ground-notes, or shine a certain light, like stars that can be used for navigation.

As you become more aware of the boat, and where it's moving, as you become more aware of your choices, the stances you are taking, the effects of your actions on others, the co-creation of the fabric of your shared experiences, you become more attuned to the guidance that is there for you.

It speaks through little voices in your head, saying "move to the left," "try this now," "you are needed over there." To follow such guidance you need to know your own strengths, you need to know how to maintain a balance in your body and mind, and you need to be willing to follow at some times and lead at others.

The energies of the teachers resonate from a level where

all movements are in harmony, in balance. This does not mean
that every message you receive from a teacher or guide is perfect, balanced or correct. Often such messages become quite
garbled as they enter your atmosphere, or get translated into
your linear verbal languages. What it does mean is that you can
learn to tune into this level from which we speak, and find your
own awareness of harmony, balance.

Tuning into guidance provides you with a larger perspective. It allows you to see temporarily beyond your own personal woes, to feel the power and strength of the larger community of beings. It helps you remember your own membership in
this community, which in its turn can help you to participate
more joyously in other shared communities: the very human,
mundane communities which inhabit this boat of yours.

The level of the teachers is a stratum of your own divine
being. It is the place where you, along with the other humans
of the planet, sit down to co-create larger movements and possibilities. We assure you that your intentions before coming
into body were not to capsize the boat and drown all inhabi-
tants in the undifferentiated zones of being. Your intention was
to create motion to this boat, and movement, so that you could
each learn a deeper form of balance. Your intention was to create disorder, missed communications, so that you could have
an arena in which to learn communication, and work out a
more profoundly satisfactory order.

Why do a group of land-dwellers take to sea in a boat? In
order to go somewhere, for the adventure of it, because they
are running away from or toward something. You and your fellow humans are in body at this time for one or all of these reasons. Can you step back from your fears for a time and appreciate the sheer exuberance of all this life force and human
effort?

*Communication will weave a web that will act as a
safety net in these times. It will also spread awareness of
the dangers. It is like a bright light that heightens your
perception of details, while also making the flaws and
shadows more apparent.*

So as you stand on your boat you have three resources
which can help to keep it from capsizing. You can listen in to
a level where plans are shared and created, and act in accordance with the awareness you learn there. You can communi-

cate with others, letting them know your intentions, reflecting your perceptions of them. And you can abstain from screaming and panic.

You can learn not to obstruct efforts of your wiser self to help you find balance, and learn not to obscure the voices of others, seeking to communicate their creative solutions. You can learn to lead and follow in accordance with your nature and the opportunities presented to you. You can learn to balance your powers, know them from within, and teach only those things you truly understand and are gifted to teach.

If you wish to change the world, and help it, then choose any problem you see and make whatever contribution you can. The power you have is in your own tiny contributions, moment by moment. Work with issues—addiction, mental illness, war and conflict, pollution—within yourself and your own life. Work to awaken yourself. And as you do, you become a beacon which can perhaps make the going a bit easier for others.

But if you focus repeatedly on the problems, exclusively on the problems, and let yourself be enmeshed in their energy, then you will lose track of your joy, of your light, of the immediate less-dramatic circumstances of your life. You will fall asleep to your own placement.

Place yourself in the light, in your light, and illumine your own life. That lights the people close to you, which awakens the people close to them. Many links down the chain it is this reinforced web (or your own awakened self) which brings aid to the poor victims, who then have a better chance of waking up, of being helped.

Have compassion, but make some choice about the quality of light you put forth, about the beacon of light you become. From that centered and empowered state, you may well have the chance to work some miracles you couldn't have worked in any more direct effort.

There is no single savior for this boat. There is only a community of beings, each listening inward, communicating, awakening, learning not to obstruct, and learning to choose actions and take on roles which can more and more lead this boat to a dynamic and moving equilibrium.

The Turning Wheel

It would be foolish for us to try to fit all changes to a single pattern, and yet all change shares certain characteristics that are the characteristics of your nature, of your energy, of your reality. The more you understand about your energy and about your nature, the more accurately you will recognize what is happening to you.

We have pointed out many times in this book that all energy has an in-out pulse. It is seen in the pumping of the heart, the ebb and flow of the tides, the rise and fall of pistons that drive an engine. You can also see an ebb and flow of energy as you try to make a change in your life.

Ancient earth religions worked extensively with the movement of the seasons, of the earth in the cosmos, and with the models in nature to understand their reality. Physical models are coded into your understanding and mental arrangements of time. Why does a day seem like a significant unit of time? Because within a 24-hour time period you complete one rotation of the earth, you complete one cycle of light and dark.

Why is a week significant? Because the number seven was a natural grouping of time. It was one quarter of a moon cycle, it corresponded to the seven directions (north, east, south, west, above, below, within), it was a time period in which the moon exerted a certain kind of pull or energy that was discernible in the behaviors of plants and animals.

Why was a month or year significant? For similar reasons. In their original forms, they conformed to the cycles of the moon around the sun, and were a clear model of the travel of consciousness through various stellar influences.

Those of you today who live in a bustling city context, who no longer navigate by the stars, or trust your life to the sea, are not as clearly in touch with these rhythms. When you have the possibility of growing things out of season in a greenhouse, or altering your environmental temperature with the flick of a button, that drumbeat of the cosmic energies may feel like superstition or quaint folklore.

But we would like to assure you that the teachings of the

earth in its cycles offers you a glyph of consciousness: *you were designed on the same pattern as the natural world you can observe*. Thus to recognize its cycles is to gain insight into the flow of your own energetic consciousness.

We do not wish to be heavy-handed here, we are not suggesting that you try to correlate all you do with the seasons. However, like riding a horse, your progress in life will be considerably less bumpy if you are able to coordinate your efforts with the movements of the energy flow within and around you. Your progress in life will be considerably more fruitful if you learn to work with energy as it ebbs and flows, and do not try to force your changes.

Let us give you an example. We met recently a man who had awakened one morning to realize that he had been growing a paunch from sitting in his office all day with no exercise. He decided to get back in shape, and promptly signed up for a six-month membership at a nearby health club.

At the club, he set up a routine to follow: a certain number of minutes lifting weights and working the Nautilus machines, and then a certain amount of swimming each day. His plan was not entirely foolhardy. He intended to start out with lighter weights and work his way up to heavier ones, start with fewer laps and increase to swimming a mile a day. He committed an hour and a half of his after-work time to accomplish this goal.

The only problem with this plan was that there was no room for his true energetic rhythms. At first, carried away by determination and visions of his new waistline, he joyously and faithfully pursued his plan. He pushed himself to keep working, even as the unused muscles began to complain with the new efforts. He kept going, even when he found, at the end of a few days, that he was sore, tired, and ready to drop with exhaustion by the time he reached home.

He continued until he reached a point of release: the exercise started to feel easier. He felt new energy and vitality. He noticed a difference in the fit of his clothes. And then one day he hit a wall. He was bored. He had something else he wanted to accomplish after work. He felt satisfied with his progress so far, but had lost his motivation to continue.

This story ends differently for different individuals. Some will push to fulfill their original plan, no matter how bored or busy they feel. Others will start to miss days at the gym occasionally, and finally stop going altogether when an excuse comes up. Still others will injure themselves and have to take a break. Most people, using this approach to change, feel failure as they quit and go back to their old ways. They notice, a year down the line, that they have fallen into the same state as before. A few keep up their discipline, but it is a discipline that frequently displaces other things in their life: they have less time for their family or friends; they are fit, but not really relaxed and at home in their bodies somehow; they get attached to the muscles and the look in a way that makes their ego more rigid in its understandings.

None of this is particularly dire. Perhaps our friend will adjust to having a paunch and realize he feels perfectly happy with limited activity in his life. But for many people the dwindling returns of such efforts, the death of hope, the sense of failure, subtly undermine their future efforts with change. They say: "What's the point? It's just one more discipline to keep up, one more project that probably won't lead anywhere."

Now, imagine our friend, in recognizing his discontent with his body, had also recognized that his problem stemmed from lack of significant physical activity in his life. What if he had noticed that the way he had organized his job and his family life excluded the physical realm to such an extent that he was falling out of touch with his body. Imagine he realized that change is like planting seeds in fertile soil. So he needed to do some things to plant the seeds and some things to fertilize the soil.

This mythical man looked at the way he had constructed his day, and looked for ways to integrate more physical activity into it. He decided to take the bus to work whenever he wouldn't need his car, and try to walk to work from the more distant bus stops when he could afford to take the time. He started taking the stairs instead of the elevator, when he could. He decided to go knock on people's doors at the office, rather than picking up the phone. He invited various co-workers to join him for a fifteen-minute walk at lunch times, and tried to take some of his coffee breaks on his feet, moving about the building, or even going outside for a stroll.

He learned to fidget. When he was sitting alone in his office, he would tune into his physical energy, and let his arms swing for a time, his legs move from side to side. He took up pacing, when he could do so subtly, and tried to just tune into his body and its energetic needs from time to time throughout the day. He changed his attitudes toward his work a bit, using the slack times to place more emphasis on his personal needs and interests.

He also joined a health club, and tried to find two or three times a week to drop in and swim. At home, he invited his family members to go for evening walks with him, instead of dawdling over dessert, or getting caught up in television programs. He bought himself a treadmill machine, and occasionally used it as he watched TV.

He looked for games and sports he could do with his family and friends. He looked for occasions to take his family bowling, swimming, or cross-country skiing. He let himself nap after work when tired, and then tried to do something to re-energize his body afterward: dancing, a short walk, stretches, rough-housing with the kids....

The amount of activity ebbed and flowed in his life. At first, with all the new efforts, he felt energized and optimistic. Then came the day he didn't feel like taking the stairs or walking on his coffee break. Instead of forcing himself, he let himself be lazy for a while, and discovered, a week or so later, that there was an intramural volleyball team forming at work. So he signed up for it, letting that be his outlet for a time. Later that year, when a conflict in scheduling arose, he quit the team, but found that fortunately, it was getting to be spring, and there was grass to mow, gardening to take care of.

Our point in all of this is that our first friend set himself up for failure by trying to address his problem with a single solution that required discipline and a fixed amount of time. Our second friend chose to work with his use of his body in all that he did, and through a series of attempts, gradually learned which activities would work for him in which circumstances. He could look back after a year and see that he had frequently been quite a bit more active than in the past, and also recognize that all his efforts had given him more insight into his whole relationship to his body, to movement and rest, to effort and laziness.

Whether or not he got rid of his paunch was not the issue. He came to understand the choices he was making about using and not using his body, and was learning to harness his natural motivations, rather than forcing himself to do things he didn't particularly enjoy. He was more aware of his body and the uses and abuses he subjected it to. He learned, with time, to enjoy being more active, because it had become an integrated part of his life.

When you want to make a specific change, it almost always requires a reorganization of your thinking, your use of time, and your activities. If you want to stop smoking, you need to do more than not smoke. You need to find other ways to calm yourself, occupy your hands, gratify your oral needs, gradually shifting your needs so they are not so oral.

When you want to quit a specific project, you need to re-balance your use of energies and time, sometimes reworking the emotional or social checks and balances in your life. With some kinds of changes, it is not always apparent what the source of the problem is, or what form resolution might take. You need to give yourself time and permission to explore, to make false starts, to work from the inside out. This is difficult if you have announced to your friends that you will stop see-ing your partner, or stop a bad habit, or get in shape, or learn a new skill. It is hard not to succumb to the pressures of the fin-ished product with which you symbolically represent your change.

A change is never a finished product. It is a shift in the way you move through life. It is an alteration of attitudes, beliefs, feelings that affect your choices. It is a movement in a particular direction, which takes your life into new territory and new dramas, each presenting their own new challenges to you. Change is a turning wheel which carries you into new realms one inch at a time.

On page 277, we have given you a picture of how the turn-ing wheel of change might look. We correlated it to the wheel of the year, not because all changes take a year, but to reinforce our point that change and consciousness move through sea-sons. You may find it useful as a guide to help you recognize the ebb and flow of energies within a change, the many phas-es you might go through.

We are not pretending that all change will conform to this pattern. The pattern here is actually the pattern energy takes within you as you grow and live your lives. It is the canter of the horse beneath you. Can you feel it?

We have, as in the earth religions, divided our wheel of the year into two larger tides: the waxing tide, when energy of the sun is growing stronger and brighter, and the waning tide, when the influence of the sun is receding. We have placed smaller mind over at the beginning of the cycle, near #1, and placed larger mind at the opposite side, at about the point where you have completed one tide of energy in your change. This is the point where you generally have enough data and experience to be more clearly mapping your progress.

We have alternated the spokes of the wheel to represent the in-breath and the out-breath, the positive and the negative. It is characteristic of most change that you would feel these alternating currents of build-up and release, of hope and let-down, of expansion and contraction, of use and conservation, of active and passive, of being energized and feeling lazy. Although the forms we suggest for each spoke vary from individual to individual, it might be fruitful for you to explore how you experience the *positive* energy flows in your life, and how you experience the *negative* energy flows, or the receding of the life pulse. Knowing that the life force pulses makes it much easier to tolerate the letdowns, the delays, the obstructions, and the small deaths that are part of every turning wheel.

In the waxing tide, energy is heightened and growing, and change often takes a more outward form. In the waning tide, the change is more internal, being integrated into your feelings and understanding. The positive energy is turned inward: to thought, reflection, re-evaluation. The negative energy often feels like murky confusion.

It is during the waning tide of a change that many people feel they have been unsuccessful and give up. But think about the year. You do not despair of planting a garden just because there are fallow months in the winter. And the winter is not just a day or two long. It lasts through a quarter to a half of the year. Thus the hidden and internal parts of change also last longer than is comfortable. The break-down and de-constructive parts of consciousness have a tide that is as long as the build-up and achievement.

Watch the wheel turning in your life. Appreciate that it is carrying you forward. Learn to recognize and value each of the spokes which make up this wheel. They each have their interest. They each serve their purpose. They each help you to grow.

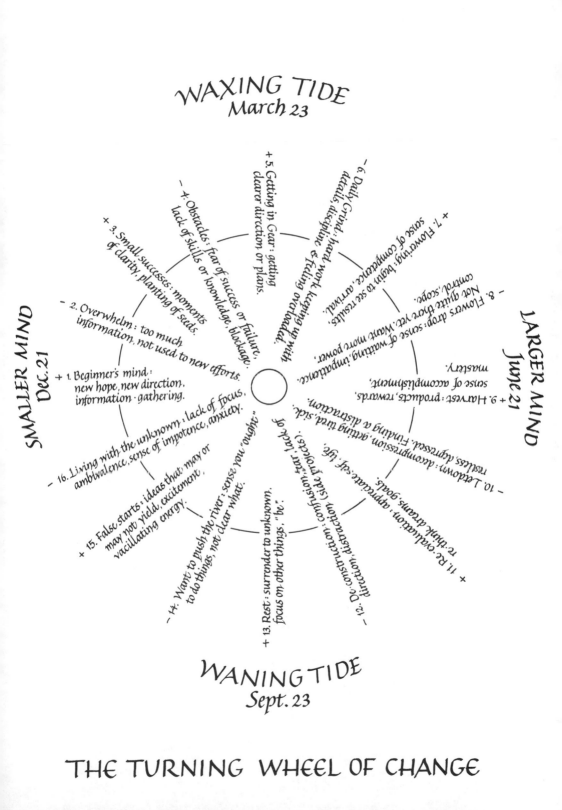

WAXING TIDE
March 23

+ 5. Getting in Gear: getting clearer direction or plans.

– 4. Obstacles: fear of success or failure, lack of skills or knowledge, blockage.

+ 3. Small successes: moments of clarity, planting of seeds.

– 6. Daily Grind: hard work, keeping up with details, discipline & feeling overloaded.

+ 7. Flowering: begin to see results, sense of competence, arrival.

– 8. Flowers drop: sense of waiting, impatience. Not quite there yet. Want more power, control, scope.

SMALLER MIND
Dec. 21

– 2. Overwhelm: too much information, not used to new efforts.

+ 1. Beginner's mind: new hope, new direction, information-gathering.

+ 9. Harvest: products, rewards, sense of accomplishment, mastery.

LARGER MIND
June 21

– 16. Living with the unknown: lack of focus, ambivalence, sense of impotence, anxiety.

– 10. Letdown: decompression, getting tired, sick, restless, depressed. Finding a distraction or distraction.

+ 15. False starts: ideas that may or may not yield, excitement, vacillating energy.

– 14. Want to push the river: sense you "ought" to do things, not clear what.

+ 11. Re-evaluation: appreciate self, life, re-think dreams, goals.

– 12. De-construction: confusion, that lack of direction, absorption. (side projects)

+ 13. Rest: surrender to unknown, focus on other things, "be."

WANING TIDE
Sept. 23

THE TURNING WHEEL OF CHANGE

Related Readings

The following list is in no way complete or even thorough. It merely represents some starting points for individuals who wish to read other books that express, embody or evoke the wisdom of the wiser self.

Bartholomew. *I Come as a Brother*. Taos, New Mexico: High Mesa Press, 1986.
Reflections of an Elder Brother. Taos, New Mexico: High Mesa Press, 1989.

Goldstein, Joseph, and Jack Kornfield. *Seeking the Heart of Wisdom: The Path of Insight Meditation*. Boston: Shambhala, 1987.

Greer, Mary K. *Tarot for Yourself: a Workbook for Personal Transformation*. North Hollywood, California: Newcastle Publishing Company, 1984.

Harman, Willis, Ph. D. and Howard Rheingold. *Higher Creativity: Liberating the Unconscious for Breakthrough Insights*. Los Angeles, California: Jeremy P. Tarcher, (An Institute of Noetic Sciences Book), 1984.

Mariechild, Diane. *The Inner Dance: A Guide to Spiritual and Psychological Unfolding*. Freedom, California: The Crossing Press, 1987.

Nhat Hanh, Thich. *Peace is Every Step: The Path of Mindfulness in Everyday Life*. New York: Bantam Books, 1991.
The Miracle of Mindfulness: A Manual on Meditation. Boston: Beacon Press, 1975, 1976.

Noble, Vicki. Motherpeace: *A Way to the Goddess through Myth, Art and Tarot*. San Francisco: Harper and Row, 1983.

Ridall, Kathryn, Ph. D. *Channeling: How to Reach Out to Your Spirit Guides*. New York: Bantam Books, 1988.

Roberts, Jane. *The Nature of Personal Reality: A Seth Book*. New York: Bantam Books, 1974.

Rodegast, Pat and Judith Stanton. *Emmanuel's Book: A Manual for Living Comfortably in the Cosmos*. New York: Friend's Press, 1985.
Emmanuel's Book II: The Choice for Love. New York: Bantam Books, 1989.

Roman, Sanaya. *Living with Joy: Keys to Personal Power and Spiritual Transformation*. Tiburon, California: H. J. Kramer, 1986.

Roman, Sanaya and Duane Packer. *Opening to Channel: How to Connect With Your Guide*. Tiburon, California: H. J. Kramer, 1987.

About the Author

Ellen Meredith has worked for the past nine years as a spiritual counselor and healer. With over 1500 clients in the U.S. and abroad, she has helped individuals to hear their own inner teachers, and taught courses in spiritual development and healing. For several years she was adjunct faculty at John F. Kennedy University in Orinda California, advising master's thesis writers and teaching graduate-level courses in the Department of Consciousness Studies. A three-year visit to Geneva, Switzerland offered her the opportunity to write this book.

Ellen has a Doctor of Arts degree in Writing and the Teaching of Writing from the University of Michigan. She won two major Hopwood Awards, for a novel and short fiction, and received grants from the Edna St. Vincent Millay colony and the Helene Wurlitzer Foundation of Taos, New Mexico.

Ellen lives near Northampton, Massachusetts with her partner, stepdaughter, and three aging cats.

Index

Order Form

Postal Orders: Please send order form and check or money order to: Horse Mountain Press, P.O. Box 446, Haydenville, MA 01039-0446.

Telephone Inquiries: Call 413-268-0276, Monday through Friday between 9:00 am and 5:00 pm Eastern Standard Time.

Fax Inquiries: 413-268-7279.

HORSE MOUNTAIN PRESS
P.O. Box 446 Haydenville, MA 01039-0446

Please send me _____copies of
Listening In: Dialogues with the Wiser Self

I am enclosing a check or money order for US $ _____ (drawn on a U.S. bank*) to cover the book price and shipping costs.

NAME _____

ADDRESS _____

CITY_____STATE_____

PHONE _____ZIP_____

Cost per book: $14.95 plus shipping.

Discount For 2 – 4 books: 20% off

For 5 – 9 books: 30% off

Sales tax: Massachusetts residents please add 5% ($.75 per book)

Shipping (within U.S.): **Book Rate:** $2.00 for the first book and $.50 for each additional book. Surface shipping may take three to four weeks.

First Class Mail: $3.50 for the first book and $1.00 for each additional book.

*European readers may send a Eurocheck for US $, payable to: Ellen Ilfeld. Airmail shipping costs are $12.00 for the first book and $4.00 for each additional book.